The Culture of Connectivity

THE CULTURE OF CONNECTIVITY

A Critical History of Social Media

José van Dijck

OXFORD
UNIVERSITY PRESS

Oxford University Press is a department of the University of Oxford.
It furthers the University's objective of excellence in research,
scholarship, and education by publishing worldwide.

Oxford   New York
Auckland   Cape Town   Dar es Salaam   Hong Kong   Karachi
Kuala Lumpur   Madrid   Melbourne   Mexico City   Nairobi
New Delhi   Shanghai   Taipei   Toronto

With offices in
Argentina   Austria   Brazil   Chile   Czech Republic   France   Greece
Guatemala   Hungary   Italy   Japan   Poland   Portugal   Singapore
South Korea   Switzerland   Thailand   Turkey   Ukraine   Vietnam

Oxford is a registered trade mark of Oxford University Press
in the UK and certain other countries.

Published in the United States of America by
Oxford University Press
198 Madison Avenue, New York, NY 10016

Library of Congress Cataloging-in-Publication Data
Dijck, José van.
The culture of connectivity : a critical history of social media / José van Dijck.
    p. cm.
Includes bibliographical references and index.
ISBN 978-0-19-997077-3 (hardback)—ISBN 978-0-19-997078-0 (pbk.)
1. Social media—History. 2. Online social networks—History. I. Title.
HM742.D55   2013
302.30285—dc23   2012029884

9 8 7 6 5 4 3 2 1

Printed in the United States of America
on acid-free paper

CONTENTS

ACKNOWLEDGMENTS

For academics in the humanities, writing a book used to be a pretty isolated activity, the author spending hours, days, weeks in virtual isolation in archives and libraries or sitting behind a desk. Over the past decade, writing has become an intensely social venture at all stages of the process: researching, archiving, communicating ideas, contacting sources, and, of course, endless chatting over different kinds of online media. Research never stops and writing happens everywhere; it fills all pockets of time and space. Writing a critical history of social media is bound to be an endless, dynamic adventure. Every time I look at my screen, the world of social networking and online sociality has changed and begs to be reinterpreted. There are two reasons to pause and put a full stop to this infinite stream of information, even if the halt is wistfully provisional. First, you realize that another tweaked interface or new app is not going to solve the world's real problems or change the basics of the history you have already assembled. Second, you find yourself doing more socializing online than offline, even inside your house or office.

This book was written in continuous conversation with many people on three continents, and listing them all would mean adding another chapter. Therefore, I would like to thank a few people who have given this book an extra dimension or made its production possible. After I served a term as a dean, it was a real treat to spend a sabbatical doing research. I am grateful to my employer, the University of Amsterdam, for allowing me precious time off from administration and teaching. Thanks to Liduine Bremer and the support staff at the Bungehuis for keeping me sane during the hectic years of my deanship. My colleagues in the Department of Media Studies are the best academic home to return to after serving years of duty: Patricia Pisters, Richard Rogers, Christoph Lindner, Jeroen de Kloet, Julia Noordegraaf, and Theo Thomassen. A special thanks to my longtime colleague Frank van Vree, who has graciously taken over the dean's desk.

The first draft of this book was written in California; as always, Santa Cruz has proven to be a locus of inspiration, not just because it is close to Silicon Valley, but because of the many friends making life social: thanks to Craig, Woutje, Mary Ellen, Katherine, Paul, Linda, Karen, and Quentin; and to Dan and Lynn for a wonderful housing exchange. The second draft of this book owes much of its sculpting to Australia, where I spent three months as a Distinguished Visiting Professor at the University of Technology in Sydney. I would like to thank Dean Theo van Leeuwen and Catriona Bonfiglioli for their perfect hospitality. Many ideas in this book have drawn on discussions with students and staff at UTS, and these debates were an impetus to revise the arguments presented in these chapters. A special word of thanks to Bert Bardoel and Caroline Spaans, whose friendship turned Sydney into one of the warmest and most comfortable places on earth. To all members of DutchLink who attended my presentation on social media and engaged in heated debates afterward, both online and offline: your contributions are greatly appreciated!

Back in my native habitat, I count myself lucky to work with so many smart and enthusiastic graduate students. A special word of thanks to Sabine Niederer, with whom I coauthored an article on Wikipedia, and to David Nieborg for coproducing an article on Wikinomics; both articles have been published by *New Media & Society* and have served as input for chapter 7. I want to express my deep gratitude to the collaborators in our research group on social media at universities in Amsterdam and Utrecht: Eggo Muller, Mirko Schaefer, William Uricchio, Ginette Verstraete, Thomas Poell, and David Nieborg. Thomas and David, I owe you both for being such supportive and critical readers of the first and second versions of the manuscript. Without your insightful comments, this book would have resembled a collection of tweets. The same holds for the three anonymous referees of this manuscript: their perceptive comments and critical remarks were extremely helpful and have led to substantial revisions. I would like to pledge allegiance to the academic peer review system: without the elaborate comments and high-quality work of many scholars in response to articles and chapters written in preparation for this manuscript, there would have been no book.

Books may soon be a relic of the past, but in whatever material form they survive, I hope publishers will sustain their support for this archaic format of sentences, paragraphs, and chapters, if only to remind students that there are cultural forms requiring a longer attention span than tweets, entries, and blog posts. With the much-appreciated help from my friend and colleague Karin Bijsterveld, I found a true believer in books at Oxford University Press. Norman Hirschy has been the most dedicated editor an author could probably wish for. His encouraging words and alert e-mails turned this process into a smooth ride. Richard Isomaki has proven to be a superb editor with a keen eye for detail.

What makes writing a book a truly social experience, though, are the emphatic responses of loved ones. It is not the first time that Ton has put his superb editorial skills and keen criticism at the service of one of my projects. I am greatly indebted to his generosity and loving partnership. This book is dedicated to my three sisters, who made my life "social" long before online media began to introduce the practices of friending and sharing. Loes, Bernadet, and Kitty: you are my role models of courage and sanity; our genetic bond is one of the great gifts of my everyday life.

Amsterdam
June 15, 2012

The Culture of Connectivity

CHAPTER 1

Engineering Sociality in a Culture of Connectivity

1.1. INTRODUCTION

Meet the Alvin family. Pete is a 45-year-old biology teacher whose hobby is paragliding. He has a Facebook page, although lately he has been negligent in maintaining his network of "friends." Through LinkedIn, Pete keeps up his professional profile and occasionally hooks up with other members from the national teachers union. An early adopter of social media, he became an enthusiastic contributor to Wikipedia in 2004, and still adds infrequent entries about his specialty, lizards, to the online encyclopedia. Pete also used to be a member of a paragliding group on YouTube, which, back in 2006, actively communicated via short videos of spectacular glides; the group later dissipated, and he only sporadically checks the site for interesting glides. Pete's wife Sandra is a former journalist who now makes money as a freelance publicist specializing in food. She has over 8,000 followers on Twitter and keeps an elaborate blog that also serves as her personal public relations site. An active family of "netizens," the Alvins order books via Amazon and download music via iTunes; Sandra uses Skype to have video chats with her brother in Hong Kong; their 16-year-old daughter Zara is a fanatic Facebook user—456 friends right now—and she also uses Pinterest for "pinning" and sharing photos; and their 12-year-old son Nick is a devoted gamer, who has recently discovered CityVille, a social network game developed by Zynga.

The Alvins represent a middle-class family in an average American town in the year 2012. Over the past decade, their professional and personal lives have gradually become inundated with social media platforms. Platforms like Facebook, YouTube, Wikipedia, and many others enable people like the Alvins to make connections by sharing expressive and communicative content, building professional careers, and enjoying online social lives. In fact, the widespread presence of platforms drives people to move many of their social, cultural, and professional activities to these online environments. Teenagers like Zara Alvin cannot imagine a life without Facebook, and Sandra has become primarily dependent on Twitter for maintaining customer relations. Pete, however, has become less active on—and more critical of— the sites he used to frequent several years ago.

Now multiply the Alvins. Every single day, millions of individuals interact through social media. In December 2011, 1.2 billion users worldwide—82 percent of the world's Internet population over age 15—logged on to a social media site, up from 6 percent in 2007.[1] Within less than a decade, a new infrastructure for online sociality and creativity has emerged, penetrating every fiber of culture today. Social media, roughly defined as "a group of Internet-based applications that build on the ideological and technological foundations of Web 2.0, and that allow the creation and exchange of user-generated content" (Kaplan and Haenlein 2010: 60), form a new online layer through which people organize their lives. Today, this layer of platforms influences human interaction on an individual and community level, as well as on a larger societal level, while the worlds of online and offline are increasingly interpenetrating. Originally, the need for *connectedness* is what drove many users to these sites. When Web 2.0 first marshaled the development of so-called social media, in the early years of the new millennium, participatory culture was the buzzword that connoted the Web's potential to nurture connections, build communities, and advance democracy. Many platforms embraced this rekindled spirit when they started to make the Web "more social."

With the rapid growth of social media platforms came the incorporation of sites by existing and new information companies. Companies often appeared less interested in communities of users than in their data—a by-product of making connections and staying connected online. *Connectivity* quickly evolved into a valuable resource as engineers found ways to code information into algorithms that helped brand a particular form of online sociality and make it profitable in online markets—serving a global market of social networking and user-generated content. Large and influential platforms such as Facebook, Twitter, YouTube, and LinkedIn exploded in terms of users and monetizing potential, alongside countless smaller profit and nonprofit sites. As a result of the interconnection of platforms, a new infrastructure emerged: an ecosystem of connective media with a few large and many small players. The transformation from networked communication to "platformed" sociality, and from a participatory culture to a culture of connectivity, took place in a relatively short time span of ten years.

This chapter's argument focuses not on a descriptive account of how social media affected one family, but on the need for a *critical history* of the rise of social media. Such a history is needed to comprehend current tensions in the ecosystem in which platforms and ever-larger groups of users operate. By exploring technical, social, economic, and cultural perspectives on social media, we can elucidate how recent changes in our global media landscape have profoundly affected—if not driven—our experience of sociality.

1.2. FROM NETWORKED COMMUNICATION TO PLATFORMED SOCIALITY

The invention of the World Wide Web in 1991, when Tim Berners-Lee managed to connect hypertext technology to the Internet, formed the basis of a new type of networked communication. Weblogs, list-servers, and e-mail services helped form online communities or support offline groups. Until the turn of the millennium, networked media were mostly generic services that you could join or actively utilize to build groups, but the service itself would not automatically connect you to others. With the advent of Web 2.0, shortly after the turn of the millennium, online services shifted from offering channels for networked communication to becoming interactive, two-way vehicles for networked sociality (Castells 2007; Manovich 2009). These new services, which opened up a myriad of possibilities for online connections, were initially perceived as a new global infrastructure, like water pipes or electricity cables, analogues to the Web itself.

It is a truism to say that media have historically coevolved with the public that uses them, as well as with the larger economy of inscription. The world's complex constellations of media, in the view of Lisa Gitelman, should be conceived as the "socially realized structures of communication, where structures include both technological forms and their associated protocols, and where communication is a cultural practice, a ritualized collocation of different people on the same mental map, sharing or engaged with popular ontologies of representation" (2008: 7). Over the past two centuries, media technologies matured as part of everyday social practices. Generic technologies like the telephone and the telegraph developed in conjunction with communicative routines or cultural practices, such as chatting on the phone or sending short messages over the wire. As a medium coevolves with its quotidian users' tactics, it contributes to shaping people's everyday life, while at the same time this mediated sociality becomes part of society's institutional fabric. Media histories and archaeologies provide ample evidence of this complex coevolution, relating technologies to users and organizations to infrastructures (Winston 1998; Kittler 1999; Zielinski 1999; Marvin 1988).

With Web 2.0 maturing into a functional infrastructure, users moved more of their everyday activities to online environments; these activities were not simply channeled by platforms, but *programmed* with a specific objective. This move shifted the emphasis from providing a utility to providing a customized service—a transformation akin to the change from delivering water through pipelines to distributing bottled Evian water or to a water-filtering system. Whereas before, websites were generally operated as *conduits* for social activity, the new platforms increasingly turn these conduits into *applied services*, rendering the Internet easier to use but more difficult to tinker with. Social media platforms, as they are now commonly called, epitomize the larger conversion from all-purpose devices to linear applied services—a development that Jonathan Zittrain (2008: 104–7) has persuasively touted as "appliancization." When companies started to build their platforms on the generic Web 2.0 infrastructure, they often presented themselves as utilities transmitting communication and information data. But even if many big platforms still want people to think of them as such, this layer of applied platforms is anything but a neutral utility exploiting a generic resource (data): they built on the "ideological and technological" foundations of Web 2.0, as Kaplan and Haenlein suggest in the definition quoted above.

Indeed, most Web 2.0 platforms started out as indeterminate services for the exchange of communicative or creative content among friends. These services often emanated from community-bound initiatives—a group of college students, photo aficionados, video enthusiasts—who adopted a specific niche of online interaction and developed a mediated routine practice. It is a common fallacy, though, to think of platforms as merely *facilitating* networking activities; instead, the construction of platforms and social practices is mutually constitutive. Sociality and creativity happen while people are busy living their lives. Michel de Certeau, in *The Practice of Everyday Life* (1984), proposes that people use *tactics to negotiate* the strategies that are arranged for them by organizations or institutions. That is precisely what happened with the development of social media platforms and the apps built on top of them: users "negotiate" whether and how to appropriate them in their quotidian habits.

Many of the habits that have recently become permeated by social media platforms used to be informal and ephemeral manifestations of social life.

Talking to friends, exchanging gossip, showing holiday pictures, scribbling notes, checking on a friend's well-being, or watching a neighbor's home video used to be casual, evanescent (speech) acts, commonly shared only with selected individuals. A major change is that through social media, these casual speech acts have turned into formalized inscriptions, which, once embedded in the larger economy of wider publics, take on a different value. Utterances previously expressed offhandedly are now released into a public domain where they can have far-reaching and long-lasting effects. Social media platforms have unquestionably altered the nature of private and public communication.

From the late 1990s onward, Blogger (1999), Wikipedia (2001), Myspace (2003), Facebook (2004), Flickr (2004), YouTube (2005), Twitter (2006), and a wide array of ensuing platforms began to offer web tools that sparked old and new online communication tactics. Most organizations operating these platforms aimed at penetrating a particular online activity with their coding technologies, and, ideally, their brand name would become the marker for a specific mediated activity. Brands such as Twitter, YouTube, MSN, and Skype have become synonyms for microblogging, video sharing, chatting, and videoconferencing—novel communicative interactions these platforms either co-developed or helped redesign. The pinnacle of a company's success in permeating a social activity is when a brand turns into a verb. The earliest example of such coding and branding phenomena in the online world is the evolution of "googling," now a synonym for online search. Googling, following Gitelman's definition above, could be called a "ritualized collocation" that developed in a "larger economy of inscription." Online searching—for example, looking up the meaning of a word, checking for the latest movies, or finding a specific scholarly source—has become part of an everyday routine. Simultaneously, this routine nested itself in the heart of a larger online economy of inscription, where search engines form the valves of content distribution. Few platforms have reached the stage where their brand has turned into a verb; at this point in time, "skyping" and "tweeting" perhaps come closest.[2]

Evidently, social media platforms, rather than being finished products, are dynamic objects that are tweaked in response to their users' needs and their owners' objectives, but also in reaction to competing platforms and the larger technological and economic infrastructure through which they develop (Feenberg 2009). In the year 2000, the Web that would come to sustain online sociality and creativity was still a vast unexplored territory, where boundaries between different mediated activities had yet to be demarcated. It was a new frontier, a bonanza where rules and laws from the "old" territories no longer applied and new ones had not crystallized yet.

The earliest cultivators of this new land were search engines, browsers, and web directories; of the many search engines that sprang up around the turn of the millennium, Google Search—including its many specialized services— has emerged victorious, leaving a few small engines trailing behind.[3] Like web browsers, search engines tend not to be presented as applications built to search, navigate, and connect information on the WWW, but they are conspicuously equated to the Web itself.[4] Over the past decade, there has been an unprecedented proliferation of social media platforms as each one of them tried to occupy the largest possible chunk of this new terrain. Whereas some have succeeded (Facebook, YouTube), others have waxed and waned (Flickr, Myspace), and yet others have quietly disappeared (remember Xanga?). On top of this layer, millions of application program interfaces (APIs) and services have been built that depend on the services of Facebook, Google, Twitter, and so on, for their success, and new ones emerge every day. The entire ecosystem of interconnected platforms and applications has been in flux and will remain volatile for some time to come.

While it would be virtually impossible to inventory all platforms and their individual evolutions, it makes analytical sense to distinguish various *types* of social media. A major type involves what is called "social network sites" (SNSs). These sites primarily promote interpersonal contact, whether between individuals or groups; they forge personal, professional, or geographical connections and encourage weak ties. Examples are Facebook, Twitter, LinkedIn, Google+, and Foursquare. A second category concerns sites for "user-generated content" (UGC): they support creativity, foreground cultural activity, and promote the exchange of amateur or professional content. Well-known UGC sites are YouTube, Flickr, Myspace, GarageBand, and Wikipedia. On top of these, we can add the category of trading and marketing sites (TMSs): these sites principally aim at exchanging products or selling them. Amazon, eBay, Groupon, and Craigslist come to mind as noteworthy examples. Another distinctive category consists of play and game sites (PGS), a flourishing genre with popular games such as FarmVille, CityVille, The Sims Social, Word Feud, and Angry Birds. This classification of social media platforms is far from exhaustive, and integrating the various types into a single book-length argument would be undoable. For this reason, I will focus primarily on SNS and UGC sites here as the main grounds on which online sociality and creativity have developed.

Important to add here is that there are no sharp boundaries between various platform categories because carving out and appropriating one or more specific niches is part of the continuous battle to dominate a segment of online sociality. Facebook, whose prime target is to promote social networking, also encourages its users to add creative products such as photos or short videos. YouTube, a site primed to generate creative content by users, can also be considered a social network site because communities share specific postings (e.g., anime videos). Despite Google's keen attempts to turn YouTube into an SNS, it has remained primarily a site for UGC, prompting the search company to start its own social networking service, Google+, in May 2011. Meanwhile, Facebook and Google try to expand their existing platforms with commercial and game services through partnerships and takeovers, making them also major players in the TMS and PGS branches.

Sharply delineating various types of social media platforms is impossible, and yet identifying their objectives is key to understanding how platforms build different niches of sociality and creativity or, for that matter, commerce or entertainment. What we have seen over the past ten years is that many platforms started out in one particular domain (e.g., online search or social networking) and gradually encroached upon each other's territory while trying to contain users inside their own fenced-off turf. Therefore, it is instructive to track how a few rapidly growing platforms began to dominate online sociality, occupying as many niches as possible. Google and Facebook each conquered a sizable chunk of this layer, to such an extent that new developers are increasingly dependent on these platforms for building new applications. We can only gain insight into the mutual shaping of platforms and apps if we view them as part of a larger online structure where every single tweak affects another part of the system. Or, to put it more in general terms, the online ecosystem is embedded in a larger sociocultural and political-economic context where it is inevitably molded by historical circumstances.

1.3. MAKING THE WEB SOCIAL: CODING HUMAN CONNECTIONS

To get a better sense of the ecosystem's emergence, we need to go back a bit further in history. In the early 1970s, computers and information technology had a dubitable reputation as instruments of control, mostly wielded by Orwellian bureaucratic governments or by giant corporations. The counterculture, born in the 1960s and matured in the early 1970s, paired values of community and collectivity with the imperative of personal freedom and empowerment—values that clashed with lingering associations of oppression and compromised individuality still hovering around information technology. It was not until the late 1970s when computers began to be seen as potential instruments of liberation rather than oppression. In a lucid account of the gradual convergence of the counterculture with "geek" cyberculture, Fred Turner has demonstrated how visions of computer networks gradually became linked to visions of "peer-to-peer adhocracy" and "expressions of the true self" (2006: 3). A famous ad campaign for Apple computers in 1984 showcased the Macintosh as a tool for user empowerment, casting the company as a rebel amid powerful computer industries and, by implication, positioned the Mac customer as a denizen of the counterculture. The ultimate irony of this promoted image, as pointed out by biographer Walter Isaacson, was that the Macintosh was a closed and controlled system, "like something designed by Big Brother rather than by a hacker" (2011: 162). But the rebel-geek image of working in the interest of the public good rather than in the interest of Big Money or Big Government was a significant precursor to the communal spirit later adopted by advocates of web culture.

The invention of the World Wide Web in 1991 gave a new impetus to the liaison between geek culture and counterculture. As the WWW consortium began to build a global standardized infrastructure, communities of enthusiastic users began to churn out applications for the Web. The period when users purportedly helped construct a new public space, outside corporate control, only lasted a few years, however. Commercial developers like Google, AOL, and Amazon, at the turn of the millennium, incorporated the Web 1.0 and, virtually overnight, replaced dot.communism by dot.commercialism. However, the spirit associated with egalitarianism and community cocooning was rekindled in the early 2000s with the advent of Web 2.0. The growth of social media platforms was (and still is) often innocuously conflated with the rise of Web 2.0, and the participatory potential of social media was sometimes erroneously attributed to the Web's technological design. Its built-in capacity for two-way communication supposedly rendered online media infinitely more democratic than the old (one-way) media.[5] Words like "interactivity" and "participatory" described Web 2.0.'s potential to "talk back" and send messages instantly, whereas previous media had wielded power over their one-way publishing or broadcasting channels.

When new interactive platforms entered the scene, such as Blogger, Wikipedia, Facebook, and YouTube, they promised to make culture more "participatory," "user centered," and "collaborative." Between 2000 and 2006, quite a few media theorists claimed that Web 2.0 applications exponentially enhanced the natural human need to connect and create, and they declared early victory for the user. Henry Jenkins in 2006 welcomed us to the world of convergence culture, a world "where old and new media collide, where grassroots and corporate media intersect, where the power of media producer and the power of the media consumer interact in unpredictable ways" (2). Media theorist Axel Bruns (2008) hailed a new class of "produsers"—creators who were also users and distributors. Wikipedia was recurrently held up as a model of collaboration of selfless users who collectively developed a unique product—an ever-expanding online encyclopedia—for the common good by exploiting a communal space. The year 2006 turned out to be the apex of user euphoria when *Time* magazine selected "You" as the Person of the Year, trumpeting the world-changing potential of connected users: "It's a story about community and collaboration . . . about the many wresting power from the few and helping one another for nothing and how that will not only change the world, but also change the way the world changes."[6] For many early adopters, belief that Web 2.0 was a communal and collaborative space inspired their endeavors to build platforms, and echoes of this early idealistic spirit resound to this day.

To some extent, the triumph of users over conventional mass media proved to be justified, as Web 2.0 offered unprecedented tools for empowerment and online self-communication, but outsized expectations nourished a premature winning mood among the web idealists. Perhaps a symbolic rebalancing of *Time*'s earlier veneration of the user was the designation, four years later, of Mark Zuckerberg as *Time*'s Person of the Year.[7] When Facebook's CEO in 2010 took over the badge of honor from "You," he promised to make the world more open and transparent, echoing the utopian spirit that had previously galvanized users. Platform owners eagerly adopted similar rhetoric in their corporate mantras and promotional slogans, such as "Do no evil" (Google), "Making the Web more social" (Facebook), and "Share your pictures, watch the world" (Flickr-Yahoo). Web companies tirelessly underscored their company's mission to benefit the common good. Zuckerberg has repeatedly stated that Facebook "wants people to find what they want and connect them to ideas they like online."[8] Today social media companies still seem eager to align the benevolent halo of early web technology with their "alternative" corporate ethos.

Rather than simply accepting or rejecting this ethos, I am interested in deconstructing what meanings developers *impute* to their platforms' goals and functions—meanings that peculiarly reflect rhetorical attempts to absorb utopian Web 2.0 connotations into corporate missions. The very word "social" associated with media implies that platforms are user centered and that they facilitate communal activities, just as the term "participatory" emphasizes human collaboration. Indeed, social media can be seen as online facilitators or enhancers of *human* networks—webs of people that promote connectedness as a social value. Individuals' ideas, values, and tastes are contagious and spread through human networks, but these networks also affect what individuals do and think (Christakis and Fowler

2009). By the same token, social media are inevitably *automated systems* that engineer and manipulate connections. In order to be able to recognize what people want and like, Facebook and other platforms track desires by coding relationships between people, things, and ideas into algorithms. The meaning of "social" hence seems to encompasses both (human) connectedness and (automated) connectivity—a conflation that is cultivated by many CEOs—and its deliberate ambiguity will play a major role in the further elaboration of this book's argument.

Companies tend to stress the first meaning (human connectedness) and minimize the second meaning (automated connectivity). Zuckerberg deploys a sort of newspeak when claiming that technology merely enables or facilitates social activities; however, "making the Web social" in reality means "making sociality technical." Sociality coded by technology renders people's activities formal, manageable, and manipulable, enabling platforms to engineer the sociality in people's everyday routines.[9] On the basis of detailed and intimate knowledge of people's desires and likes, platforms develop tools to create and steer specific needs. A button that shows what your friends watch, hear, read, and buy registers your peers' tastes while concurrently shaping them. Users, in general, also tend to emphasize human connectedness when explaining a platform's value in their lives. Facebook helps its members to make and maintain contacts, but for many ordinary users it is difficult to recognize how Facebook actively steers and curates connections. Moreover, it is far from transparent how Facebook and other platforms utilize their data to influence traffic and monetize engineered streams of information. And yet connectedness is often invoked as the pretense for generating connectivity, even now that data generation has become a primary objective rather than a by-product of online sociality.

Besides the term "social," concepts like "participation" and "collaboration" get imputed a peculiar new meaning in the context of social media. Users of content are supposedly "collaborators" who "co-develop" creative products and thus enrich communities. Notions of community and group-think abound in the rhetoric of platforms, and their echoes resounded particularly during the years 2004 to 2007. Indeed, many platforms, such as YouTube and Flickr, started out as community initiatives; they were carried by a group of video buffs and photo fans, respectively, eager to share their creative products online. After their takeover by Google and, in the latter case, Yahoo, the sites' corporate owners kept nurturing the image of collectivity and user-centered operation long after their strategies had transmogrified to the commercial realm. Photographic and video content became instrumental to the automated collection of data about meaningful social relationships, propelled by such questions as, Who shares which images with whom? What images or videos are popular among which groups? Who are the leading tastemakers in these communities?

A similar conflation of human connectedness and automated connectivity happens when social activities are translated into algorithmic concepts. In the offline world, people who are "well connected" are commonly understood to be individuals whose connections are gauged by their quality and status rather than their quantity. In the context of social media, the term "friends" and its adjunct verb "friending" have come to designate strong *and* weak ties, intimate contacts *as well as* total strangers. Their significance is commonly articulated in one indiscriminate number. The term "followers" has undergone a similar transformation: the word connotes everything from neutral "groups" to "devotees" and "believers," but in the context of social media it has come to mean the sheer number of people who follow your twit stream. From the technological inscription of online sociality we derive that connectivity is a quantifiable value, also known as the *popularity principle*: the more contacts you have and make, the more valuable you become, because more people think you are popular and hence want to connect with you.

What goes for people also holds for ideas or things that can be "liked": likability is not a virtue attributed consciously by a person to a thing or idea, but is the result of an algorithmic computation derived from instant clicks on the Like button.[10] However, there is no quality assessment built into these buttons: online quantification indiscriminately accumulates acclamation and applause, and, by implication, deprecation and disapproval. The choice for a "like" button betrays an ideological predilection: it favors instant, gut-fired, emotional, positive evaluations. Popularity as a coded concept thus not only becomes quantifiable but also manipulable: boosting popularity rankings is an important mechanism built into these buttons. People who have many friends or followers are touted as influential, and their social authority or reputation increases as they receive more clicks. Ideas that are "liked" by many people have the potential of becoming trends. Friending, following, and trending are not the same functions, but they derive from the same popularity principle underpinning the online economy of social media.

Key terms used to describe social media's functionality, such as the "social," "collaboration," and "friends," resonate with the communalist jargon of early utopian visions of the Web as a space that inherently enhances social activity. In reality, the meanings of these words have increasingly been informed by automated technologies that direct human sociality. Therefore, the term "connective media" would be preferable over "social media."[11] What is claimed to be "social" is in fact the result of human input shaped by computed output and vice versa—a sociotechnical ensemble whose components can hardly be told apart. The norms and values supporting the "social" image of these media remain hidden in platforms' technological textures. Not coincidentally, the same assumptions supporting the goal of making the Web more social—or, if you wish, of making sociality more technical—also support the ideology of making online sociality *salable*.

1.4. MAKING SOCIALITY SALABLE: CONNECTIVITY AS RESOURCE

Mark Zuckerberg's promise to "make the Web more social" is inextricably intertwined with his professed desire to "make the world more transparent." Essential to the narrative of the social Web rendering a transparent world was the implied assumption that if users proffer their true identity when sharing personal data, platforms, for their part, would also carry a robust ethic of openness and sharing.[12] The rhetoric of transparency and openness was supposedly rooted in and certainly inspired by the rhetoric of community-based online sociality, which flourished during the first six years of the new millennium. Most of these online groups, though, preferred to conduct their activities in a noncommercial, public space where they could communicate free of government or market constraints. When corporations took over online platforms, they were eager to co-opt the rhetoric and spice their corporate image with values more commonly attributed to the public sector. Indeed, companies liked to present themselves as pioneers of a joint public-private endeavor.

Legal and economic scholars further advanced these hybrid ideological foundations. The networked information environment, as Yochai Benkler asserted in 2006, would give rise to a flourishing nonmarket sector of information and creative production. Web 2.0 strategies challenged both market and state economies as they enabled the development of a cooperative nonmarket, peer-production system that served communicative and creative needs through networks of like-minded individuals. This "networked public sphere" was fundamentally different from the existing public sphere and would "emerge *alongside* the commercial mass-media markets" (Benkler 2006: 10, emphasis added). In line with media theorists' assessments at that time, we can discern a victorious appraisal of Web 2.0's potential to promote community over commerce, or, at the very least, afford their peaceful coexistence. Among many examples of cooperative endeavors, Wikipedia stands out as the poster child for the networked public sphere—a model of nonprofit, nonmarket peer production emerging alongside commercial encyclopedic products, rather than in competition with them.

Between 2000 and 2005, most platforms thrived on the enthusiasm of users as they ran and operated their new virtual spaces, which were often regarded as experiments in online citizenship and a reinvention of the rules for democratic governance. The peaceful coexistence of market and nonmarket peer-production, as divined by Benkler, gave social media platforms the image of being alternative spaces, free from corporate and government constraints, where individuals could pursue their communicative and creative needs and could regulate their own social traffic. In the early years of YouTube, Wikipedia, and Flickr, user communities invested much time and effort in keeping "their" channels clean from pollution by filtering out pornographic and racist content. The promise of self-regulation and community-supported surveillance worked well as long as the platforms were relatively small and uniform in their user base.

As user bases began to explode after 2005, the investment required of users became too big, and the focus of most platforms was diluted. At the same time, many platforms were taken over by big media corporations or were otherwise incorporated; the spirit of "nonmarket peer-production" soon dwindled. During the ensuing years, between 2005 and 2008, corporate owners remained cautious about exposing their profit motives to user communities, and in many instances kept nourishing the image of platforms as peer-production structures that put users before profits. Because user bases were still immersed in a participation spirit, platform management had to walk a tightrope between a growth scenario—luring more customers to sites—and pleasing its original, often assertive, users, who were keenly aware of the value they added to the site's market position (Clemons 2009; Potts 2009). The development of business models, balancing user participation against for-profit strategies, posed a real challenge to the digital media industry (Vukanovic 2009). A corporate management demanding returns on investment faced the risk of being confronted by user protests or boycotts. Platforms had to navigate between Silicon Valley's venture capitalist culture, which pushed for quick turnovers and speedy IPOs, and the original participatory spirit, which had caused the platforms to grow in the first place. The safest strategy for many managers seemed to be expeditious growth while conducting careful experiments with monetizing schemes.

Tapping into academics' celebratory rhetoric of a new public sphere of nonmarket collaboration, business managers and marketers glorified the potential of mixed public-private entrepreneurship by absorbing Wikipedian-style peer-production into their for-profit business models. More precisely, they borrowed one particular element of Wikipedia's innovative model—user participation—squeezing it into a for-profit business and corporate governance structure. "Wikinomics," an Internet business concept launched by economists Don Tapscott and Anthony Williams (2006), fostered the immanent merger of the market and nonprofit sector in a networked information environment.[13] They applauded Google and Yahoo for creating "new public squares, vibrant meeting places where your customers come back for the rich and engaging experiences"; echoing the slogans of credit card companies, the authors significantly add: "Relationships, after all, are the one thing you cannot commoditize" (Tapscott and Williams 2006: 44).

Perhaps ironically, commoditizing relationships—turning connectedness into connectivity by means of coding technologies—is exactly what corporate platforms, particularly Google and Facebook, discovered as the golden egg their geese produced. Besides generating content, peer production yields a valuable by-product that users often do not intentionally deliver: behavioral and profiling data. Under the guise of connectedness they produce a precious resource: connectivity. Even though the term "connectivity" originated in technology, where it denotes computer transmissions, in the context of social media it quickly assumed the connotation of users accumulating *social* capital, while in fact this term increasingly referred to owners amassing *economic* capital. Ten years after its start, Wikipedia is perhaps an uncomfortable reminder of what the Web could have been, as it is currently one of the few main sites that have not been co-opted by big business. A quick look at today's palette of the 100 biggest social media platforms reveals that the overwhelming majority (almost 98 percent) are run by corporations who think of the Internet as a marketplace first and a public forum second—Wikipedia being the most notable exception.[14] And yet the rhetoric of a new public sphere was (and still is to some extent) gratefully appropriated by businesses to salvage the virtues of the corporate sphere. An endorsed fusion of nonmarket and for-profit principles breathes the spirit of public collectivism, a spirit espoused by those who regard the Web's technical infrastructure as an opportunity for opening up unimpeded social space.

Not surprisingly, the rapid rise of social media has also triggered a standoff between social media adepts and staunch critics in academic circles. On the one hand, we find early enthusiasts who, in Benkler's and Jenkins's footsteps, rejoice at the potential of Web 2.0 to empower users to wield their new digital tools to connect and create, while developing a new public sphere or a fused public-corporate sphere in the process. Social scientists and journalists have argued that social media open up a new private sphere or are at least an exciting experiment in mixing private and public.

For instance, communications scholar Zizi Papacharissi (2010) argues that social media platforms have introduced a space where boundaries between private and public space have become fuzzy, claiming that this imprecision opens up new possibilities for identity formation. Jeff Jarvis (2011) also cheers the ambiguity; he attributes its redeeming potential to Facebook's and other sites' ideal of openness and connectedness.[15]

On the other end of the spectrum, we find two types of detractors. Political economists assailed the incorporation of social media, labeling them as failed experiments in democratic participation or dismissing them as dependent on a naive belief in the possibility of developing a new or alternative public sphere alongside the existing public, private, and corporate spheres (Milberry and Anderson 2009; de Peuter and Dyer-Witheford 2005; Skageby 2009). The incorporation of platforms, some critics contend, hampered the development of Web 2.0's full potential as an instrument for participatory culture, self-regulation, and democracy. Instead, commercial platforms introduced new modes of surveillance, bartering privacy for the accumulation of social capital (Cohen 2008; Haythornthwaite and Kendall 2010). Other critics of platforms object to users' being doubly exploited, both as workers—deliverers of data to UGC and SNS platforms—and as consumers forced to buy back their own processed data by relinquishing privacy (Terranova 2004; Petersen 2008). More profoundly, some observe that the selling of privacy may be mistakenly viewed as the natural consequence of users' eagerness to connect and promote the self, rather than being understood as the corollary of a political economy deeply rooted in audience commoditization (Fuchs 2011a).

In addition to adepts in political economy, a number of legal experts and consumer groups have censured Facebook and other platforms for violation of privacy laws as they cultivated their newfound digital territory. Offsetting the benign rhetoric of fading or fuzzy boundaries, courts and lawyers often recognize a sharp dichotomy between private and public in their affidavits when taking on cases against new media corporations. Legal scholars have called for a recalibration of traditional juridical concepts in response to social media platforms deliberately exploiting the fissures of virtual space (Solove 2008; Nissenbaum 2010; Grimmelmann 2009). Privacy experts consistently defend the boundaries between private, corporate, and public space to protect the rights of citizens against platform owners' calls for more "transparency"—a term that often appears to apply to users only. Although my argument takes a nonjuridical perspective, I share legal experts' concerns about privacy in social media.

As often happens with debates on contentious and multifaceted phenomena, the issue gets mired in a myriad of polarized debates. Over the past decade, connective media have often been framed as a confrontation between users and owners. *Time* magazine's triumphant dictum about the "many wresting power from the few" had it backward; according to some, the new media were about the "few (platform owners) wresting control from the many." Even though I sympathize with the criticism of political economists that a forfeiture of privacy is a direct result of social media's commoditization, I often find the users-versus-owners standoff to be unproductive as an explanation. The resulting picture is mostly one of victims versus perpetrators, of the powerless versus the powerful. Obviously, social media services can be both intensely empowering and disturbingly exploitative; sociality is enjoyed and exercised through precisely the commercial platforms that also exploit online social activities for monetary gains.

Going back to the Alvin family, introduced at the beginning of this chapter, we can see these two profoundly different views on user agency mirrored in Pete and Sandra. Sandra represents the many users for whom social media platforms provide a means not only of pleasure but of profitable business: Blogger has been instrumental to her blog-publishing activities, and without Twitter and Facebook, she would not have had an extensive network of followers and friends through whom she acquires paid assignments. Like many (mostly young) entrepreneurs, she is taking advantage of those platforms that monetize connectivity, while taking their sometimes-obscure commercial strategies for granted. Pete Alvin exemplifies those users who are disappointed with mainstream platforms taking over the community spirit they initially cherished and nurtured. He feels uncomfortable giving away so much personal information while gaining little transparency in return. The perspectives Sandra and Pete represent are driven by different ideologies or worldviews; however, they are not mutually exclusive or incommensurate. Users can enjoy connective media and still be critical of their functioning, for instance by taking a vocal stance on privacy issues or data control. Users are citizens as well as consumers, professionals as well as assertive voters. Platform owners and app developers are producing agents and social forces; they can exercise economic and political power to change or sustain existing hierarchies and deploy their technologies to do so. In sum, the heterogeneity of actors warrants a treatment of sociality more complex than that of simply confirming the standoff.

1.5. THE ECOSYSTEM OF CONNECTIVE MEDIA IN A CULTURE OF CONNECTIVITY

Academic discussions on social media generally mirror public debates, often zooming in on breach of privacy laws, the assessment of viable business models, and an analysis of users' pleasures or of their exploitation.

Although these debates are all valid and highly relevant, the aim of this book is to focus not on privacy or commoditization as such, but on the *historical and cultural* convolutions underpinning these tensions. In exploring the short but rich history of social media platforms and the online sociality that came along with their evolution, I want to expose the changing cultural norms and values on which these legal and economic challenges are staked, as well as the technological, ideological, and socioeconomic structures through which they are wagered. Privacy and commercialization concerns are emblematic of the larger battle for control over personal and collective information. Who can own someone's profiling and behavioral data? Who is allowed to interpret, aggregate, and sell information derived from personal data? How do various platforms infiltrate everyday communicative and creative habits, and what power do users and owners have to shape online sociality?[16]

Social media constitute an arena of public communication where norms are shaped and rules get contested. Norms, as Michel Foucault (1980) has theorized, constitute the social and cultural cement for grounding laws and legal regulations. The power of norms, in the area of sociality, is much more influential than the power of law and order. Contemporary methods of power are methods whose "operation is not ensured by right but by *technique*, not by law but by *normalization*, not by punishment but by *control*" (Foucault 1980: 89, emphases added). In less than a decade, the norms for online sociality have dramatically changed, and they are still in flux. Patterns of behavior that traditionally existed in offline (physical) sociality are increasingly mixed with social and sociotechnical norms created in an online environment, taking on a new dimensionality.[17] For instance, the norms for "sharing" private information and for accepting personalized advertisements in someone's social space were very different in 2004, in the early stages of Web 2.0 space, than in 2012. Changes were implemented gradually, and while users got habituated to new features, the norms for privacy and accepting monetization were stretched accordingly. It is precisely these changes I am interested in: how they occur through specific platforms and how they affect online sociality as such.

Normalization occurs detectably, through various levels of adjustments, including technology features and terms of use. But it mostly happens imperceptibly, through gradual transformations of user habits and changing levels of acceptance. In addition, norms are diffuse, as they have strikingly different effects on individual users, particularly users from different generations. Pete and Sandra showed dissimilar levels of appropriation; their children's experience of online sociality, for their part, is also very different from their parents'. For Nick and Zara, the use of social media is fully "normalized" in their everyday lives; not having gone through the early evolutionary stages, they accept these platforms as *conditions* for social interaction and are less likely to challenge their underpinnings. Once new technologies and their use have gained a naturalized presence, it is much harder to identify underlying principles and thus question their raison d'être.

Hence, new norms for sociality and values of connectivity are not the outcome but the very *stakes* in the battle to conquer the vast new territory of connective media and cultivate its fertile grounds. Instead of identifying how Facebook violates privacy laws or how Google's legal transgressions correlate with its monetizing schemes, my aim is to trace disputed definitions of *what counts as* private or public, formal or informal, collaborative or exploitative, mainstream or alternative—arguments that are part of an ongoing clash between user tactics and platform strategies (van Dijck 2011). The battle described and analyzed has implications for society and culture at large. Norms are part and parcel of a larger culture that is infused with historical circumstances and political conditions. Legal scholar Julie Cohen suggests that culture "is not a fixed collection of texts and practices, but rather an emergent, historically and materially contingent process through which understandings of self and society are formed and re-formed." To underscore the relevance of the ideological forces at work in this dynamic and the theoretical thrust of its essential openness, she adds:

> The process of culture is shaped by the self-interested actions of powerful institutional actors, by the everyday practices of individuals and communities, and by ways of understanding and describing the world that have complex histories of their own. The lack of fixity at the core of this conception of culture does not undermine its explanatory utility; to the contrary, it is the origin of culture's power. (Cohen 2012, 17)

The "explanatory utility" of the culture of connectivity is to help us understand social media's historical expansion, the disputes arising in the process, and the normative changes in which they result, even if the outcome is transitory.

Several aspects of this culture will be highlighted in this book. First and foremost, it is a culture inundated by coding technologies whose implications go well beyond the digital architectures of platforms themselves. Sociality is not simply "rendered technological" by moving to an online space; rather, coded structures are profoundly altering the nature of our connections, creations, and interactions. Buttons that impose "sharing" and "following" as social values have effects in cultural practices and legal disputes, far beyond platforms proper. Second, it is a culture where the organization of social exchange is staked on neoliberal economic principles. Connectivity derives from a continuous pressure—both from peers and from technologies—to expand through competition and gain power through strategic alliances. Platform tactics such as the popularity principle and ranking mechanisms hardly involve contingent technological structures; instead, they are firmly rooted in an ideology that values hierarchy, competition, and a winner-takes-all mind-set. And third, the culture of connectivity evolves as part of a longer historical transformation characterized by a resetting of boundaries between private, corporate, and public domains. The steady weakening in recent decades of the public sector and its gradual takeover by corporations forms a necessary backdrop for understanding the momentum for fast-growing connective media. Historically, neoliberal clashes with social-democratic ideologies often revolved around questions of the freedom of individuals and corporations vis-à-vis the responsibilities of communities and states. Platform owners' calls for more transparency and openness, for maximum sharing and frictionless online traffic, are entrenched in a neoliberal political agenda often advocating a downsizing of the public sector.

The struggle to define networked sociality and to impute new norms and meanings to this space began roughly in 2001 and still "lacks fixity," to reprise Julie Cohen's words. For practical reasons, May 2012 serves as the provisional endpoint of this study. If the aim is to understand how, in the intervening period, online sociality evolved, it is not enough to study individual platforms; rather, we need to apprehend how they coevolved in a larger context of interpenetrating platforms and to dissect the cultural logic undergirding this process. Therefore, I propose to look at distinct platforms as if they were *microsystems*. All platforms combined constitute what I call the *ecosystem of connective media*—a system that nourishes and, in turn, is nourished by social and cultural norms that simultaneously evolve in our everyday world. Each microsystem is sensitive to changes in other parts of the ecosystem: if Facebook changes its interface settings, Google reacts by tweaking its artillery of platforms; if participation in Wikipedia should wane, Google's algorithmic remedies could work wonders. It is important to map convolutions in this first formative stage of connective media's growth because it may teach us about current and future distribution of powers.

Over the past ten years, several (groups of) academics have taken on the study of singular platforms and reviewed their varied manifestations. Needless to say, Google, Twitter, Facebook, and others have been the subject of numerous laudatory "inside" stories—mostly attempts to translate a platform's commercial power to interested users or small businesses, or to satisfy people's curiosity about how things work inside "the plex."[18] Some platforms have received ample academic attention from scholars analyzing their technological and operational complexities.[19] Furthermore, there have also been a number of general critical studies that examine the Web's technological specificities (Galloway 2004) or look at media ecologies as emergent technical, sociopolitical, or historical systems (Fuller 2005; Lovink 2012; Gitelman 2008). Last but not least, there are a few excellent studies mapping the political and economic significance of social media and focusing on how they leverage power at the levels of grassroots activists, governments, and corporations (Morozov 2011; Castells 2009; Fuchs 2011b). All these studies, as well as a score of others, provide valuable input for the argument developed in this book.

The particular approach adopted in *The Culture of Connectivity* is aimed at providing a critical history of roughly the first decade of connective media, relating the analyses of five specific platforms to the larger ecosystem and the culture in which it evolved. Rather than recounting or discounting the success of these platforms, I try to articulate their specificities as well as their differences by tracking their evolution. Dissecting these platforms to find the principles of their anatomy, I will be looking for differences and similarities in the way they function and operate. How did individual platforms code and brand specific niches of everyday life? What specific user functions did they develop, and how did users respond to a platform's changing technologies? How are the tactics and mechanisms of individual platforms interrelated? On what ideological or political assumptions do they operate? What social and cultural norms underpin the ecosystem of connective media, how have they changed, and what role did (and still do) users and owners play in this transformation? Such questions require not just a comparative analysis of single platforms but also a connective approach. Designing such an approach partly forms the challenge of this study.

The ecosystem of connective media, as it has progressed since the turn of the millennium, has comprised hundreds of players, engaged millions of users, and affected both local and global normative and legal schemes. To this day, the larger technological infrastructure on which social media platforms are built is still volatile, and few, if any, platforms have yet attained a stabilized meaning or standardized use in the context of this unstable ecosystem (Feenberg 2009). I do not pretend in any way to cover the territory in its entirety, but by tracing the fortunes of five prominent platforms—Facebook, Twitter, Flickr, YouTube, and Wikipedia—I hope to offer a systematic framework for understanding their interdependent development.[20] The last chapter will particularly address the connections between microsystems and ecosystem: how do all platforms interconnect in an infrastructure that is increasingly compartmentalized? And how do they live up to promises of making the Web more social and the world more transparent? As we look into the future, the trend of engineered platforms permeating our everyday lives will only gain significance with the dazzling expansion of mobile apps and devices. The ecosystem, too, adds importance in the wake of technological developments such as "Big Data" processing. The year 2012 configures a momentary link between the first decade of maturing platformed sociality and the next decade of a projected Semantic Web with automated connectivity at its core.[21]

Notwithstanding the Alvins, this book does *not* depict the microbehaviors of users or the quotidian activities of families at one moment in history. It is rather about the ways in which social media have permeated manifestations of sociality and creativity in the (Western) world over the past decade. Teenagers and young adults can no longer imagine organizing their social lives without Facebook at its center; news organizations have accepted Twitter as one of their principal sources of breaking news; a pop band that ignores the potency of YouTube's viral videos might as well denounce its fan base; Flickr and Facebook have become global distribution centers of digital snapshots; and few students would still be able to write a term paper without access to Wikipedia—or Google Scholar or Search, for that matter. *The Culture of Connectivity* aims to offer an analytical model to elucidate how platforms have become central forces in the construction of sociality, how owners and users have helped shape and are shaped by this construction; in other words, it wants to enhance a historical understanding of social media's impact on the everyday lives of families like the Alvins.

When critically examining the history of platforms and the ecosystem through which they evolve, we need to create a functional anatomical instrument, a multilayered analytical prism that allows us to see more than just a technological platform deployed by users and run by owners. Since there is neither a ready-made analytical model nor a clear-cut theory to tackle this phenomenon consistently and systematically, the next chapter sketches the outlines of a multilayered approach to social media.

CHAPTER 2

Disassembling Platforms, Reassembling Sociality

2.1. INTRODUCTION

When Steve Jobs introduced iTunes in January 2001, he knew it was not just a piece of music-management software that turned the computer into a digital hub.[1] Eight months later, the advent of the iPod incarnated a whole new social routine of playing and listening to recorded music—a major leap from the listening experience introduced by the Sony Walkman in the 1980s. Apple showed the advantages of integrated development of hardware and software when it came to controlling the end-user experience. The iPod/iTunes ensemble also inaugurated a new cultural form, the first since the long-play album: the single song became the preferred unit of music recording because the device favored user-compiled playlists and random "shuffles" over traditional artistic forms. In other words, the development of technology—hardware, software, and design—was intricately intertwined with a changing user experience and a restyling of content.

In hindsight, iTunes and the iPod inducted a major transformation of the music industry, including its conventional monetizing schemes. When the MP3 player turned out to be a big consumer hit, the iTunes Store opened its virtual doors in 2003. Apple's CEO went to great lengths to cajole artists, the content industry, and copyright holders in the music business to join his effort to counter the exploding practice of illegal downloading promoted by systems like Napster. As a result, a new business model saw the light: for 99 cents per song, consumers could download as many favorites as they wanted to their mobile devices, causing a turnaround in the consumer culture of online listening. In the ensuing years,

UGC-services and online distributors, which besides iTunes also included Myspace (2003), Spotify (2006), SoundCloud (2007), Google Music (2011), and a large score of smaller platforms, totally changed the scene of music production and distribution. They competed not only with each other but also bartered new relationships with old-style music industries, artists, and consumers. Ten years after its start, the iTunes platform has become the world's leading vendor of popular music.

The short history of this microsystem exemplifies why the development of new technologies is inseparable from the emergence of user practices and content, while at the same time it is impossible to disregard the platform's organizational level. iTunes and the iPod might have easily proved a failure without Apple's simultaneous reformation of its socioeconomic context: a business model and an online "store" concept to regulate mass distribution while customizing user profiles. In the process of developing its platform, Apple also helped change the economic and legal conditions for music production and distribution. iTunes procured itself a new niche amid a number of other emerging platforms. One microsystem turned out to have a profound impact on the larger ecosystem of connective media; competing platforms adapted to innovative schemes of content production and distribution, and their new business models in turn affected other fields besides music, most notably publishing, television, and news.

The mutual shaping of microsystems and ecosystem constitutes the nucleus of this study. A multifaceted phenomenon like social media offers quite a challenge to existing models for media analysis, which, as I explained in the previous chapter, tend to separate user-technology interaction from the organizational socioeconomic structure. The intimate intertwining of both levels, as well as the dynamics between microsystems and ecosystem, is hard to pinpoint in a single theory or analytical framework. Two theoretical approaches that inspired this book, actor-network theory and political economy, offer valid perspectives on the transformation of technology and society, and their combination informs the design of a heuristic model. This model comprises of two configurations. The first helps to *disassemble microsystems*. By taking apart single platforms into their constitutive components, we may combine the perspectives on platforms as techno-cultural constructs and as organized socioeconomic structures. But disassembling platforms is not enough: we also need to *reassemble the ecosystem* of interoperating platforms in order to recognize which norms and mechanisms undergird the *construction of sociality and creativity*.

A connective approach aimed at disassembling platforms and reassembling sociality can hardly succeed if we fail to take into account the larger cultural matrix in which this assemblage emerged. Every tweak in a platform sends ripples down the entire ecosystem of incumbent and novel media players, as evident in the iTunes example. Surely, even if a multilayered analysis is applied, it can never result in a complete scrutiny of the entire system, as each model generates its own myopia. And yet, if we do not choose such integrative analytical approach—if we restrict our perspective to one or two specific elements or one or two specific platforms or companies—we can hardly grasp the mutual shaping of social media and the culture of connectivity.

2.2. COMBINING TWO APPROACHES

When it comes to studying the complex dynamics of media constellations, actor-network theory (ANT) and political economy are seldom regarded as harmonious bedfellows because they operate on different levels: the first concentrates on coevolving networks of people and technologies, whereas the second accentuates the economic infrastructure and legal-political governance as conditions for networks to evolve. ANT, developed by Bruno Latour, Michel Callon, and John Law, supports a view of platforms as sociotechnical ensembles and performative infrastructures. ANT does not examine "the social" as such, but aims to map relations between technologies and people and tries to explain how these relations are both material and semiotic. Another major asset of ANT is that it acknowledges both human and nonhuman actors whose agencies help shape the interactive process, a process characterized by contingency and interpretive flexibility. Platforms, in this view, would not be considered artifacts but rather a set of relations that constantly need to be performed; actors of all kinds attribute *meanings* to platforms. According to ANT principles, a study of social media platforms incites questions such as these: "Which agencies are invoked? Which figurations are they endowed with? Through which modes of action are they engaged? Are we talking about causes and their intermediaries or about a concatenation of mediators?" (Latour 2005: 62). For these reasons, ANT is a useful source of inspiration when examining sociality in this formative stage of connective media's evolution.

Notwithstanding its amenities, ANT is also limited in terms of its *analytical* scope. For one thing, a Latourian perspective refuses an a priori distinction between technologies and their social dimension (user agency). While I certainly subscribe to this view on an ontological level, for analytical purposes it is often functional to distinguish between these actors if only to explain their indivisible yet changing relationship. In addition, ANT pays scarce attention to content or cultural form as a meaningful force in the construction of technology and users. In the context of social media, content and form are a significant factor, as we learn from the iPod example above: the single song and the random shuffle could simultaneously be regarded an attribute of technology, usage, *and* content. Finally, critics have objected that ANT hardly accounts for preexisting power structures in terms of the economic and legal matrix from which technologies arise; although I do not entirely agree on this point of contention, I do think that in the case of social media platforms it is inevitable to integrate economic and legal structures as formative factors from the very onset.[2]

Proponents of a political economy approach choose organizational (infra) structures as their main focus: they regard platforms and digital networks as manifestations of power relationships between institutional producers and individual consumers. Drawing upon economics, law, and political science, sociologist Manuel Castells (1996, 1997, 1998) theorizes the political-economic context in which informational networks could grow into powerful industrial players. In his later work, Castells (2009) contends that Web 2.0 is shaped by a clash between users asserting communicative and creative freedom and owners curbing users' newly acquired technological power. His analysis engages more with institutional agency than with user activity when he recommends that theory identify the "concrete social actors who are power holders" and "examine their global networking and their local workings" (Castells 2009: 430). Institutional actors may involve governments or corporations engaged in economic schemes (takeovers, mergers) or legal processes (lawsuits, regulation), but also political grassroots groups using social media as a means to counter power. The struggle to dominate the realm of social media is led by power holders called "programmers"—those who program networks and platforms—and "switchers"—those who have the ability to connect and ensure cooperation of different networks. In other words, individuals, groups, and organizations can all resist power holders.

Castells's political economy of networks complements ANT at precisely the economic-legal junction. Yet despite the fact that Castells's approach accounts for preexisting power structures, his approach lacks the ability of ANT to expose how power is executed from technological and computational systems, for example, interfaces or coding systems for file sharing. Whereas actor-network theory provides the analytical armamentarium necessary to understand both the technology itself and its integration with human interaction, Castells's political economy goes straight to the institutional level of power wielding.[3] Moreover, Castells's theoretical apparatus, for all its benefits, could never leverage insight into the question of sociality: What is "social" about social media? How do platforms shape and penetrate different kinds of sociality? What does it mean when "power holders" claim they want to make the Web more social and that privacy is just an evolving norm? How do "programmers" actually encode sociality, and how do users resist or bend imputed meanings? In other words, institutional power structures *alone* do not yield insights into how platforms evolve in tandem with their users and content; mutatis mutandis, sociotechnical ensembles *alone* do not explain the larger power relationships vital to their development. ANT offers sublime insights on the sociotechnical level, but limits its scope of actors to technologies and users while disregarding content and organizational structures. Political economists, for their part, focus on socioeconomic power struggles between owners and users, but technologies and content are likely to escape their radar. Moreover, both approaches tend to understate the significance of cultural values and social norms that build a scaffold for the struggle for dominance in this arena.

Which brings me back to the focus of this book: understanding the coevolution of social media platforms and sociality in the context of a rising culture of connectivity. Actor-network theory and the political economy approach each by itself offer a partial analysis of the dynamic intricacies of platforms. However, combining these perspectives and complementing this symbiosis with several additional elements may help inform the multilayered model proposed in this book. The first part of this model concentrates on the dissection of individual platforms (microsystems) as both *techno-cultural constructs* and *socioeconomic structures*. Each level will spotlight three constitutive elements or actors—elements systematically followed throughout all case studies. Approaching platforms as sociotechnical constructs, we need to analyze technology, users, and content in close alignment; highlighting platforms as socioeconomic structures, we will scrutinize their ownership status, governance, and business models (see figure 2.1).

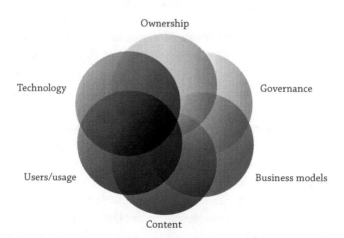

Figure 2.1: Disassembling platforms as microsystems

Before we systematically connect the level of microsystem to the larger ecosystem, the next two sections describe each of these six constitutive elements in more detail.

2.3. PLATFORMS AS TECHNO-CULTURAL CONSTRUCTS

Technology

The term "platform," as Tarlton Gillespie (2010) lucidly explains, carries multiple meanings: platforms are computational and architectural concepts, but can also be understood figuratively, in a sociocultural and a political sense, as political stages and performative infrastructures.[4] Borrowing terminology from actor-network theory, a platform is a *mediator* rather than an intermediary: it shapes the performance of social acts instead of merely facilitating them. Technologically speaking, platforms are the providers of software, (sometimes) hardware, and services that help code social activities into a computational architecture; they process (meta)data through algorithms and formatted protocols before presenting their interpreted logic in the form of user-friendly interfaces with default settings that reflect the platform owner's strategic choices.

As far as the first part of the definition is concerned, this book will primarily focus on the software and services turning social activities into computational architectures, paying scarce attention to hardware or design.[5] Software studies experts have repeatedly underscored the social and cultural importance of coding technologies. Matthew Fuller (2008) and David Berry (2011) emphasize that understanding code requires sensitivity to its changing manifestations as well as to its historically changing technical milieu.[6] As software increasingly structures the world, "it also withdraws, and it becomes harder and harder for us to focus on as it is embedded, hidden, off-shored and merely forgotten about" (Berry 2011: 4). The challenge is to make the hidden layer visible and show *how* software is increasingly quantifying and measuring our social and everyday lives; software helps translate our social actions into computer language and, vice versa, execute computer language into social action.[7] For instance, Amazon codes customer's taste preferences and buying behavior, and LinkedIn codes connections between professionals or job seekers and employers; next, both platforms translate these encoded social activities into programmed directives to steer user behavior.

If we take apart the second part of the above definition, we can distinguish five significant concepts that help unpack the technological dimension:

(meta)data, *algorithm*, *protocol*, *interface*, and *default*. These terms have in common meanings that carry beyond the technological realm into the social and the cultural.[8] Basic resources for coding technologies are *data* and *metadata*. Data can be any type of information in a form suitable for use with a computer, for example, text, image, sound, and numbers. Data may also be personal profile facts, such as name, gender, date of birth, and zip code, commonly provided by users following a site's protocol for registering and entering. Metadata contain structured information to describe, explain, and locate information resources or otherwise make it easier to retrieve, use, or manage them.[9] Examples of manually provided metadata are tags that YouTubers attach to their video entries, such as keywords on content and genre. Automatically derived metadata include geospatial and time stamps—information that is transmitted when pictures from digital cameras are downloaded to Flickr, Picasa, or other online photo sites. Metadata also derive from cookies planted without a user's consent; cookies may mine behavioral data relating to search histories or browse strategies, and connect these data to specific IP addresses.

At least some technical comprehension of data and metadata is required to conceive of the huge legal, social, and political implications of coding technologies in the context of social media. Automated or embedded metadata continue to be a source of legal battles over consumer rights versus owners' rights. For instance, some national laws now require music CDs to carry a layer of metadata containing name of artist, genre, copyright owner, and recording dates, so these can be automatically recognized when illegally downloaded. Control over (meta)data is often the cause of heated debates over user rights; for example, are sites such as LinkedIn allowed to sell to advertisers, employers, governments, or intelligence agencies data (un)consciously delivered by their members? If Twitter's uploads contain automatic geostamps and time stamps, is the site allowed to use them for tracking users' whereabouts, for instance by yielding information to help law enforcement? And what say do Facebook users have over profiling data the platform requires all of its users to make public? These are just a few examples of how platforms can use (meta)data to encode sociality at the same time and by the same means that they may exploit them.

Apart from their ability to collect (meta)data, the computational power of social media platforms lies in their capability to include *algorithms* for processing data. An algorithm, in computer science, is a finite list of well-defined instructions for calculating a function, a step-by-step directive for processing or automatic reasoning that orders the machine to produce a certain output from given input. For instance, Amazon deploys algorithms that aggregate millions of pieces of (meta)data—customer's profiling data,

data about buying behavior, and content they bought—to calculate the relations between taste and buyer's preference. Amazon's recommendation system—famous through its marketing slogan: "Customers who bought this item, also bought . . ."—is the direct result of algorithmic processing. But the taste recommendation system Amazon employs comprises more than automated output: algorithms infiltrate a social (trans)action by means of computational data analysis, upon which the outcome is translated into a commercial-social tactic. Algorithms are often proprietary trade secrets, akin to patents or other kinds of intellectual property.

Besides deploying algorithms, a platform's coded architecture makes use of *protocols*. Protocols are formal descriptions of digital message formats complemented by rules for regulating those messages in or between computing systems. According to American media theorist Alexander Galloway (2004: 121), protocols are technical sets of rules that gain their usability from how they are *programmed* and how they are *governed* or managed by their owners. Governing protocols provide a set of instructions that users are forced to obey if they want to partake in the mediated flow of interaction. For instance, because Facebook wants you to share information with as many people as possible, the platform scripts actions such as joining lists, groups, and fan pages. Facebook's protocols guide users through its preferred pathways; they impose a hegemonic logic onto a mediated social practice. However, users may also subvert or resist this inscribed logic, for instance by tinkering with a platform's software or designing subversive apps. Protocological control by platform owners often meets protocological resistance from defiant users—a subject I will return to shortly.

Protocols hide behind invisible or visible *interfaces*. Internal interfaces are concealed from the user, who can only see the front end, or the visible interface. An invisible, internal interface links software to hardware and human users to data sources (Fuller 2008: 149). Platform owners, evidently, control the internal interface; changes they make to the internal interface do not necessarily show in the icons and features visible to users. Some platforms, like Flickr and Twitter, allow users or third parties free or paid access to their data sets in order to develop so-called application program interfaces (APIs)—a set of codes that specifies protocolized relations between data, software, and hardware. Visible user interfaces commonly contain technical features (e.g., buttons, scroll bars, stars, icons) as well as regulatory features (e.g., the rule that a personal profile is required before entering the site), and these features actively steer connections between users and content. Interfaces, both internal and visible, are an area of control where the meaning of coded information gets translated into directives for specific user actions.

Finally, interfaces are commonly characterized by *defaults*: settings automatically assigned to a software application to channel user behavior in a certain way. Defaults are not just technical but also ideological maneuverings; if changing a default takes effort, users are more likely to conform to the site's decision architecture. A notorious default is Facebook's setting to distribute a message to everyone, rather than to friends only (Lipford, Besmer, and Watson 2008; Stutzman and Kramer-Duffield 2010). Presets are thus conscious efforts to cajole users into a certain routine: setting a default to sharing all pictures with everyone or preselecting a certain browser embodies the owners' interest.[10] Defaults are often the literal stakes in the battle for social meanings, most prominently in legal disputes over privacy or in disputes with users over information control.

From the description of these features it becomes clear that, in line with ANT contentions, technology and user agency can hardly be told apart, given that they are inseparable. Media theorist David Beer calls the powerful, oblique, and only partially visible information apparatus that has come to produce everyday life the "technological unconscious." He points to the potent, active technological environments that operate "without the knowledge of those upon whom they are taking an effect" (Beer 2009: 990). Algorithms, protocols, and defaults profoundly shape the cultural experiences of people active on social media platforms, and although it is true that users are often insufficiently aware of the mechanisms upon which their communicative practices are predicated (Skageby 2009), they are not "dupes" of technology or uncritical adopters. To adequately describe these tensions, it is functional to regard user agency not as an actor distinct from technology, but as an analytical category that requires delineation on its own terms.

Users and Usage

User agency, in the context of social media, is a complex and multifaceted concept, not least because it encompasses both conscious human activity and the "technological unconscious." In addition, users are recipients and consumers, producers and participants of culture; they may be considered amateurs and citizens as well as professionals and laborers (van Dijck 2009). Debates concerning the distinct contribution of users to online communities and identity formation via platforms pertain to ideological debates on issues: Do social media platforms stimulate active participation and civic engagement, or has collectivity become a synonym for automated connectivity? To what extent are users empowered or constrained by platforms to fashion their unique identity and stylize their self-presentation? Rather than solving these ideological debates here, I explore the leverage of user agency in shaping online social norms. Similar to a platform's coding strategies, user agency is a negotiated and embattled concept, and the power of users to control their actions is an important stake.

Online sociality has increasingly become a coproduction of humans and machines. Analyzing user agency as a techno-cultural construct requires a conceptual distinction between implicit and explicit user participation (Schaefer 2011: 51). *Implicit* participation is the *usage* inscribed in the engineer's design by means of the coding mechanisms described in the previous section.[11] *Explicit* use refers to how real or actual users interact with social media. However, the term "explicit users" may be operationalized in a number of different ways. First, it refers to a demographic or statistical conception: websites, for instance, publish facts and figures about their user intensity (e.g., unique monthly users), their national and global user diversity, and relevant demographic facts (gender, age, income class, nationality, etc.). A second type of explicit user is the experimental subject. For instance, a number of users may be selected to perform tasks so researchers can observe their ability to control privacy settings (Leon et al. 2011). Third, explicit users figure as ethnographic subjects: their usage of social media may be observed and analyzed in situ; they may also be interviewed about their habits or practical use (boyd and Ellison 2007; Cox, Clough, and Marlow 2008; Stutzman and Kramer-Duffield 2010). This book does *not* actively pursue the acquisition of demographic, experimental, or ethnographic data on users and their behavior, although it respectfully incorporates results of academic research involving these types of users.

In light of this book's central project—understanding the coevolution of social media platforms and sociality in the context of a rising culture of connectivity—I will concentrate on one specific type of user agency: articulated user *responses*. Over the past decade, users have actively responded to changes in social media, often publicly communicating these reactions through web publications, blogs, or social media content.[12] Most commonly, these responses are spontaneous comments of users reacting to platform changes that affect their online experience. Pleased users tend to comply with platform-imposed alterations, leaving few remarks, but critical responses may take many forms. Manually changing a default setting could be regarded the mildest form of defiance, just like filling out false profiling information. By actively tinkering with applications or hacking the site, users modify their technical environment as a form of social protest. Users' ultimate leverage is to quit the site altogether or join a competing platform. Each single user exploit is an act of appropriation or one of defiance. The confrontation between implicit usage and explicit use embodies part of a negotiation process between platform owners and users to control the conditions for information exchange; such struggle also bares disputed norms and values. Technology shapes sociality as much as sociality shapes technology; we can partly trace this process through user reactions.

During the first decade of social media's rise, users fiercely debated platforms' power to reconfigure sociality and to influence identity formation. Users value UGCs and SNSs as means to express themselves and present themselves to others; platforms empower individuals by enabling them to connect with lots of friends, control their self-presentation or make them belong to a community. Comparative studies of platforms have shown how different sites' architectures cultivate distinct styles of connectedness, self-presentation, and taste performance (Papacharissi 2009; Luders 2008). By the same token, platform's architectures are engineered to control user agency: most platform owners have a vested interest in knowing users' "true" identity, their preferences, and behavioral data. Most major SNSs prohibit the use of fake names or anonymous identities (Facebook, Google+), even though there are also sites (e.g., Last.fm) that encourage the deployment of aliases, pseudonyms, and multiple identities, resulting in different configurations of identity or self-representation (Baym 2010; Haythornthwaite and Kendall 2010). Notions of individuality, privacy, community, and identity are often expressed in user responses, making them rather relevant to the larger battle over information control.

The analytical case studies in this book also highlight explicit users as they respond to issues of platforms' changing ownership status or monetizing strategies—elements that will be further elaborated in the next section of this chapter. Changes in ownership status or management, especially of those platforms that were initiated by user communities, have elicited emphatic user reactions over the years. Responses often contain explicit judgments on what counts as "collective" or "exploitative" if users compare newly introduced business models or revamped privacy rules to older ones. Altered terms of use often give rise to reassessment of a user's relationship with a platform, thus revealing more about the stakes involved in users' and owners' negotiation of norms and values. User engagement may also manifest itself in a claim to partial ownership of contributed content or a claim to control one's data. In short, explicit user responses to specific platform changes articulated over the years provide relevant source material, serving a historical analysis of platforms.

Content

Content is often overlooked as a constitutive element in social media, and yet it is an important element to distinguish, even if its manifestation is often tied up with technology and user agency. Between 2000 and 2006, when social media platforms first evolved, user-based UGC sites were generally welcomed as vehicles for expansive creativity and amateur-produced cultural content. UGC platforms like YouTube, Flickr, and Myspace gave an unprecedented boost to the online production and distribution of multimodal content—videos, photos, text, and music. Platform-channeled content inspired new genres and forms, such as the "webisode" for online video. The sharing of content enhances connectedness between people and also helps many acquire a (global) stage for public viewing. More than anything, *cultural* content—whether text, music, or videos—draws out opinions on what people like or dislike, what they covet or loathe, what interests them and what does not. And while common tastes and desires can be deployed to harness bonds and discover group affiliations, they also provide precious information on social trends and consumer preferences.

Users and owners share the objective of having "good content" flow sinuously through the ecosystem's arteries, but their interests also diverge. First of all, where users favor multiple forms and formats, platforms prefer standardization of content and uniform deliverance. YouTube and Facebook, for instance, allow users to upload videos of limited length, Twitter administers a 140-character restriction upon its users' verbal expressions, and LinkedIn imposes a chronological CV layout on every member's home page. Some degree of standardization is important to facilitate connectedness—helping people find content—but also to enhance connectivity: algorithmic steering works better if input is uniform. When looking at social media platforms developing over time, we can discern gradual changes in the presentation of content through the implementation of interface features. In their responses, users often comment on the pros and cons of these imposed changes, revealing value judgments and thus insights into the politics of cultural form.

Debates on content's specific cultural form are staked on claims about its materiality: user-generated content is considered unfinished, recyclable input, in contrast to the polished finished products of mainstream media. Implied in these debates is the distinction between amateur and professional content. Definitions of content's status often figure in legal clashes concerning copyright and intellectual ownership; beneath these legal challenges are normative debates between users, creators, platform owners, and industrial producers that give us insight into *what counts* as content, who *owns* and *controls* it. For many platform owners, content is just another word for data; they are particularly interested in the quantity of data streams that flow through their channels, which they can treat as aggregated and computational resources.

Technology, user agency, and content are three fibers that platforms weave together in order to create the fabric of online sociality. As evidenced by the description above, these techno-cultural actors can hardly be separated from the socioeconomic structure through which a platform operates, so let us look more closely at three elements that constitute this layer: ownership status, governance, and business models.

2.4. PLATFORMS AS SOCIOECONOMIC STRUCTURES

Ownership

A platform's ownership model is a constitutive element in its functioning as a system of production. While a number of platforms were commercial adventures from the beginning, the ownership status of many social media platforms, as described in the previous chapter, changed over time from nonprofit, collectively owned, user-centered organizations to for-profit, corporate owner-centered enterprises. On one end of the spectrum, we can identify sites launched by small start-ups that rapidly grew into global firms, for example, Facebook and Twitter. Facebook's initial public offering (IPO) in May 2012 signified an important change in ownership status: the company's leaders now have to yield power to investors, likely at the expense of users who loathe the growing pressure to increase the site's profitable prospects. Twitter is still contemplating the move to "go public." On the other end of the spectrum, there are sites that are nonprofit and nonmarket; a few sites have tried an in-between status.[13] Each microsystem's analysis will raise specific questions with regard to its ownership status and structure: How did a brand evolve in the market or in the nonprofit realm? What image of their platform do owners cherish, and does this image live up to users' evaluation and appreciation of their platform?

Ownership status is a significant bargaining chip in the volatile ecosystem of networked media. New start-ups are added every day, and successful ones are bought and sold by "established" companies—the term seems to apply awkwardly in an industrial sector that is itself barely older than a decade—for sometimes staggering sums.[14] A large, active, and demographically interesting user base is usually a platform's most precious asset. The value of a social media company is often articulated as value per customer—a price that is often speculative and always volatile.[15] Besides expanding their user bases, companies like Google and Facebook constantly fish for takeover bait to annex engineering expertise or valuable algorithms and patents owned by other companies. In the case of Google, the vertical integration of search engines, operating systems, browsers, user-based software systems, online advertising systems, content providers, and a host of other functions guarantees more control over the end-user experience and hence over user data.[16]

Although mergers and takeovers are part of the dog-eat-dog culture in Silicon Valley, a new variant of the takeover is partnership. Partnerships are agreements between platforms and other digital media companies or API-based services to implement the other's buttons and get access to the other's data stream. Facebook, for instance, announced partnerships with music-streaming site Spotify and video-chatting service Skype to promote a seamless user experience; obviously, these partnerships are also aimed at making databases mutually profitable. Another type of partnership can be noticed in terms of vertical integration: online social media teaming up with "old media," particularly in the publishing and television industries, such as Facebook's alliance with NBC during the Olympic Games in London in 2012. Tracing connective corporate moves and partnerships can often be quite a challenge, as companies seem reluctant to release details about their corporate governance; nevertheless, it is important to trace power relationships in the ever-expanding ecosystem of connective media to identify how institutional structures control social enactment.

On the nonprofit end of the scale, it is equally important to dissect a platform's operational management. Ownership status—whether a platform is or should be publicly governed, community based, nonprofit based, or corporately owned—is a bone of contention in the debate over who controls social processes. Just as genes and herbs used to be common resources squarely belonging to the public sphere before they were appropriated by biotech and pharmaceutical industries, all kinds of sociality are currently moving from public to corporate space; even as little as ten years ago, the coding of social actions into proprietary algorithms, let alone the branding and patenting of these processes, would have been unthinkable. Today, Facebook, Google, Amazon, and Twitter all own algorithms that increasingly determine what we like, want, know, or find. Battles over ownership of software and hardware are at the heart of much more profound debates on what constitutes public, nonprofit, or corporate space, especially at a time when distinctions between those spaces are ideologically besieged.

To analyze the governance structure of a social media site, one needs to understand *how*, through what mechanisms, communication and data traffic are managed. In the early days of Web 2.0, users often patrolled their own sites, relying on few rules. The majority of platforms, once taken over by corporations, gradually implemented professional and (semi)automated forms of governance. Content management systems consist of technical protocols, as described in the previous section, and *social* protocols—implicit or explicit rules to manage user activities. Explicit rules also serve to regulate claims in the realm of property, privacy, and acceptable behavior and are commonly articulated through end-user license agreements (EULAs) or terms of service (ToS).

A EULA or ToS is a contractual relationship that users enter into every time they log on to a platform, and these contracts impose restraints and obligations. They touch upon a real-world realm where social norms concerning property rights, identification, privacy, and sanctions for misconduct are inscribed into laws. And yet EULAs and ToS are not laws. They constitute a gray area where interested parties are engaged in (re)setting the norms for privacy, property, and proper behavior, such as prohibiting the posting of explicit sexual and racist content or unilaterally denying service to users who deviate from certain rules. Like algorithms and user agency, a site's terms of service are an arena for setting and contending social norms, a struggle that may eventually affect legal rulings (Grimmelmann 2009). Such focus triggers the question of how control is performed: How are norms inscribed in ToS clauses? How are they negotiated and disputed?

EULAs and terms of service are often left unread before users click-to-agree; users enter into numerous online actions per day, and yet they barely know the traffic regulations (Madejski, Johnson, and Bellovin 2011). Facebook's privacy policy, for one thing, is known to be more complicated and longer than the U.S. Constitution. Even without reading the rules, though, Facebook users encounter changes in governance through altered interfaces, usually without formal notice from the platform's owner—a tactic that has angered users and consumer groups. Modifications in governance are thus intricately intertwined with changes in technology, user agency, and content. A site's governance rules are not set in stone: they are a constant target of negotiation, for instance when protesting user groups have a rule withdrawn or when they subvert particular policies.[17]

Besides privacy and proper behavior, terms of service also rule the use of metadata by service providers and third parties. Most terms of service include clauses about the platform owner's right to use or sell (meta)data provided by users; few terms of service define the rights of users to access their data. In fact, by logging onto the site, users commonly agree to surrender their data for mining and reselling. Since online platforms are a relatively new space for social traffic, the law does not yet cover all corners of this territory; consequently, the boundaries of what the law allows and what users accept are constantly tested. Complicating the issue is that laws arise in national and thus culturally specific contexts. Germany, for instance, has tougher privacy laws than the United States. Of course, terms of service are routinely adjusted to national customs, but the global reach of most platforms gives owners a vast advantage over states when it comes to regulation. Control over ToS is primarily in the hands of owners, who can adjust conditions at any time, without users' prior consent.

Business Models

What holds for governance also pertains to business models: they are *mediators* in the engineering of culture and everyday life. Over the past decade, the emphasis in the cultural industry sector has shifted from products to services, pressing media companies to develop new ways of monetizing online creativity and sociality. During most of the twentieth century, the cultural industry sector thrived on the mass production of standardized consumption goods, such as books, records, and films. Traditionally, there were three main ways of making money on cultural products: profits derived from sales of reproduced goods (CDs, books, DVDs), profits from viewing or subscription fees (TV programs, cinema, video rental), and profits derived from advertising, which is basically the selling of audience attention juxtaposed to, or interspersed with, cultural or entertainment content.

With the advent of the Internet, and particularly the arrival of Web 2.0 platforms, the industrial logic of mass-reproduced cultural goods was radically uprooted; products became virtual, and downloads were a hard sell because they did not fit the conventional definition of "product." Apple's iTunes was one of the first attempts to actually sell downloads of songs as commodities, also pricing them as products. It took some arguing from the side of the industry to define (legal) downloads as salable objects, just as CDs were initially considered of lesser value than vinyl records. The value of content's materiality is relative and changes with the advent of new digital incarnations: downloads are in turn regarded as more "tangible" and thus more vendible than streamed content.

More problematic was social media's revamping of business models based on viewing or subscription fees—a model that ill suited a culture mired in user participation and accustomed to free content and services. Some UGC-sites experimented with subscription models, charging a (low) monthly fee for unlimited access; other sites introduced the so-called free-mium model, running a "free" model sustained by advertising alongside an advertising-free subscription model for "premium" users. As economist Clemons (2009) rightly points out, social media's business models are a delicate harmonizing act between users' trust and owners' monetizing intentions. If users feel that they are being manipulated or exploited, they simply quit the site, causing the platform to lose its most important asset.[18]

The model of free user services and free content was only sustainable through advertising—a model earlier developed by traditional broadcast media and firmly grounded in the attention economy. However, economies of scale became economies of scope, forcing media companies and advertising agencies to reconsider the very principles undergirding the attention economy (Vukanovic 2009; Doyle 2002). Conventional advertising strategies appealing to mass audiences no longer applied to a world dominated by user-generated content and social networking; in online social environments populated by "friends," users neither expected nor tolerated commercial activities. So for the first few years, online platforms avoided the use of pop-up ads, out of fear for massive user discontentment.

Yet the same technologies that impeded mass advertising also enabled the development of automated customization and personalization. The perusal of (meta)data computed into customized taste profiles rendered advertising more effective and targeted than previous models of mass media advertising. Customized ads appearing as banners or running in sidebars became popular rapidly, but were about the least innovative strategies introduced by social media. More insidious were personal recommendations by contacts and "friends": having a product recommended by a friend, after all, is more effective than a product promoted by advertising. Seeking out "influencers"—people with a large network of connected followers and friends—to promote products online is now a common marketing strategy. Ad culture is gradually turning into a recommendation culture, as new tactics still appear every day.

Besides selling virtual products, subscriptions, and advertising models, digital media companies explore a score of other business models relating to the exploitation of data and metadata. Platform owners have become acutely aware of the valuable resource that streams through their pipelines everyday. Sophisticated mathematical models for analyzing aggregated data and predicting social trends are turning the incessant flow of data into a potentially lucrative connective resource. It is important, though, to view monetizing strategies not as static models of exploitation, but as dynamic mediators in the process of shaping sociality and creativity.

As social media platforms evolve, business models are constantly tweaked and changed to test their evolutionary strength (Potts 2009). Platforms try different models in response to other players in the ecosystem while also experimenting to find out how much intrusion of their online social space users still find acceptable. Obviously, the norms for how much commercial activity users tolerate are gradually stretched and expanded to include new tactics and business models. Many users are well aware of a platform's commercial motives and profit-driven strategies, yet they still make calculated decisions whether to utilize it based on how much they will benefit. Therefore, for analytical purposes, we need to take into account not only the design and purpose of specific monetizing strategies, but also their effects on users as articulated in actual user responses.

2.5. CONNECTING PLATFORMS, REASSEMBLING SOCIALITY

The model for analyzing platforms as microsystems, as introduced in the previous sections, distinguishes two layers and six constitutive elements. However, the model's explanatory power lies not in these single elements, but in the connections between them. The interdependence of elements and layers shows, for instance, in the algorithms that inscribe user interaction, in terms of service that calibrate content, and in business models that steer interface architecture. Each platform implements an intricate scheme of coding and branding strategies to shape specific niches of online sociality. Only by taking apart a platform's constitutive elements does one start to see their integral performance. But decisions to change interfaces or to try new business models are hardly stand-alone choices; instead, platforms owners wield them as strategic instruments to carve out a niche vis-à-vis competing platforms. A company shapes its platform(s) as part of the larger constellation of competing and collaborating platforms. Therefore, it is important to scrutinize how microsystems respond to each other in the context of the larger ecosystem of connective media as well as of traditional media (television, music recording, media entertainment).

What characterizes the ecosystem most is the *interdependence* and *interoperability* of platforms. If the six constitutive elements are analyzed consistently throughout all platforms, we may reveal specific patterns in the ecosystem. Buttons for sharing, trending, following and favoriting are distinctly different, but they also share a common logic; the ubiquitous implementation of a competing platform's button signals not just a technological alignment but a strategic maneuver to boost user traffic and infiltrate user routines. For instance, the integration of Twitter's "trending" button in many platforms as well as traditional media such as television news and entertainment profoundly influences journalists' professional practices and user habits. Cross-platform integration of technologies and the mutual shaping of users and content indicate that microsystems can hardly be studied separately.

The interdependence of industries is played out on the socioeconomic level as well. Competition and collaboration are two, perhaps paradoxical, defining forces in the ecosystem of connective media. From the political economy perspective, competition has been related mostly to corporate structures of networks in order to explain processes of commodification.[19] Competition has also been associated with global information and communication market developments to describe processes of innovation (Cowhey and Aronson 2009). But competition and collaboration are not just restricted to the corporate or governance levels, but play out interchangeably on the level of technology and users. Reciprocal data exchange or mutually excluding coding features may ultimately shape distribution channels and fluidity of traffic or, for that matter, may define what content is accessed by whom. Identifying these patterns in the global dynamics of interdependent microsystems is a must for governments and citizens as they define their policy and legal strategies.

First dissecting specific platforms and then recombining their constitutive elements to detect larger patterns in the ecosystem is also crucial because it fosters broader questions concerning the shaping of sociality and society. Computer codes and business models reconfigure social norms; conversely, changing social norms also reshape how networking sites operate. Platforms engineer connectedness and connectivity by coding and branding online social activities, but these processes do not leave any of the agents involved intact. Users and owners are not the same in 2013 as they were in 2006 or 2002; business models and content have transformed along with governance policies and interfaces. Each single platform adjustment taps into a larger scheme of normative and regulatory change. What sort of private, public, and corporate space do these platforms occupy vis-à-vis each other, and how does their intersection affect our relative concepts of these spaces? How do various platforms' architectures and regulatory protocols influence society's legal norms, such as trust or privacy? How do platforms respond to each other's changes in monetizing schemes, and what are the mechanisms for sharing data? In short, this analytical model, rather than revealing what online sociality *is*, has been designed to explain how platforms and sociality mutually constitute each other.

One obvious problem with studying the phenomenon of social media is that it involves a multitude of probing angles that each bring along a different academic expertise. If we take the above questions seriously, we need insights from at least six disciplinary perspectives—information technology, social science, humanities, economics, law, and political communication—to open up a panoramic view onto social media. This could well lead to each perspective highlighting one single aspect of the phenomenon. Information scientists are intent on exploring large data sets provided by, for instance, YouTube or Flickr, in order to analyze and design algorithms; social scientists study data to detect patterns of user behavior; academics from the humanities commonly set their minds to examining content and cultural form; economists and MBAs zoom in on business models; legal scholars focus on issues of privacy and intellectual property; and political scientists or sociologists are concerned with social media's implications for the larger information order. Indeed, many of these disciplinary perspectives yield important research results and fascinating insights.[20] The problem, however, is that each discipline moves around in its own orbit of mutually incompatible vocabularies and methodologies.

I have proposed a combination of theoretical approaches, partly experimental, partly based on proven insights, to tackle the complex phenomenon of social media as they evolved; this blend of Latourian techno-cultural and Castells-inspired political economy views, resulting in a multilayered analytical model, may trigger objections of incongruity and inadequacy. Some might object that this approach is eclectic or methodologically daring. However, as legal scholar Julie Cohen (2012) fittingly observes: "In any serious study of the role of law in the networked information society, methodological eclecticism is not an indulgence; it's a necessity" (20). The proposed model is neither perfect nor all encompassing. And yet my preference for eclecticism is warranted by the need for a pragmatic analytical approach, a model that may offer economists, lawyers, policymakers, and information scientists a lens through which they can see the *cultural* presumptions and changing norms in which many debates are entrenched.

In the remainder of this book, I will put the multilayered model to work, first to disassemble five single platforms in their multiple dimensions—Facebook, Twitter, Flickr, YouTube, and Wikipedia—only to reassemble them in the context of their mutually sustaining surroundings and the culture of connectivity through which they advanced. By scrutinizing the construction of platforms in hindsight, we should attain a comprehensive view of how online sociality has evolved over the past decade. The ecosystem of connective media, as discussed in the last chapter, is not simply the sum of individual microsystems, but is rather a dynamic infrastructure that shapes and is shaped by culture at large. Such analysis is neither neutral nor arbitrary: it provokes questions pertinent to the ideology and politics underpinning this ecosystem. This investigation of the culture of connectivity will, I hope, clarify and sharpen the big questions regarding information control in the geographies and politics of networked space.

CHAPTER 3

Facebook and the Imperative of Sharing

3.1. INTRODUCTION

In May 2010, Mark Zuckerberg told *Time* reporter Dan Fletcher that Facebook's mission was to build a Web where "the default is social" in order to "make the world more open and connected." Other senior managers publicly underlined the company's ideal. Barry Schnitt, Facebook's director of corporate communications and public policy, revealed in an interview: "By making the world more open and connected, we're expanding understanding between people and making the world a more empathetic place." And Sheryl Sandberg, Facebook's chief operations officer, in an interview with the British *The Guardian* proclaimed: "We have really big aspirations around making the world a more open and transparent place; we define our aspirations more in terms of that mission than in terms of the company's aspirations." Facebook's mantra, that their mission is not just a corporate one but one pursued in society's interest, was endlessly repeated in the run-up to the company's initial public offering (IPO).[4]

With a claimed 835 million users worldwide in March 2012, Facebook is the largest social network site in the United States and in Europe, with the highest penetration among Internet users.[5] Size and dominance are certainly the most important reason for choosing Facebook as the first platform to dissect; what makes this choice even more compelling is that owners and users have been very outspoken in articulating norms for online social networking. The values of openness and connectedness are quintessentially reflected in the word favored most by Facebook's executives: *sharing*. In the context of connective media, sharing is an ambiguous term: it relates to users distributing personal information to each other, but also implies the spreading of that personal information to third parties. The social meaning of sharing is often pitched against the legal term "privacy," which Mark Zuckerberg peculiarly refers to in the same *Time* interview quoted from above as "an evolving norm." Used in contrast to openness, the word "privacy" connotes opacity, nontransparency, and secrecy. If analogized to connectedness, the term connotes individualism and a reluctance to share. Counter to Zuckerberg's claim, I argue that *sharing*, rather than privacy, is the evolving norm. This norm is not simply "out there" in society and reflected online. Instead, owners and users have been negotiating the meaning of sharing from the very start of the Harvard-based college network in 2004 up to its Nasdaq debut in 2012.

But how did a specific ideological meaning of sharing—along with "friending" and "liking"—become dominant during this period? Analyzed through the multilayered prism of six interdependent elements, the transformation of these terms becomes apparent. By implementing various coding technologies and interface strategies, Facebook inscribed how online social interaction should be conducted. Users, from the very onset, countered this steering with a mixture of compliance and resistance. In the ensuing struggle, formatted content, governance policies, and business models appeared prime tools for intervention. Facebook's ideology of sharing pretty much set the standard for other platforms and the ecosystem as a whole. Because of its leading position in the SNS segment, the platform's practices substantially influenced the social and cultural norms that bolster legal values such as privacy and control over data.

Changing the meaning of sharing turns out to be vital to altering legal rulings concerning privacy and to accepting new forms of monetization. Whereas the term "privacy" commonly refers to the judicial realm, "sharing" involves social as well as economic norms, cultural as well as legal values. Therefore, the mass adoption of Facebook as the preferred Western engine for social networking deserves close scrutiny: How did the platform contribute to the normalization of a specific notion of sharing before this meaning becomes ubiquitously accepted and "legalized"? Looking at Facebook's powerful position in the ecosystem, one can hardly underrate its impact on networked manifestations of sociality.

3.2. CODING FACEBOOK: THE DEVIL IS IN THE DEFAULT

Technology

From a technological point of view, the two meanings of "sharing" relate to two different types of coding qualities. The first type relates to *connectedness*, directing users to share information with other users through purposefully designed interfaces. Facebook's interface allows its members to create pro-files with photos, lists of preferred objects (books, films, music, cars, cats), and contact information; users can also join groups and communicate with friends by means of chat and video functions. Several features channel social interaction, including News Feed, for updates of stories from people and pages, the Wall for (public) announcements, Poke for attracting attention, and Status for informing others about your whereabouts or for announcing changes in your (relational, professional) status. Features such as People You May Know (PYMK) help you find friends; Facebook automatically signals which other people you may be interested in contacting and adding to your list—suggestions based on algorithmically computed relationships. Tagging names to people in pictures helps identify and trace "friends" across the net-work. The second type of coding features relates to *connectivity,* as they aim at sharing user data with third parties, such as Beacon (now defunct), Open Graph, and the Like button.

Distinguishing between the two types of sharing and their coding struc-tures serves to address the issue of information control: who is allowed to share what data to what ends? Platform owners have a vested interest in complete openness on the side of users; the more they know about users, the more information they can share with third parties. By aggregating and processing data into targeted personalization strategies, they create value from data. Users, for their part, may deploy the platform to invest in maxi-mum connectedness: the more connections users make, the more social capital they accumulate (Ellison, Steinfeld, and Lampe 2007). In many ways, Facebook's connective functions provide empowering and enriching social experiences. However, users' interest is not always served by com-plete openness; users may want to control third parties' access to the infor-mation they voluntarily or involuntarily entrust to Facebook. As a result, Facebook has a stake in promoting the first type of mechanism while diverting attention from the second type: the more users know about what happens to their personal data, the more inclined they are to raise objec-tions. Owners' power over coding technologies thus gives them a distinct advantage over users in the battle for information control.

The transformative meaning of sharing becomes poignantly discernable in Facebook's history of coding features, both of the first and of the second kind, but for the purpose of this chapter, I will concentrate mostly on the second. During the first years after its inception, when the site was launched at the Harvard campus, Facebook's virtual space overlapped with the rela-tively protected space of educational settings. Sharing information by default meant sharing your information with designated friends and with other students. Starting in 2005, Facebook opened up the site to users other than students and cautiously began to place (banner) advertisements in that protected social networking environment. The introduction of Beacon, in November 2007, caused quite a stir because it explicitly promoted the sharing of user information with commercial agents. Forty-four commercial websites, including Fandango, the *New York Times*, and TripAdvisor signed on to Beacon, allowing Facebook to send automated updates on purchases from these sites to a buyer's friends listed on Facebook. Users were enrolled in Beacon by default, and initially they were not offered an opt-out option. Only after vehement protests did Facebook give in to users' demand. Zuckerberg issued apologies, and in September 2009, the company shut down the service altogether.

The problem with Beacon was not that Facebook was not open enough about its sharing intentions; the problem with Beacon was that the company was *too explicit* about the intentions inscribed in its protocol. Users easily detected the conflict of interest arising from their personal purchasing data being distributed to all their friends and beyond. A second miscalculation was to openly identify the commercial agents involved in this scheme; by implication, Facebook was seen as serving the interests of companies rather than its users. But, most of all, it was a mistake to implement Beacon as a default in a social networking environment that, back in 2007, had not yet accepted "sharing with third parties" as a common standard. Facebook quickly adapted its strategies. Instead of conforming itself to the reining norm, it started to work on *changing* the very norm, replacing the narrow meaning of "sharing" with a more expansive one. Part of this new strategy was to open up the platform's technical potential to other companies interested in connecting with Facebook's users. Through the launch of Facebook Platform, in 2007, the company provided a set of APIs and tools that enabled third parties to develop applications supporting Facebook's integration across the Web, which they massively did. Since then, developers have generated millions of active applications connecting Facebook to other services and platforms. The contextual meanings of "connectedness" and "sharing" thus shifted from interaction *inside* the social network site to interaction with all virtual life *outside* Facebook's territory.

In May 2010, Zuckerberg announced two new features that formed a natural next step in this process: the introduction of Open Graph and the Like button. Both new interface features implied a definite move from the first to the second meaning of sharing. The Open Graph API allows external websites to deploy user data collected on Facebook to create personalized experiences on their own websites. Social plug-ins, as they are called, aim at connecting disparate corners of the Web and pulling them all together. Part of this integral effort to identify and align heretofore incongruent objects, people, and ideas is the development of a standard to give every object—whether human or nonhuman, concrete or abstract—a unique ID: the OAuth 2.0 authentication standard, which Facebook adopted in collaboration with Yahoo and Twitter. The standard allows users to share their private resources (e.g., photos, videos, contact lists) stored on one site with another site without having to supply their credentials, typically username and password.

Connecting people, things, and ideas is also the principle behind the much-debated Like button, a feature that lets users express their instant approval of a specific idea or item and share it. For instance, if you discover a movie via a movie database, you can tag it there and this preference automatically appears on your Facebook friends' News Feeds. Three months after its introduction, more than 350,000 external websites had already installed the feature, much to its inventor's benefit. All user data collected on these external sites, including IP addresses, are automatically routed back to Facebook. In fact, Facebook records *any* user's presence on a site with a Like button, including nonmembers and logged out users; a Like box allows Facebook to trace how many users and which of their friends have pushed the button. The visible part of the interface calls attention to user-to-user interaction, suggesting that information stays within the first meaning of sharing. However, invisible algorithms and protocols execute the programmed social task of "liking." Personal data are turned into public connections, as the Like function is ubiquitously dispersed to many items on the Internet. Because of its omnipresence, symbolized in the generic thumbs-up icon, Facebook is no longer seen as the exclusive owner of this feature. Unlike Beacon, the massive adoption of the Like button has turned personal data sharing by third parties into an accepted practice in the online universe; hence, the Like button epitomizes the profound modification of a social norm.

Underlying these features are proprietary algorithms EdgeRank and GraphRank, which filter data produced by users and shape them into a meaningful stream of information for that specific user. In a detailed analysis of EdgeRank, media scholar Tania Bucher (2012a) shows that the algorithm favors certain users over others; for instance, friends with whom a user interacts on a frequent basis or on a more "intimate" level (e.g., via the Chat function) count more than friends you contact infrequently or who merely appear on your Wall. EdgeRank provides a filter that implicitly ranks the importance of friends. The problem is that users cannot know exactly how this filter works. All features added to Facebook have resulted in mostly invisible algorithms and protocols that, to a great degree, control the "visibility" of friends, news, items, or ideas. The objective is obviously to personalize and optimize one's online experience; but the aim may also be to promote something or someone, although that aim may be hard to trace. You have to look under the hood, into the technical specifics of features, to understand the implications for users and society at large. This has not always been easy because Facebook has been reluctant to share information about its proprietary algorithms.

At the press conference announcing the Like button and Open Graph, Zuckerberg explained their rationale in terms of sociality, rather than in terms of technological progress or market value. He said: "The Web is at a really important turning point right now. Up until recently, the default on the Web has been that most things aren't social and most things don't use your real identity," adding that introduction of these changes would lead to a Web that is "smarter, more social, more personalized, and more semantically aware."[6] The term "default" in this explanation does not refer to technological or economic potential, but to social attitude. Indeed, the ubiquitous implementation of software entails a cultural rather than just a technological transformation (Fuller 2003). Facebook produces tools because people expect the Web to serve its users in a personalized way, helping them connect to all things they want and like, and to all people they know or would like to now. Underneath this user-centered rationale of connectedness is the owner-centered logic of connectivity: Facebook's interface foregrounds the need for users to be connected, but partly hides the site's mechanisms for sharing users' data with others.

Users

Facebook's unique selling point over the years has been its rapidly growing user base, not only in terms of sheer numbers but also in terms of diversity and global reach.[7] Behind these impressive numbers hides a more complex story of who these users are: their demographics, national and global distribution, and their online behavioral patterns. As explained in the previous chapter, this book is not concerned with actual users as empirical subjects, but tries to track how the usage inscribed in platforms triggers explicit users' responses. Over the past eight years, Facebook users have manifested themselves on the Web, commenting on their site and reacting to the changes implemented in its interface. How have users appropriated the normative architecture of Facebook's coding technologies? Did they support or criticize the (changing) social norms of sharing inscribed in the platform's interface? Let me first explain users' motivations for joining and enjoying Facebook before turning to various modes of resistance.

The steadily growing masses of users signing up for the service are proof of the site's becoming a centripetal force in organizing people's social lives. The principal benefits for users are, first, to *get and stay connected* and, second, to *become (well) connected*. Even though human contact through Internet sites has never replaced offline sociality, SNSs have arguably replaced e-mail and the phone as the preferred media of interaction for the younger generation (Raynes-Goldie 2010). "Getting in touch" and "staying in touch" are now activities completely centered on SNSs; the services facilitate the bridging of space and time and help people to keep updated on their friends' lives. Facebook's design makes subscribing feel like hooking up to a utility. Once a member, the social push to stay connected is insidious, especially for young people, because *not* being on Facebook means not being invited to parties, not getting updated on important events, in short, being disconnected from a presumably appealing dynamic of public life. SNSs, as researchers confirm, have become a leading space for accumulating social capital (Valenzuela, Park, and Kee 2009).

By the same token, Facebook has become a primer for promoting the self as the center of an extensive network of friends; the notion of "friending" relates to bonds that may also exist in real life, but equally refers to weak ties and latent ties. In online environments, people want to *show* who they are; they have a vested interest in identity construction by sharing pieces of information because disclosing information about one's self is closely linked with popularity. Psychology researchers Christofides, Muise, and Desmarais (2009) have argued that "identity is a social product created not only by what you share, but also by what others share and say about you. . . . The people who are most popular are those whose identity construction is most actively participated in by others" (343). Since Facebook is the largest social network, it offers the best potential for what Castells (2009) calls "mass self-communication."[8] In contrast to other mass media, SNSs in general—and Facebook in particular—offer individual users a stage for crafting a self-image and for popularizing this image beyond intimate circles. Popularity and disclosure are two sides of the same coin, and they mirror the double meaning of "sharing" as argued above.

The verb "friending" has become virtually synonymous with Facebook's demarcation of online friendship, and, as is the case with "liking," the concept is ambiguous and embattled. As described in the previous section, friendship is not only the result of spontaneous, human-based (inter) actions, but also the result of programmed sociality—relationships suggested by PYMK buttons and friends-of-friends algorithms. This "friendship assemblage" of technology and user thus defines "who our friends are, what they have done, and how many of them there are" (Bucher 2012b).

However, if we look at concrete users' articulation of friendship and their perception of online relationships on Facebook, researchers find that users actively engage with the site, building social capital by smartly playing out the various levels of friendship as well as exploiting the site's potential for self-expression and self-communication (Ellison, Steinfield, and Lampe 2011: 888). As Ellison and her colleagues conclude, users differentiate between Facebook friends and "actual" friends when gauging the quality of friendship. Indeed, even if users are aware of the fact that Facebook actively steers their online experience of friendship and converts their social capital into economic capital, they may still enjoy it.

The meaning of "friending" as inscribed in the interface is thus not simply accepted but also appropriated and contested by users. While a majority of Facebook users comply with the site's protocols for online sociality—which after all benefit their self-interests—a substantial part of its membership shows concerns about how data are used.[9] A small but vocal group of users have explicitly objected to the site's changing interface features. As briefly mentioned earlier, the company was flooded with protests when Beacon was introduced. Action group MoveOn.org organized a petition, and less than two weeks after Beacon's announcement, 50,000 users had joined a collective protest. In 2008, a class action suit was filed against Facebook and some of the 44 corporations enlisted in the Beacon scheme, resulting in the shutdown of the service and a settlement in court. User protests have occurred pretty regularly since the Beacon debacle, but never have had the same impact. When Facebook made substantial changes to its News Feed feature in 2009, over one million users joined the "Change Facebook back to normal!" group.[10] But whereas 50,000 protesters in 2007 still formed a substantial percentage of all Facebook users, one million protesters in 2009 represented only a small minority of the site's exploding user base. The protest caused only a ripple, and News Feed remained as implemented.

Another form of resistance favored by Facebook users critical of the company's data control strategies was to intervene at the technological level. There have been a number of attempts to thwart Facebook's control policies. For instance, hackers found out that Facebook distributes cookies to track user preferences even when users are logged out or haven't subscribed to Facebook.[11] Other forms of resistance include what Galloway (2004) would call "counter-protocological attacks": users write scripts that intervene with Facebook's interface design and intentionally block protocols. An example of such intervention is an app, offered on the site userscripts.org, that allows users to dismantle all Like buttons.[12] Yet another kind of manifest intervention is the site UnFuck Facebook, run by a college student who deploys the Facebook Platform to publicize scripts that help users to remove ads and lists of recent activities from their log files. Facebook, needless to say, immediately strikes down challenges to its default settings. As the founder of UnFuck Facebook intimated on his site on November 15, 2010:

> I'm fairly certain Facebook has been intentionally breaking this script. Every time I release a fix a few days later Facebook changes to break the script. I did this several times and I'm just tired of fighting them.[13]

Resisting or subverting default settings requires both technological ingenuity and persistent motivation. Facebook has every interest in preserving its default settings that make information as open as possible.[14] The fight with defiant users over information control is played out over the tiniest technological details.

A subtler form of Facebook criticism is for journalists to discover and disclose strategic technical details of the platform's invisible tactics. For instance, in October 2011, *USA Today* journalist Byron Acohido was able to compile from interviews with senior Facebook staff technical details about how the social network keeps tabs on its users.[15] He found out that Facebook tracks loyal users as well as logged-off users and nonmembers by inserting cookies in your browser. These cookies record the time and date you visit a website with a Like button or a Facebook plug-in, in addition to IP addresses. Correlations between personal data and web-browsing habits could be used to reveal consumers' political affiliations, religious beliefs, sexual orientations, or health issues. When confronted with these findings, Facebook claimed it was using these tactics for security reasons, but, obviously, tracking these kinds of correlations could also become a tempting business model.

Some users disgruntled with Facebook's strategies decided to quit the site altogether, either as individuals or as a collective sign of protest. But quitting Facebook by unsubscribing is easier said than done. Etched into the engine's default is a protocol that sends deserters a number of automated messages containing pictures of "friends" who say they will miss you if you deactivate your account. Few users are resistant to such guilt-tripping, but even if they are, it is not sure they will be able to quit the site for good. To delete your account, you have to really search to find the suitable links, and if you merely push the "deactivate" button—rather than opt out of getting e-mails by pushing "delete" buttons—you can still be tagged and spammed through Facebook.[16] A group of vocal resisters called for collective action when they named May 31, 2010, Quit Facebook Day.[17]

The pledge was posted by users who deeply cared not only about privacy issues but also about the future of the Web as an "open, safe and human place." More than one year later, almost 40,000 users had actually resigned their membership—a number evaporating in the face of the site's monthly accumulation of users.

Over the course of eight years, there have been regular skirmishes between Facebook owners and users over the control of the site's default settings. Whereas Facebook has given in to some demands (Beacon), it has ignored others; the platform pushes three steps forward before users' demands force them to take one backward. What becomes clear is that coding technologies and user appropriations are tools to promote one meaning of sharing over the other. Facebook wants its preferred meaning of sharing, implying complete openness and maximum exchange of data with third parties, to become the "shared norm." Some users have publicly and vocally disputed this interpretation. Even though most protests are framed in the press as privacy concerns, the responses signal a wider scuffle between users' and owners' interest in information control.

Content and Cultural Form

The gradual shift from user-centered connectedness to owner-centered connectivity brought along a change in the organization of Facebook's content from a *database* structure into a *narrative* structure. In the platform's early years, content was generally organized around user connections, news and friends updates, and active discussions. Facebook's interface, as British researcher Garde-Hansen (2009: 141) observed, was presented as a database *of* users and *for* users where "each user's page is a database of their life, making this social network site a collection of collections and collectives." For some users, their page presented a personal archive, a way to share life histories and memories with selected others or open it up to the public at large. For others, SNSs appeared to be a "stage for digital flâneurs," a place to "see and be seen" (boyd 2007: 155). Content diversity allowed users to appropriate the site to suit their own purposes. Over the course of several years, the platform's owners clearly strove toward more uniformity in data input and began to introduce specific narrative features in the interface—a transformation that culminated into the implementation of Timeline in 2011.

With the advent of Timeline, every single piece of data previously uploaded on Facebook—text, picture, video, sound, but also Likes, Pokes, and so on—was automatically transferred onto the new compulsory format upon opening it. The new interface no longer looked like a random database (Manovich 2001) but is, rather, organized as a biography chronicling one's life up to the present. The resulting narrative is a construction in hindsight, a retroactive chronological ordering of life events. Starting with the most recent months, months are slipping into years when you scroll toward the bottom. The entire left side of the page is filled with events, "stories of your life" in the form of pictures, posts to friends, music that you like(d), recipes you exchanged, all your likes and pokes, updates, maps of the places you have been, and a lot more. The narrative presentation gives each member page the look and feel of a magazine—a slick publication, with you as the protagonist. With the introduction of Timeline, Facebook has crept deeper into the texture of life, its narrative principles imitating proven conventions of storytelling, thus binding users even more tightly to the fabric that keeps it connected.

Users responding to Timeline noticed this effect and commented on how memory and emotion are made part of the Facebook experience. The Timeline format cues members to post pictures from the pre-Facebook days of their youth—a baby picture, family snapshots, school classes, old friends, college years, wedding pictures, honeymoon—and thus experience content in terms of their life's story. As one blogger explains:

> Years-old memories flashed before me—old friends, old places, things I hadn't thought about in ages. I got sucked back into the past the same way I would have in front of my mother's old cedar chest, a trunk packed full of childhood tchotckes and pictures that holds our family's history. This innocuous social web tool had just made a powerful and convincing bid for more than my information or my time. Facebook was grasping at my emotions by way of my memories, and it was doing a damn good job.[18]

But while the transformation to Timeline caused enhanced feelings of intimacy, memory, and connectedness in some members, it roused suspicion and discontent in others, especially with regards to the release of more personal information. When switching to Timeline, every formerly inserted piece of data was set by default to "public," even if you had previously set it to "friends only." Users received a grace period of seven days to make decisions about their content's revamped presentation.[19] With every piece of data—both new and old—one had to decide to whom it would be accessible: to friends, a wider circle, or the general audience. And while research has demonstrated that Facebook users have gradually become more skilled in the techniques of audience appraisal (Marwick and boyd 2011), it is still likely that a large number of users accepted the automatic conversion of their privacy settings, either because they did not know how to modify them or because they did not care. Critical users expressed their discontent mostly on account of involuntary loss of privacy; for some users the transfer to Timeline was also a wake-up call that "brought home to me *just how much* I had shared in the way of status updates, photographs, groups I had joined and Likes I had made."[20] Users also voiced concerns about the consequences if identity thieves used this feature to cajole information out of naive users.[21]

Facebook's new content architecture smoothly integrated the principle of narrative with the principle of connectivity. Apart from the fact that the narrative structure of the site's interface renders users' content presentation more uniform, the architecture also streamlines user input of data, thus facilitating data management and enhancing the application of algorithms. For instance, unified data input makes it a lot easier for companies to insert personalized advertisements for diapers in the Timelines of women with babies and toddlers. Another feature Facebook released simultaneously with Timeline, which received much less attention, was its Page Insight Data. The feature enables marketers to access real-time analytics that measure the effectiveness of their ads interspersed in Facebook's Timeline moment by moment. Leveraging these insights, companies can make decisions about what works and what does not, subsequently tweaking ads in order to optimize their effect. The introduction of Timeline, more than any other feature after Beacon, exposed content presentation as a bone of contention between owners and users. With an IPO nearing, Facebook's rolling out of Timeline caused worries that its move would trigger negative concerns, but as with most previous changes, Facebook soothed resistance by leveraging strategies at various levels. On one level, it offered users a chance to reorganize their content and reconsider their strategies to open up and hide information. On a different plane, Facebook offered advertisers and third parties more and uniformly accessible user data.

During the first eight years of the platform's evolution, technologies, users, and content mutually shaped one another. In 2012, none of these elements were the same as they were in 2004. Coding and content features affected user behavior, while user behavior and explicit responses prompted Facebook to adjust its strategies. Features such as the Like button and the Timeline format also had a profound impact beyond the platform proper, affecting online sociality as such. But before returning to the site's bearing on sociality, we first need to look at Facebook's strategies to establish a brand—a trademarked service that governs its user base while monetizing its resources.

3.3. BRANDING FACEBOOK: WHAT YOU SHARE IS WHAT YOU GET

Ownership

How does the ideology of sharing play out at the level of corporate owner-ship? When Facebook was launched in 2004, it was competing with several other platforms, such as Friendster, Myspace, and Xanga, to become users' preferred brand for online social networking. Eight years later, most early competitors have vanished from the scene or are left behind as "failed" sites with dwindling numbers of users. Few companies have experienced such a meteoritic rise as Facebook. From 2004 to 2012, the platform has remained in the hands of its initial owner, Facebook Inc. The company refused several offers by moguls like Microsoft and Google, and soon became too big to serve as takeover bait. With 2,000 employees and 15 offices worldwide, the company's size was surprisingly modest in relation to its net worth of almost 100 billion dollars at the time of its initial public offering in May 2012.

The branding of Facebook as *the* social network experience has grown steadily over the years. Size brings convenience for users and more adver-tising potential for owners, as Tim Wu (2010) has pointed out. Informa-tion companies vie to monopolize a niche from where they can comfortably try to encroach on other areas. As Facebook grew exponentially, it quickly outpaced competitors' user numbers through a winner-takes-all effect; Facebook's global reach often came at the expense of smaller (national) social network services.[22] The platform has played an important role in spreading (American) social norms into other national user communities worldwide. Because of their size and global reach, players like Facebook are not only frontrunners in terms of trying to beat the competition, but also in terms of defining mediated social habits in that particular niche.

Although Facebook quickly defeated its early rivals in the SNS market—by 2009, only Myspace was still holding a foot on the threshold—the com-pany faced major challenges from large Internet corporations dominating other niche areas, such as search. In 2011, Google attempted to dethrone Facebook from its comfortable position by launching Google+. Strategically counteracting Facebookers' dissatisfaction with the site's privacy policy, Google+ introduced the features Circles and Hangouts in its interface—features that offered a more refined system for "sharing the right stuff with the right people," according to its website's promotional rhetoric.[23] In doing so, Google literally branded its new service to tackle its opponent's weak spot: the criticism about its contested default settings. Facebook almost immediately responded by adding the features Group Chats and Video Call-ing, enabling live communication through a corporate partnership with

Skype.[24] With the seamless integration of other apps, such as Spotify, users can choose to let everyone see what they are listening to.

At the corporate level, "sharing" has been assigned the additional connotation of *frictionless sharing*, a term again played out on two levels simultaneously: first, to accommodate users' convenience when they move from Facebook to other platforms without hitting another key or needing an extra click; second, to please platform owners by connecting Facebook to third-party applications and make all data available to all parties. In the words of Facebook's CEO: "Every app is going to be social. If we build the best service, there's massive value there. If we don't, somebody else will."[25] According to Zuckerberg, making everything social is a corporate ideology that is increasingly shared by other social media platforms as well as third parties. Apps, like people, are connectors that boost overall data traffic so all companies can benefit from the "massive value" generated by expanded connectivity. Facebook's strategy of enhancing its power in the ecosystem of connective media thus has a double focus: Zuckerberg counters (potential) competition by pointing at the inevitability of a changing norm ("everything is going to be social") before he invites competitors to join Facebook in their endeavor to create a "truly open and connected space."

In the venture capitalist economy of Silicon Valley, partnership deals, even with competitors, are as important as beating the competition: all companies have a common interest in making the online ecosystem uniformly accessible and shareable. Particularly in the last three years, Facebook has enlisted partners in other niches (games, video chatting, streamed music) in pursuit of promoting overall data traffic and enhancing connectivity in the name of a smoother user experience. Uninhibited data flows between platforms are vital to companies like DoubleClick (owned by Google) and Advertising.com (AOL) selling targeted personalized messages. Facebook also pushed for global acceptance of its narrative form: enforcing Timeline's architecture not just on individual members but also on companies and advertisers, Facebook drives them to sell brands through stories, for instance via personal tales of a product experience. By joining the ecosystem's bandwagon, many platforms attuned their corporate strategies to Facebook's normative definitions of sharing and openness.

In the months preceding its IPO, Facebook Inc was careful to craft its corporate image not as a multinational working in the interest of shareholders, but as a user-centered business that wants to share ownership with the people who made it grow.[26] To "sharing" was hence ascribed another ambiguous meaning in the context of shareholder ownership. The contentious relationship between owners, users, advertisers, and shareholders painfully showed in the wake of the company's going public: not only did

General Motors withdraw its advertising account two days before the IPO, but a group of disgruntled users also filed a lawsuit against Facebook, accusing the company of misusing the Like button for sponsored stories without prior consent or even knowledge of users. The lawsuit was settled a month later, but it did not help to boost the company's public image. Three months after its IPO, Facebook shares had lost almost half their value, disappointing owners and shareholders alike. Obviously, the company's public status increased pressure on its owners to render the site more profitable, at the risk of further upsetting loyal users who are wary of increasing commercialization. This friction also shows at the level of governance.

Governance

Facebook's expanded norm of sharing is not only coded in its interface and user scripts, but is also crafted in its terms of service (ToS). The site's policies regulating online traffic are an eclectic combination of do's and don'ts, claimer and disclaimer, rights and responsibilities, and contractual agreement. Since 2007, Facebook's terms of service have been a constant bone of contention for its users. Complaints concerned the level of control over privacy settings, surveillance, and data mining, as well as the length and complexity of the company's terms. Objections have come from government agencies, advocacy groups, and users alike. Perhaps as a result of this criticism, the company has changed its ToS frequently. Since users are never explicitly notified of changes, it is difficult to keep up with policy adjustments. The majority of users never bother to read the terms they have to click-to-agree; most users tend to stick to defaults or are apathetic about privacy settings (Stutzman and Kramer-Duffield 2010; Madejski, Johnson, and Bellovin 2010). Nonetheless, Facebook's terms are a vital ploy in the battle to define what sharing is.

If we look more closely at Facebook's governance, the first thing to notice is that there are at least five different ToS levels: Facebook Principles, Statement of Rights and Responsibilities, Privacy Policy, Data Use Policy, and Platform Policy.[27] All policies are derived from Facebook Principles. The fundamental ambiguity of "sharing" is etched in the opening statement, which carefully crafts the company's mission:

> We are building Facebook to make the world more open and transparent, which we believe will create greater understanding and connection. Facebook promotes openness and transparency by giving individuals greater *power to share and connect*, and certain principles guide Facebook in pursuing these goals.

Achieving these principles should be constrained only by limitations of law, technology, *and evolving social norms*. We therefore establish these Principles as the foundation of the *rights and responsibilities* of those within the Facebook Service. (Facebook Principles, emphases added)

The statement articulates the company's service entirely in terms of users' needs rather than the company's interests; "evolving social norms" are explicitly mentioned as a constraining force—a force outside Facebook's reach—but in fact, Facebook's rules are a major factor in steering these very norms.

In the remainder of the Principles text, the double meaning of "sharing" stands out in the first two principles, titled "The Freedom to Share and Connect" and "Ownership and Control of Information." Whereas the first principle marks one user's right to connect to another and to exchange data "as long as they both consent to the connection," the second principle actually undermines the platform's own declaration that people should "own their information" and should have the freedom "to set privacy controls to protect those choices," adding the following disclaimer: "Those controls, however, are not capable of limiting how those who have received information may use it, particularly outside the Facebook Service." This last phrase obviously relates to all third parties and companies connecting to Facebook— connections actively pursued by the company. Over the years, Facebook has indeed allotted its users more technical control over their data by adding privacy settings; but these settings do not cover "sharing" in the second meaning of the term, so the effect of these buttons is illusory if you take into account the disclaimer added in the second principle.[28]

This sustained ambiguity in the meaning of sharing has sparked legal dissent over the lawfulness of the platform's ToS, stemming not only from users but also from government agencies and consumer groups. In 2009, after Facebook had announced it would now treat users' names, profile photo, friends list, gender, and other profile data as publicly available information, the Electronic Privacy Information Center (EPIC), along with the American Library Association and several consumer rights advocacy groups, asked the American FCC to look into these changes. A lawsuit filed in Los Angeles in August 2010 claimed that Facebook's Like button intentionally exposes minors to unsolicited advertising; a similar concern was raised by Canada's Privacy Commissioner and the German state of Schleswig-Holstein, contending that all federal agencies should remove the Like button and similar plug-ins from their websites because it breaches national data protection laws.[29] And in August 2011, the German-based "Europe vs. Facebook" group called for legal and political action after it found out that Facebook keeps enormous amounts of data on file for a long time, even though Facebook claims to have removed it.[30]

Facebook's response to lawsuits and other allegations over its privacy policies has been to listen to user complaints and make amends when required by law. As described in the previous section, the debacle over Beacon resulted in a court settlement, requiring Facebook to spend $9.5 million on the establishment of a Privacy Foundation, with appointed users as board members.[31] After the complaints filed by EPIC, Zuckerberg issued a press release announcing the need for "companies like ours" to develop new models of governance: "Rather than simply reissue a new Terms of Use, the changes we're announcing today are designed to open up Facebook so that users can participate meaningfully in our policies and our future."[32] In a purported move toward online democracy, Facebook created two user groups to help it draft what would eventually become Facebook Principles and Facebook Bill of Rights and Responsibilities. All users could log into the "ballot page" to issue their vote on what these principles and bill of rights should entail—not unlike a virtual town hall meeting. An interesting caveat issued by Facebook was that the process needed to be finished within 30 days and would need to draw at least 30 percent of active Facebook users if its results were to be binding—a totally unrealistic goal considering the fact that the site already had over 200 million subscribers in 2009. Not unexpectedly, the attempt at "open governance" failed in its intentions, but nevertheless became included as Principle 9: "Facebook should have a town hall process of notice and comment and a system of voting to encourage input and discourse on amendments to these Principles or to the Rights and Responsibilities." Despite the specified rule, it is unclear to this very day how the company conducts "town hall meetings" or how it plans to muster "open governance" in future policy amendments.

Perhaps most remarkable in Facebook's deployment of its governance model as an instrument in the struggle over information control is the company's strategy of cementing the notion of sharing in user-to-user traffic. Putting the onus on user involvement while de-emphasizing Facebook's interest in commercial exploitation, the company's claim to transparency included in Facebook Principles is conspicuously one-sided. Transparency and openness apparently apply to users who are pushed to share as much information as they can, but does not pertain to owners reluctant to reveal information about their plans to share data for commercial purposes. As long as there is little openness about the platform's commercial strategies, the company's gesture to establish a semidemocratic governance structure remains entirely symbolic. So how open has the company been about its monetizing intentions?

Business Models

To better understand Facebook's monetizing capacity in the wake of the ideology of sharing, we need to return to the double logic of connectedness versus connectivity, a logic that is mirrored by users' interests in mass self-communication vis-à-vis the owners' interest in mass customization. Online social networks generate two more potential economic values besides connectivity: *attention* and *popularity*. In the "attention economy," attention means eyeballs or (unconscious) exposure, and this value is an important part of Internet advertising in the form of banners, pop-ups, and paid ad space on websites. Gaining popularity is important to people who want to boost their public reputation; identifying popularity is relevant to companies that want to seek out influential people or recognize prevalent trends. And yet popularity is not simply out there, ready to be measured: it is, rather, engineered through algorithms that prompt users to rank things, ideas, or people in relation to other things, ideas, or people.

Although popularity has no relation to values such as truth, trust, objectivity, or quality, it is often equated with these values. For instance, users trust their private profiling data to Facebook because they are invited to join the network by a friend, often as part of a preexisting offline network community, and to join other circles of friends while online. Users gain popularity when they get involved in more groups and make more contacts; having many friends on Facebook, after all, enhances your individual market value. The PYMK button uses the popularity principle by culling name suggestions from automated data and cookies. In other words, popularity rooted in *relative* connections between people on the basis of trust is translated into an automated, quantifiable commodity. When communities of users continuously push Like and Poke buttons, issue recommendations, forward favorite items, or state preferences on what's hot and what's not, information garnered through informal networks generates real value on the commodity exchange floor.

The values of attention, popularity, and connectivity have gradually and carefully been mixed to constitute the basis of Facebook's business model. Since 2010, Facebook has progressively opened up user data to extract more value out of the site, risking a serious loss of users through a steady erosion of privacy and trust (Nussbaum 2010). Economic success is highly dependent on a mixture of social media as meeting places (places to make contacts and socialize) and marketplaces (places to exchange, trade, or sell goods). Facebook's owners carefully nourished the site's reputation: a site needs many visitors and a high level of connective activity before it can monetize either one of these values. And yet because SNS sites are meeting places and not just marketplaces, they are different from conventional media. Network communities that collectively define popularity may be used for their evaluative labor or as deliverers of metadata, but they cannot be held captive to the attention industry. When users are no longer interested or when they feel manipulated, they may simply leave (Clemons 2009). In other words, the long-term viability of Web 2.0 platforms depends on a pristine equilibrium between attracting and exploiting communities, between entertaining users and making them participate (van Dijck 2009). The power of users rises above the normal capability of consumers to abstain from consumption because they are also value creators; users have the ability to exercise competent choices, grounded in their understanding of competing and even conflicting incentives and motivations. This strategic power of users thus poses a major challenge to Facebook's business model.

Not surprisingly, the platform waited several years to build a large and loyal member base and to test which values could render the site profitable. Whereas Facebook members, in 2007, were still reluctant to accept advertising in their informal socializing environment, tolerance for commercial infiltration of their social space expanded over the years. Since the Beacon debacle, the company has tried a mixture of strategies to monetize connectivity while building its brand. Banner advertisements appearing on a side bar are the most common tactic; like Google's AdSense, Facebook makes use of personalized targeted ads, connecting specific Facebook users to advertisers based on content interests.[33] Open Graph connects the company to an enormous quantity of data generated outside of its own service through Like buttons and similar apps, giving them access to a vast reservoir of marketing data, data on users' interests, and demographics. The Like button, as we now know, is vulnerable to Like-jacking and personalized spamming; users may regularly find recommendations on their News Feed or Wall that are ostensibly sent by "friends" but are in fact propelled by third parties using an unwitting friend's Like as an advertising ploy. Sponsored stories, as part of the company's narrative strategy, are claimed to be almost 50 percent more effective than targeted ads.[34] Users automatically approve this tactic by signing the ToS.

Advertising aside, Facebook has ventured into several other profitable business models, such as selling pages to major and minor brands. Virtually all multinationals, from Coca-Cola to BMW, are using Facebook for marketing and so-called "mouth-to-mouth at scale" promotion. They pay influential Facebook connectors—people with many friends—to promote their brand through the many intersecting groups and networks they are involved in. As Facebook owns an unprecedented reservoir of customized (meta)data, advertising and public relations are becoming a mixture of science and statistics, and therefore a lucrative business model. Facebook's strategy also includes integrated pay services. Granting members of the site access to online games or apps such as CastleVille or Words with Friends, Facebook receives one-third of these sites' revenues. Besides being a social network, Facebook thus increasingly serves as a gateway and identity provider to selected services and goods. The platform becomes a closed membership alliance whose members' data represent valuable marketing and advertising niches to which companies can buy access (Turow 2006).

Facebook's business model is most certainly a contentious balancing act between stimulating users' activity and exploiting it; its success ultimately depends on customers' willingness to contribute data and to allow maximum data mining. Some economists have hailed this value as the corporation's most valuable resource, even though the specificities of its mining methods are far from clear.[35] At the other end of the spectrum, critics contend that platforms like Facebook are turning the Internet into a proprietary space where control over tools and services is firmly held by a small number of media corporations who are "pushing for control and exclusion as a means to exploit and reorient online users as consumer" (Milberry and Anderson 2009: 409).[36] Over the years, information about Facebook's business model has been carefully held from the public view. Up to its IPO in May 2012, the firm was conspicuously quiet about its plans to make its gold mine more profitable; the Nasdaq offering forced the company to make its revenue streams and data capitalization more open.[37]

In the overture toward Facebook's going public, we can again observe the divergent meanings of sharing being captured in one seamless notion. In a video roadshow released several weeks before the IPO, the company pitched its bright future prospects to prospective investors.[38] Facebook's top managers and CEO, along with two of the platform's biggest advertisers (Ben & Jerry's and American Express), explain their business strategies in an almost evangelical way, professing the company's "social" mission as an economic boon. A spokesperson for the ice-cream company echoes the rhetoric of Facebook:

> Messages on Facebook spread not just from business to consumer, but from friend to friend. At Ben & Jerry's, we're not just a company, we really are a friend to people. We want a holistic relationship with our community, our customers. We engage in a large-scale conversation.

In virtually every line of text in the 30-minute promotion video, values of connectedness and community are equated with connective values, smoothly aligning business models with user interests. Clients are communities and customers equal friends, warranting the identification of a new category of "frustomers." Facebook's mantra of making the world social is presented as a win-win business proposition. The double logic of sharing, as we have seen, is not just anchored in the site's business model, but penetrates every fiber of the company's philosophy, including coding features, user practices, content and ownership strategies, and governance models.

3.4. SHARED NORMS IN THE ECOSYSTEM OF CONNECTIVE MEDIA

The struggle over the meaning of sharing does not just reflect one company's effort to code and brand sociality, but also represents a *cultural* battle to establish a new normative order for online socializing and communication. Early stages of this struggle are articulated in the way Facebook has shaped sociality at the same time and by the same means as it has been shaped by technological advances, legal codes, and market forces. But the reason that Facebook has managed to impose its ideology on a vast number of users cannot be explained exclusively by the company's technical ingenuity or its visionary poise, inspiring a young generation's lifestyle. Facebook's distribution of the sharing norm has been widespread because its buttons have been effectively exported to other platforms, promoted by the frictionless sharing stratagem. Games, pay services, employment sites, and a large number of other online facilities have partnered with Facebook to benefit from its size, in lieu of sharing data with Facebook. Most online companies absorb Facebook's connectivity principle to offer a free service, collect data about users as they use the service, and sell advertising on the basis of these data.

Perhaps more significant than Facebook's export of buttons and sharing principles is the platform's acceptance into so many people's everyday routines. What used to be informal social activities in the private sphere— friends hanging out together and exchanging ideas on what they like— have become algorithmically mediated interactions in the corporate sphere. The significance of this transition, though, gets lost in the common vernacular of sharing, friending, and liking.[39] In less than eight years, the meaning of "sharing," once understood as user-to-user information exchange, has subtly been replaced by a meaning that naturalizes the sharing of personal data with anyone on the planet. Among teenagers, the idea of "friending" as building the largest possible network of contacts—a social badge of honor informed by the popularity principle—has been steadily on the rise. The concept of "liking" pushes popular ideas or things with a high degree of emotional value, arguably at the expense of rational judgments for which there are no buttons in the online universe; "difficult but important" is not a judgment prompted by social media sites. Sharing, friending, and liking are powerful ideological concepts whose impact reaches beyond Facebook proper into all corners of culture, affecting the very fabric of sociality.

The normalization of a specific social rule at some point inevitably affects the process of legalization—of norms turning into laws. Media companies trying to change privacy laws recurrently invoke changed social norms to back up their argument. For instance, in December 2011, viewing-on-demand platform Netflix backed a bill in the American Congress that would amend the Video Privacy Protection Act, issued in the 1980s, prohibiting the disclosure of a client's personal information or consuming behavior without written consent.[40] Netflix lawyers argued that the law is outdated because people share their information all the time on Facebook and Spotify, so why can't they share information on videos they are watching? Doctors keen on keeping patients' private information confidential are puzzled to find that patients themselves publish the most intimate details of their illnesses on their Facebook pages. On a different note, job applicants have been asked during interviews to relay their Facebook passwords to prospective employers so they can check information that was intentionally set to "friends only."[41] The new norm of online sharing is thus invoked in other domains to forfeit individual rights or to push legal amendments.

And yet Facebook's normative dominance is not set in stone but is vulnerable to forces in the connective environment it helped create. Critical responses to the prevailing definition of sharing have come from individuals, legal agencies, and also from the market. First of all, a backlash from users is not unimaginable. Facebook resisters, according to the *New York Times*, are growing in number as people's worries over the platform's privacy policy increase.[42] There is a mounting awareness among users about the need to protect precious private information from the industry's calls for "openness."[43] In May 2012, with all eyes on the company's IPO, a class action suit on behalf of users was filed in a California court, claiming that Facebook improperly tracks and exploits its users. The joke "Why did Facebook go public? Because they couldn't figure out the privacy settings either" gained viral acclaim. Besides being the target of American lawsuits, Facebook's expanding definition of sharing has been the target of active monitoring by European and American watchdogs, NGOs, and consumer advocates such as the Center for Digital Democracy.

Perhaps more telling are *market* responses to the pervasive ideology of sharing. New services besides Google+ offer alternatives to people who feel uncomfortable with the principles undergirding the platform's dominance. They target Facebook's strength, which is simultaneously its weak spot: its generic user base and undifferentiated friending functions. Many smaller platforms, such as Path, FamilyLeaf, ConnectMe, Diaspora, and Pair, offer network services with specific restraints on the number of users or more user control. Other services envision a future of networked sociality in which users will be more aware of their data's value. Although studies show that many consumers care about the collection of personal data by an online company, few are willing to pay to protect it.[44] A few start-ups, such as Personal, operate on the basis of people taking control from the digital trails they leave on the Internet and sell their personal data for services they explicitly want.

Facebook's operational logic is indeed a powerful force in the ecosystem of connective media, affecting many other platforms and infiltrating many people's social lives, but there are also countervailing forces. And even if the platform seems invincible at the apex of its popularity, it is susceptible to the vagaries of the same ecosystem that helped make it big. If the world's users decide Facebook has lost its coolness, has sold out your private data, or has yielded to censoring governments, its popularity may dwindle. If lawmakers and governments get a mandate from citizens to secure more information control, Facebook's business models may become less lucrative. If competing platforms manage to attract substantial user bases and occupy new specialized niches in the social networking universe, Facebook's value may easily drop. In fact, many predicted this fate after the company lost a large chunk of its value in the first month following its IPO. The ecosystem of connective media has proven a capricious environment in which a platform's status is never secure.

But even if Facebook loses its cool as a platform, its ideology has spread so deeply into the pores of online sociality that its newspeak and mantras will reverberate for a long time. Facebook's ambition is not to be an open social network that lets its content and data be crawled by other engines, especially Google's. Instead, it wants to be a gateway to social content, a toll road to a data infrastructure that facilitates all forms of online commercialized sociality. In the video roadshow discussed in the previous section, Mark Zuckerberg elucidates Facebook as a core upon which other platforms can build: Facebook is "a *fabric* that can make any experience online social." The company's creed to make the world a more connected and transparent place has thus come full circle: if the world lets Facebook define the norms for online sociality, it will build a world powered by Facebook.

CHAPTER 4

Twitter and the Paradox of Following and Trending

4.1. INTRODUCTION

> I think Twitter is a success for us when people stop talking about it, when we stop doing these panels and people just use it as a utility, use it like electricity. It fades into the background, something that's just a part of communication. We put it on the same level as any communication device. So, e-mail, SMS, phone. That's where we want to be.[1]

When cofounder and executive Jack Dorsey prophesied Twitter's prospects at a Future of the Media panel in New York in 2009, he underlined that the company wants users and developers to shape the platform into a generic infrastructure for online communication and social interaction. Twitter first emerged in 2006, at a time when nobody really knew what microblogging was. Early adopters had experimented with several usages when Twitter really took off at a South by Southwest conference in 2007. Six years after its launch, the platform has become the world's leading microblogging service, attracting almost 500 million registered users and 88 million active users per month.[2] Over the past half decade, "tweeting" has sported multiple meanings, from sending instant short messages to creating a live stream of instant opinion. Twitter's technological design was modified several times, and while establishing its brand name, the platform experimented with various business models and governance strategies to turn connectivity into a source of sustainable income. Social constructivists would consider the platform's development to be a stage of "interpretive flexibility": a stage when a technology is still in flux and various, sometimes contradictory, interpretations are wagered before stabilization is reached (Bijker 1995; Pinch and Bijker 1984; Doherty, Coombs and Loan-Clarke 2006).

Dorsey's stated objective of turning the platform into a utility, like water from the tap or electricity from an outlet, entails a peculiar paradox. The terminology presumes Twitter to be a *neutral* platform upon which users freely interact, much like the Web itself—an infrastructure that transports streams of tweets, regardless of who its users are and indifferent to the contents they exchange. According to Twitter's founding CEO, the infrastructure itself needs to fade into the background, the way water pipes are made *invisible* and electricity cables are taken for granted. From such a perspective, Twitter presents itself as an echo chamber of random chatter, the online underbelly of mass opinions where collective emotions are formed and where quick-lived trends wax and wane in the public eye. And yet Twitter's pipelines do not just transport streams of live tweets; neither the platform nor its users are simple carriers of information. Much rather, streams of data are engineered to promote certain uses and users over others. Twitter presents the platform as a carrier, like a phone company, but this objective is simultaneously challenged by the pressure to make its content streams profitable. The paradox of enabling connectedness while engineering connectivity, of propagating neutrality while securing profitability, is played out in every aspect of the platform.

If we apply the concept of interpretive flexibility to Twitter's first six years, we can observe how conflicting meanings and divergent pressures informed the microsystem's development. The previous chapter described how Facebook gradually imputed expansive meanings to the online activities of "sharing," "liking," and "friending"; in the case of Twitter, a similar evolution took place with regards to social practices now known as "following" and "trending." Specific algorithms that inform these practices are presented as neutral, but in fact apply filtering mechanisms to weigh and select user contributions and tweet content. On the level of platform organization, Twitter had to walk a tightrope between its ambition to be an autonomous communication network and the commercial pressure to become an applied service accommodating advertisers. To understand the implications of this ambivalence, we also need to track how microblogging's development plays out in a complex Internet milieu of push-and-pull forces. How did Twitter position itself vis-à-vis its competitors in other niches? What are the implications of the following and trending logic beyond the platform itself? Posing the existential, strategic, and ecological question, this chapter probes the validity of the platform's aspiration to become a neutral utility.

4.2. ASKING THE EXISTENTIAL QUESTION: WHAT IS TWITTER?

Technology

When Twitter first arrived on the scene, nobody really knew how to define it. Touted as the "SMS of the Internet," the technology allowing users to send and receive text-based messages of up to 140 characters known as tweets was characterized as something between a short message service, a phone call, an e-mail, and a blog: less cumbersome than keeping a blog, less exclusive than talking to one person on a phone, less formal than e-mail exchange, and less elaborate than most social network sites. The initial idea was for Twitter to be "a sort of adrenalized Facebook, with friends communicating with friends in short bursts."[3] The 140-character limitation was chosen not only because of its conciseness and intensity, as we will see later on, but primarily for its technical compatibility with mobile phone SMS services. The application quickly spread via a number of other devices, such as PDAs, laptops, and desktops. Twitter's strength was its hardware versatility, as well as its capability of fitting multiple online environments.[4]

If we take Jack Dorsey's words seriously, Twitter was designed to be a multipurpose tool upon which apps could be built. During the first years after its emergence, Twitter was often called a service in search of a user application. Predictably, users and markets are always looking for one specified function to designate its value. Researchers, app developers, and journalists all tried to help answer the existential question of what Twitter really was. Journalists wondered about the technology's most evident usage, let alone its "killer app" (Arceneaux and Schmitz Weiss 2010). Information scientists "followed the hardware" to understand the motives of early adopters, who are commonly eager to tweak technologies to suit their needs or who invent needs for unspecified tools.[5] Several researchers of information and communication technology attempted to characterize Twitter by analyzing its activity streams (Krishnamurthy, Gill, and Arlitt 2008); others tried to define Twitter's user rationale by mapping network nodes in geographical space (Java et al. 2007). Researchers keenly observed that subtle hardware adjustments affected interaction between (groups of) users, and monitored the site's architectural design to suggest modifications that would strengthen the platform's collaborative functions.[6]

Twitter rapidly managed to occupy a social networking niche that Facebook and Myspace did not really serve. Over the years, a number of competing microblogging platforms carved out niches within niches.[7] Some of these services were country-specific, and some combined microblogging with other services, for instance file sharing. In contrast to its competitors, Twitter positioned itself as an autonomous brand, unconnected to one specific tool, one specific country, or one specific paired service. For one thing, Twitter steered its technological design to favor ubiquitous integrated use of its basic architectural elements; in order to interlink with as many social networks as possible, the microblogging service gradually adapted its hardware and tweaked its software to fit other services' standards. About the same time Twitter emerged, Facebook added its own microblogging tool to its already hugely popular site: News Feed highlighted information on recent profile changes, upcoming events and birthdays, and other updates. In 2007, Facebook also adopted Twitter on its site, which tremendously boosted the latter's popularity. Less than a year later, virtually every SNS provided links to Twitter, as did most major news and entertainment organizations, ensuring it a winner-takes-all position in this particular segment of the ecosystem.

So which distinctive features did Twitter's interface integrate over time? For starters, the platform firmly manifested itself as a user-centered site, a concept cemented in the idea of *following*: users may subscribe to other users' tweets, and subscribers are known as followers. "Following" in the early years meant engaging in a real-time communal dialogue, looking at and responding to comments of users you were interested in. In a very short period, the platform gained a critical mass of users, who wanted to engage in public or community debates, exchanging suggestions and opinions. The Twitter logo transmogrified into a click-on T-button that established "twittering" or "tweeting" as a ubiquitous online practice, much as Facebook's F-button did for "friending" and the thumbs-up sign for "liking." In line with Jack Dorsey's ambition, the light-blue and white T-button arguably became the kind of turn-on switch you expect to find in any social meeting place.

A significant expansion of Twitter's architecture was the implementation, in late 2008, of "trending topics"—a feature that enabled users to group posts together by topic by articulating certain words or phrases prefixed with a hashtag sign (#). From now on, users could actively trend certain topics or passively track topics. All trending topics are instantly indexed and filtered, before they become visible in the "trending" sidebar. The Retweet function was rolled out in 2009; retweeting—users reposting interesting tweets from their friends using the letters RT followed by the @ sign and a user name—became a very popular function, generating enormous amounts of traffic on Twitter. By implementing this feature, Twitter encouraged conversational tagging. Users started deploying the tag itself as a prompt to create typically short-lived, heavily retweeted topics (Huang, Thornton, and Efthimidias 2010). An important part of the push for integrated use was the promotion of Twitter's microsyntax as a new sort of currency. The symbols @ (referring to an online name) and # (denoting a searchable topic) and RT (Retweet) were quickly absorbed into everyday communication. The gradual appropriation of Twitter syntax across the Web and beyond—on T-shirts and magnets—signals its ubiquitous integration in online and offline social practices around the globe.

Most of the features mentioned so far emphasize Twitter's purpose as a generic service, developing its own techno-grammar to facilitate communication of a specific nature across platforms. Starting in 2010, twitter.com rolled out its revamped interface and presented itself as the "New Twitter," a transformation that confronted users with the site's other (corporate) ambitions. Users could now click on individual tweets to see pictures and video clips from a variety of other websites, including Flickr and YouTube, without leaving Twitter. Like Facebook and Google, Twitter started to require external developers comply with the OAuth standards. The site also inserted geospatial features, allowing users to initiate conversational interactions in a specific location or area and track them. Besides, Twitter introduced Promoted Tweets and Promoted Trends—a trending topic or widespread tweet paid for by a sponsor. Evidently, these new features promoted frictionless sharing between platforms and expanded Twitter's commercial potential, as they facilitated the introduction of new business models—an element I will return to in the next section.

An even more thorough interface redesign, also known as the "New-new Twitter," came in late 2011, shortly after Facebook had announced its Timeline feature. This revamping introduced four new buttons: the Home button, showing a "timeline" of tweets of people you follow; a Connect button, symbolized by the @ sign, displaying who and what you are following and retweeting; a Discover function, shaped like #, which forwards "the most relevant stories from your world"; and the Me button, a feature that contains your profile, direct messages, and favorites.[8] Twitter's new interface layout structured users' navigation while also rendering input more uniform and thus more accessible to advertisers. Much like Facebook's narrative Timeline structure, Twitter's New-new interface experience comes across as more streamlined than the old one. The choice of a standardized design is obviously a response to major competitors' interface strategies, not just Facebook but also Google+.

Improving the potential for interoperability and frictionless sharing across platforms, Twitter's interface overhaul reflects an attempt to weave its idiosyncratic microsyntax into the fabric of sociality: hashtags, RTs, and @replies moved to the center of each member's online experience. If Twitter were up to now largely regarded a site for technology-savvy people, the New-new Twitter helped push the site's image as a common utensil for ordinary users—one step closer to becoming a "utility." The platform's functionality as a network that helps users to connect, and to initiate and follow conversations worldwide, obviously generated a mass of tweets and twitterers. The gradual rollout of coding and design changes reveals a pattern where features enhancing user connectedness are gradually complemented by features advancing exploitation of the site's connectivity.

Users and Usage

From the onset, users and governments embraced Twitter as a tool for connecting individuals and communities of users—a platform that empowers citizens to voice opinions and emotions, that helps stage public dialogues, and supports groups or ideas to garner attention. In August 2010, Wikipedia listed nine "notable uses" for Twitter, each describing a real-life (or real-time) context in which Twitter had recently functioned as a central tool: in campaigning, legal proceedings, education, emergencies, protest and politics, public relations, reporting dissent, space exploration, and opinion polling.[9] One can read this list of notable uses as a haphazard inventory of the various social contexts in which Twitter penetrated people's everyday lives. Wikipedia's list singles out social circumstances in which *users* appropriated the tool, but that does not imply the tool itself is not a shaping force. If we examine the mutual shaping between Twitter and its users in specific social settings, we can hardly escape the ambiguous proposition inscribed in the platform: while claiming to facilitate all voices evenly, at the same time the site crafts a hierarchical structure of twitterers. I will zoom in on two specific usages to illustrate this paradox: Twitter as a tool for (community or political) organizing and as a platform for self-promotion.

Twitter users tend to be perceived as a mass of mostly young active users who feel empowered by the service in their individual contributions to dialogues or in their collective efforts to influence public debates. The platform's demographics and user dynamics reveal a more nuanced picture, though. In the early years of its existence, Twitter's user demographics stood out from other SNSs. Most social media, such as Facebook and Myspace, gained their popularity from large contingents of young, educated users—teenagers, college students, young professionals—who, at that stage in their lives, are eager to establish as many contacts as possible, at both a personal and a professional level. In contrast to competing SNSs, Twitter's initial user base largely consisted of older adults, many of whom had not used other social sites before. For the first couple of years, the microblogging network attracted users mostly in business settings and news outlets, resulting in an early adopter profile of older (35 and up) professional users.[10] Once the Twitter audience started to soar, markedly after May 2009, the group of younger adults grew at a much faster rate, resulting in a user constituency aged predominantly 35 and under.[11] As Twitter began to filter into the mainstream by catering news feeds and celebrity updates, the swing coincided with a shift in gender demographics.[12]

Along with the demographic changes came gravitation in user dynamics toward a few heavy twitterers: a small but prolific group of 10 percent of Twitter users accounts for over 90 percent of tweets (Heil and Piskorski 2009).[13] In 2010, information scientists reported from their comprehensive data analysis of all Twitter users that only 22 percent have reciprocal relationships, while 68 percent of users are not followed by any of their followings: "People follow others not only for social networking but for information, as the act of following represents the desire to receives [sic] all tweets by the person" (Kwak et al. 2010: 594). The popular RT and # buttons were exploited by few users to become influential twitterers. However, the most influential positions were not exclusively reserved for users who spawn large numbers of retweets; indeed, the most skillful users can exert substantial influence over a variety of topics, as researchers conclude: "Influence is not gained spontaneously or accidentally, but through concerted effort such as limiting tweets to a single topic" (Cha et al. 2010: 10).

Despite Twitter's image as the online "town hall" for networked communication—a mere amplifier of individual voices as well as collective opinions—the platform manifested itself increasingly as a potent instrument for routing ideas and manipulating opinions. On a self-proclaimed neutral "utility-like" platform such as Twitter, one would expect all users to be equal. But some users are more equal than others—an inequity that is partly due to the platform's architecture, as described above, and partly to users' own active steering. The ideal of an open and free twitterverse in reality comes closer to a public dialogue ruled by a small number of hyperconnected influencers skilled at handling large numbers of followers. The platform's architecture privileges certain influential users who can increase tweet volume, and whom thus garner more followers. Twitter's ambition to be an echo chamber of serendipitous chatter thus finds itself at odds with the implicit capacity, inscribed in its engine, to allow some users to exert extraordinary influence. How did this ambiguity manifest itself in specific social situations?

The first social context in which Twitter's dilemma surfaced is that of political (grassroots) activism. The Iranian uprising, in 2009, the Arab Spring in 2010, and the Occupy movement of 2011 were all considered examples of users' empowerment through social media—citizen's taking hold of their own communication and propaganda channels to challenge the power of conventional gatekeepers such as governments and news organizations. The 2009 revolt in Iran was hailed as the "Twitter revolution," stressing a view of social media as inherently liberating (Gaffney 2010; Giroux 2009). Foreign media and government officials attributed major significance to social media platforms in the Arab Spring uprisings; they considered them neutral tools, which, in the hands of prodemocratic citizens, rendered them powerful as a collective. Detractors such as Morozov (2011) and Christensen (2011) have raised serious doubts about social media's liberating potential, arguing that most platforms aggravate the grip of totalitarian regimes on protesters because actual users can be easily tracked through these tools.[14]

According to critics of the liberating view, Twitter is not a neutral platform, and all users are not equally influential. Twitter's filtering functions are constantly fine-tuned, gauging the influence of its users in order to better organize search results (Huberman, Romero, and Wu 2009). Twitterers like CNNs Christiane Amanpour or some Middle East specialists are automatically assigned more weight in the twitterverse than just anyone who offers an opinion. On top of these filtering mechanisms, the voices of protestors using Twitter during the uprisings were not all equally influential. In their thorough analysis of the protests in Tunisia, Poell and Darmoni (2012) show that twitterers at the center of the Arab diaspora networks, who were well connected with activist organizations and journalists around the world, were able to use the platform for distributing messages to international media. Just as EdgeRank filters Facebook "friends" for relevance, Twitter's algorithms, policies, and user practices consign different weight to different voices.

A second context in which to demonstrate the platform's ambiguity and its users' differentiated authority is Twitter's role as a tool for self-promotion. While Twitter boasts of its capability to resonate the "roar of the crowd," the platform savors the stardom of influential twitterers, especially of stars, politicians, and celebrities. Famous personalities profit from Twitter's followers' function as the perfect medium to organize and maintain their fans. For politicians, Twitter has become an indispensable tool with which to galvanize their electoral base because the medium allows them to control their messages—a big advantage over mainstream media, where they are dependent on journalists' framing. Not surprisingly, celebrities and politicians top the list of most frequently followed twitterers, resulting in a ranking where the top five attracts millions of followers.[15] Most star twitterers employ professional PR staff to manage their devotees, voters, or fans. Twitter, for its part, supplies consultants to keep the high-ranking influencers on top; after all, the traffic volume these stars create is quite lucrative to the company in terms of selling advertising space—a strategy I will return to in the next section.

Nursing a big following is not just a celebrity's privilege, however; for a lot of average users, Twitter has become a prime tool to advertise the self. The sheer number of followers has become a barometer for measuring popularity and influence, ascribing more power to few users in the twitterverse. Individuals quickly learned how to play the system and accumulate a lot of clout on Twitter. According to *New York* magazine journalist Hagan, the "impulse to make life a publicly annotated experience has blurred the distinction between advertising and self-expression, marketing and identity."[16] Users want large followings not just for reasons of vanity or self-esteem: they may actually cash in on their popularity rating by selling their influence to the highest bidder. Specialized sites such as Klout automatically calculate an individual's influence on the Web, using an algorithm that is largely based on Twitter followings and Facebook connections, and then sells this information to potential advertisers or companies looking for online influencers.[17] Companies and advertisers are keen to pay powerful twitterers—both celebrities and ordinary users—to distribute their brand name.

As these two social uses of Twitter illustrate, explicit users are shaping the platform's direction at the same time, and by the same means, as the platform is shaping users' behavior and social standing. The meaning of "following" initially was connecting to someone for the purpose of interaction and exchange. Gradually the term also came to signify trailing someone and "buying into" his or her ideas. To examine the equally ambiguous meaning of "trending," we will now look more closely at the content and cultural form of tweets.

Content and Cultural Form

Both the quality and quantity of tweets have been vital elements in the dispute of what constitutes Twitter's essence during the stage of interpretative flexibility. The "tweet" is arguably Twitter's most distinctive contribution to online culture; a sentence limited to 140 characters flagged by a hashtag has become a global format for online public commentary. This new cultural form has been adopted widely outside the platform proper, for instance in newspapers and on television. Its concise syntax and delimited length render the tweet virtually synonymous with a quote—a citation from a source for which authentication resides with the platform, not the journalist. Aside from figuring in the news, the tweet has emerged as a cultural form inspiring poets and literary authors. So-called "twitlit" is yet another sign of Twitter's microsyntax becoming part of globalized cultural discourse.

The quality of tweets has been subject to interpretive contestation; most discussions revolve around the question whether tweets are conversational or informational, and whether they contain essential or nonessential information. Some early critics touted the flow of tweets as verbal diarrhea, while others characterized it, in line with Twitter's ambitions, as a gush of free-floating public chatter.[18] During the first three years of Twitter's development researchers discussed whether the tool just supported everyday small talk or whether it had news-signaling significance.[19] Indeed, Tweets may be about the latest development in the Middle East or about Lady Gaga's cold.[20] But essential and nonessential content have always coexisted in older media, even in what we call quality newspapers; it is hardly surprising, then, to find these two types of content emerge side by side in a new medium. Perhaps most typical of a Tweet is not the "weight" of its content, but the message's expressive and personal nature. Researchers Marwick and boyd (2011) observe that tweets with the pronoun "I" in them tend to be well received. Politicians use tweets to wrap their political messages in personal narratives in order to exploit the intimate connotation of the medium's communicative mode. Tweets also work best to convey affective content, both in terms of gut-fired opinion and spontaneous reactions. Increasingly, politicians' and celebrities' "personal" tweets appear in the mass media as commentaries, replacing the perfunctory quote. Fitting in with Facebook's narrative strategy, the tweet's effectiveness lies in having a personalized public message enter a customized online social environment.

The most vital qualifier of the paradoxical nature of tweets, though, lies not in their quality but in their enormous quantity. The daily number of Twitter messages increased from 27 million in 2009 to 290 million in February 2012.[21] On the one hand, tweets flowing in real time are often conceptualized as a stream of (global) consciousness or a resonance room for unmediated public chatter. On the other hand, the concept of an indiscriminate flow of tweets is at odds with Twitter's efforts to structure the amorphous information stream into a usable, exploitable resource. Not every tweet is assigned the same importance: as described above, some senders are valued over others, and some tweets weigh more than others. Weight is measured in tweets per second (TPS): when intensity is high, they are assigned more impact. The algorithmic push of intensity over quality results in short periods of heavily circulated messages that may become trends. Trending topics may thus refer to streams of "surfacing content" but may also signal content-massages aimed at pushing the message to go viral and spill over into other social platforms and mainstream media. The double logic of "tracking emerging trends" and "setting a trend" poses a profound challenge to Twitter's owners. As one of the platform's CEOs, Dick Costello, rightly observed, the "danger of overstructuring information is that the user stops experiencing Twitter the way people originally came to experience Twitter as the place for free-form, serendipitous chatter."[22]

Twitter's investment in trending topics could be regarded emblematic for the platform's divergent ambitions to simultaneously measure, engineer, and mobilize the public's mood. Both the platform's coding technologies and its users help content surface while, vice versa, trending topics help certain users to become influencers. The function of a platform as a global opinion machine is hardly novel. Jürgen Habermas (1989) theorized that media channels, far from registering the free exchange of ideas, constitute a social space through which norms for communication and interaction are produced. Referring to newspapers and television news, Habermas argued that by using publicity strategies such as opinion polls, mass media infiltrated the formal public sphere, where they "corrupted" collective opinion formation by introducing mechanisms that served corporate or government interests (van Dijck 2012a). In other words, opinion polling also includes opinion engineering.

What is new in microblogging is that the tweet flow, in contrast to the programmed television flow, is conceptualized as a *live* stream of uninhibited, unedited, instant, short, and short-lived reactions—a stream that supposedly taps a *real-time* undercurrent of opinions and gut feelings. If we accept at face value the owners' claim that Twitter is a neutral infrastructure where the current gist of tweets gushes unmediated through its pipelines, this ambition is controverted by the fact that the system is engineered to manage the flow and gets manipulated by hyperconnected users who want to influence the flow. To understand the inherent paradox of Twitter's following and trending logic, it may not be enough to ask the question of what Twitter *is*; we also need to raise the question of what Twitter *wants*, meaning we have to look at its socioeconomic structure. How does the company envision its corporate strategy, including its governance policy and (future) business model?

4.3. ASKING THE STRATEGIC QUESTION: WHAT DOES TWITTER WANT?

Ownership

As stated in the previous section, Twitter's owners wanted to develop the platform as an independent microblogging service. Like Facebook, Twitter concentrated on making its service compatible with as many platforms as possible, securing the ubiquitous presence of its iconized light-blue and white T-button in all kinds of hardware (mobile phones), software (websites), and media content (TV programs, ads, newspapers). Facebook and Google have integrated Twitter in their services—likely at the expense of their own microblogging services News Feed and Buzz—because Twitter's brand name quickly attracted lots of traffic. Twitter's status as a stand-alone company, though, has been a regular subject of speculation; market analysts keep a constant eye on the site's monetizing strategy, whether as an autonomous brand or as a potential takeover target for other plat-forms.[23] So far, the company has proved able to retain its sovereign status, ostensibly anchoring its claim to neutrality in independent ownership sta-tus, but how long will the company manage to live up to its original ideals? And, learning from Facebook's IPO, would a future public offering compro-mise the owner's objectives and thwart users' enthusiasm?

One of Twitter's problems in retaining independence is related to the company's ambiguous ambitions: can Twitter be a utility that facilitates connectedness while at the same time being a company that exploits the giant stream of tweets and metadata its users generate? The answer is sim-ple: it needs to do both if it wants to survive. Twitter's position in the eco-system has always been a precarious one. Its rivals, Facebook and Google, each dominate a demarcated territory in the ecosystem: Google "owns" search, Facebook "owns" social networking. Sure, Twitter "owns" microb-logging, but its niche is not (yet) as clearly branded as that of its competi-tors. In 2011, CEO Dick Costello began to call Twitter an "information network" rather than a "social networking service" to signal the company's move toward the connectivity approach. Shying away from Jack Dorsey's earlier "utility" ambitions and attaching a new generic label to the platform may well be interpreted as a territorial defense strategy—a deliberate attempt to wall off Twitter's niche from its looming contenders' turf. "Information networking" could be considered the company's revamped corporate aim, still in the early stages of development—microblogging's period of interpretive flexibility being far from over. However, new corpo-rate goals require strategic positioning, not only toward third-party devel-opers that historically popularized Twitter by designing a large variety of apps, but also toward "old" media building on Twitter traffic mechanisms and, last but not least, toward big social media competitors.

Until 2010, the company never charged for the use of its data, and many app designers proved to be much better than Twitter itself in monetizing their daily gush of tweets. For instance, TweetDeck, a popular monitoring tool that used the Twitter API to form a sort of dashboard for trailing and redirecting online traffic, became a successful start-up. In 2011, Twitter took over TweetDeck, thus underscoring its new ambition to monetize content rather than exploit a utility. From the side of "old" media, television producers increasingly integrated microblogging tools into their professional routines for making news or entertainment. A number of newspapers signal "trending topics," based on Twitter's most popular tweets of the day, and deploy Twitter's potential to tap into near-boiling topics to anticipate and create news.[24] In addition, broadcast producers exploit Twitter's "viral looping" capacities by drawing audiences into a conversation, while the company can also provide aggregated real-time analytics that help one understand the dynamics of televised debate or detect sentiment pulses in staged entertainment (Diakopoulos and Shamma 2010). If Twitter wants to be a leading service in information networking, we should not be surprised to see partnerships with major content producers and broadcast industries emerge.

Twitter's independent position as an "information network" seems far from secure if we consider the importance of search in any setting that centers on (meta)data interpretation and exploitation. And with the increased emphasis on information and search comes a scenario in which Twitter has no choice but to team up with the giant of search: Google. Twitter's annexation by one of the big content providers may seem unlikely at this point, but the above examples of takeovers and alliances suggest that Twitter's autonomy is anything but guaranteed in the volatile ecosystem of connective media.[25] If Twitter wants to be an information company rather than a utility, this choice not only affects Twitter's ownership status but also its choice of business models.

Business Models

Up until 2009, Twitter's owners remained deliberately vague about plans to monetize their popular service; they raised enough money from venture capitalists to allow time to find a suitable revenue model.[26] At some point, though, business analysts began to ask whether Twitter's owners were interested in monetizing the service at all; just as media watchers initially called Twitter a service in search of a user application, market analysts wondered whether Twitter, four years after its launch, was still in search of a business model.[27] Like other social networking sites, notably YouTube and Facebook, Twitter relied on the strategy of building an audience of users first and finding revenue streams later. In these years, management experts were still convinced that the largest possible user base is crucial to a site's long-term sustained profitability (Enders et al. 2008). However, business models are not ready-made strategies; testing business models, building a user base, and tweaking the interface are mutually defining tactics—a dynamics that few economists recognize (Orlikowski and Iacono 2001).

When Twitter still regarded itself as a general conduit for communication traffic, it aimed at helping businesses create customer value. Hence, the company appeared mostly interested in business models that involved generating service fees from users or revenue fees from corporate clients. The first option soon turned out to be illusory—users were not going to pay for a subscription if they could use competing services for free. The second option looked more promising. From the very beginning, Twitter encouraged third-party developers to design APIs by opening up its metadata to everyone, from researchers to commercial developers, without charge. Several years into the site's existence, a number of books already explained the tool's power to "dominate your market" or how to "get rich with Twitter" (Comm and Burge 2009; Prince 2010). The company stood by and watched as outside programmers developed monetizing services and tested them in the marketplace.[28]

For the first couple of years, Twitter also resisted the business model of paid advertisements showing up next to the Twitter dialogue box. It was not until the implementation of Twitter's trending topics and geospatial features that the company started to exploit data for targeted, personalized advertising. In the spring and summer of 2010, some cautious steps in Twitter's slow-rolling business model could be observed. The site launched @earlybird Exclusive Offers, offering followers time-sensitive deals on products and events from sponsors, and introduced Promoted Tweets and Promoted Trends, a service linking keywords to advertisers in order to insert sponsored tweets into the stream of real-time conversation.[29] Geospatial features, such as Points of Interest, allowed for location-based targeted messages. Earlier that year, Twitter had bought up Summize, a successful start-up that exploits search engines linked to geo-location systems. By monetizing these new features, Twitter paved the way to include sponsored content—push-based, pull-based, or geo-based—next to Twitter messages.

It took more time for the company to figure out how to utilize the increasingly precious resource of connectivity flowing nonstop through the site's veins, especially the massive amounts of instant, spontaneous reactions to themed tweets. Indeed, Twitter had already sold the rights to include tweets in search results to Google and Microsoft in 2009, which turned out to be a lucrative deal. And by starting to charge external developers for using Twitter's data in 2010, the company recouped some of that value. Still, some Twitter watchers and market analysts became impatient with the company's slow learning curve when it came to business models:

> For those of you not familiar with the firehose, it's the data that flows through Twitter from its 175 million users and the 155 million daily tweets. That's a lot of valuable data that can be used for a variety of reasons by Twitter and third parties. Currently, Twitter charges some companies to access its data but most companies pay a modest amount or nothing to access the data stream. But as data becomes more important, the value of Twitter's firehose becomes more valuable. It means that Twitter has a huge revenue source under its nose, as long as Twitter is willing to capitalize on it.[30]

In other words, if Twitter takes seriously its ambition to become an information company, exploiting real-time user data is an indispensable means to this end. Researchers tested Twitter's effectiveness as a "social sensor" for real-time events, such as accidents or earthquakes, which could be measured almost instantly by tracking the tagged trends on Twitter (Sakaki, Okazaki, and Matsuo 2010). In addition, academics examined Twitter's potential as an instrument for "sentiment analysis" and "opinion mining" (Diakopoulos and Shamma 2010; Pak and Paroubek 2010) and for measuring the public mood with the help of "real-time analytics" (Bollen, Mao, and Pepe 2010).

Building a business model on this potential invokes the paradox explored in the previous section while also adding another one. Besides the tension between perceptions of Twitter as a neutral platform while, in reality, its mechanisms promote engineering and manipulation, the platform also faces the dilemma of what Andrejevic (2011) calls "affective economics." Sentiment analysis, mood mining, and opinion mining—all subsets of predictive analytics—largely work on the presumption that Twitter is indeed a barometer of emotion and opinion, but these methods entail more than taking the "emotional pulse" of the Internet. Complex algorithms derived from past user behavior are used to anticipate but also *affect* future behavior: The process of aggregating and disaggregating data from individual consumers may be deployed to tap into users' buzz about brands as well as to *create* brand communities based on Twitter dialogues on specific topics. As Andrejevic (2011) concludes: "Any consideration of affective economics should include the ways in which marketers seek to manage consumers through the collection not just of demographic information, but of extensive real-time databases of their online behavior and conversations" (604).

While Twitter's monetizing strategy is still open and ambivalent, the company carefully pursues various business models, rolling out changes in interface gradually—a sort of controlled experimentation with different models alongside each other (McGrath 2009). After all, every modification involves the risk of losing users—a precious asset for an "information networking" company that is completely dependent on users' willingness to transmit content. As Twitter develops its business models in close relation to coding technologies, user routines, and content, we see that the company's transforming ambitions result in a double paradox. Twitter-the-ambient-utility promoting user connectedness finds itself at odds with Twitter-the-information-network exploiting connectivity to help businesses promote their brands among users. Platform owners, users, and third parties are engaged in a precarious choreography that surfaces most poignantly at the level of governance.

Governance

In contrast to Facebook, Twitter's terms of service (ToS) have always been quite forthright in stating the rights and restrictions of users versus owners and of users versus third-party developers.[31] When Twitter started in 2006, its terms of service were very general and did not say much about the way users could deploy the tool to communicate: "We encourage users to contribute their creations to the public domain or consider progressive licensing terms." Unlike Facebook users, twitterers never fostered the illusion of privacy or intimate circles, as they use the service largely as a tool for (self)-promotion and interaction with the world at large. Twitter's policy in 2009 explicitly articulated the company's intention to offer an open service to global communities: "What you say on Twitter may be viewed all around the world instantly. You are what you Tweet!" In other words, users should control their public statements, while the platform vows to protect a users' right to express their views and own their content. As stated in the ToS: users "retain rights to any Content [they] submit, post, display on or through Twitter." Twitter users have never taken the site's owners to court for violation of privacy rules, and, to many users' surprise, the company indeed protected twitterers' freedom of speech: they even challenged a defeat in a subpoena case to hand over a specific user's tweets by taking the decision to a higher court.[32]

Users were a lot more critical, though, when Twitter announced its policy, in January 2012, of complying with each country's laws and censor tweets per region, whereas previously Twitter would only block tweets or accounts globally. From now on, a specific tweet could be prevented from appearing in a particular country or region, replaced by a gray box with a note reading, for instance, "This tweet from @username has been withheld in: Thailand." A spokesperson explained that Twitter had no choice but to abide by national laws and comply with local legal requirements if the platform were to stay in service in these countries. The example of German law prohibiting Nazi material to be published on any online platform provided an example of the kind of legal constraints the company faced. Yet Twitter users feared a censorship policy that threatened First Amendment rights in many non-Western countries. A "Twitter Black-out day" was staged on January 28, 2012, to protest this rule.[33] Using the hashtag #TwitterBlack-out, the boycott rallied support among thousands of users in various countries, gathering responses such as "Twitter starts deleting tweets, I stop posting tweets. Join the #twitterblackout tomorrow!"

While most SNSs' terms of service, particularly Facebook's, tend to regulate relationships between platform owners and users, Twitter deployed its governance terms also to arbitrate the interests of its users vis-à-vis those of third-party developers. The platform's first ToS in 2006 said nothing about the use of data by app developers or by the platform's owners for advertising purposes. In 2009, the ToS added that all data sent through Twitter may be used by third parties: "You agree that this license includes the right for Twitter to make such Content available to other companies, organizations or individuals who partner with Twitter for the syndication, broadcast, distribution or publication of such Content on other media and services, subject to our terms and conditions for such Content use." On the condition of the owner's consent, and later by paying a small fee, app developers were thus granted access to Twitter data. The introduction of Promoted Tweets and Trends led to a change in the 2011 terms of service, which now contain a line stating that "Twitter and its third party providers and partners may place such advertising on the Services or in connection with the display of Content or information from the Services whether submitted by you or others." Even if users were not very happy with Twitter's new advertising policies, they did not protest them either, apparently accepting the new norm of letting a free service be paid for by ads.

However, the inclusion of a new clause in Twitter's revised ToS policy in 2011, aimed at anchoring the platform's broadened options for data mining, raised more eyebrows, especially those of third-party developers:

> Twitter uses a variety of services hosted by third parties to help provide our Services, such as hosting our various blogs and wikis, and to help us *understand the use of* our Services, *such as Google Analytics*. These services may collect information sent by your browser as part of a web page request, such as cookies or your IP request. (Emphases added)

If before 2011, all third parties were indiscriminately allowed to develop Twitter services on the basis of its API, this clause grants this privilege to select third parties on the condition that they comply with strict rules. The statement also reveals that Twitter partners with Google to develop data-mining strategies. Instead of users lashing out at Twitter for selling out their data, third-party developers protested what they saw as unprecedented restrictions on their freedom to develop apps for a service once known as a "utility." A company spokesman defended Twitter's new rules, citing the need for a more "consistent user experience" across platforms, because "consumers continue to be confused by the different ways that a fractured landscape of third-party Twitter clients display tweets and let users interact with core Twitter functions."[34] He confirmed that third-party developers could continue to create client applications, such as content-curating or publishing tools, as long as they adhered to Twitter's ToS. Unsurprisingly, the announcement triggered furious reactions among third-party developers, who felt excluded and rejected after many years of helping the platform gain ubiquitous visibility in the vast ecosystem of connective media. As one blogger expressed his dismay:

> You [Twitter] may feel you "need" this consistency, but you don't. You want it, and are willing to make tradeoffs to get it. I just hope you realize how big those tradeoffs are, and how chilling it is for Twitter to decide that only certain kinds of innovation on the Twitter API are welcome.[35]

It is difficult not to read these ToS modifications as the next step in Twitter's new ambition to become an "information company." While Twitter's governance policy explicitly protects users' rights to express and control their opinions, the company is forced to comply with country-specific legislation if it wants to stay in business; and the company's vocal defense of users against exploitation of their data by third-party developers draw a thin veil over the company's need to team up with a data giant to help monetize Twitter's vast resources.

Within the short time span of six years, the company's ambitions transformed from wanting to be a global, neutral communication channel for citizens that might be used in defiance of governments, to wanting to be a profitable venture that must obey the laws of those countries where it seeks to attract customers. Twitter also risked its reputation as an "open" platform facilitating all potential developers by restricting access to its precious tweet flow and seeking exclusive collaboration with few powerful allies. A detailed exploration of this paradox likely does not answer the question of what Twitter wants; it rather exposes the minefield of conflicting forces in which the company operates. And this minefield of forces inevitably draws attention to the larger ecosystem of connective media in which Twitter has evolved and is bound to play a role in the future.

4.4. ASKING THE ECOLOGICAL QUESTION: HOW WILL TWITTER EVOLVE?

The gradual transformation of Twitter as an autonomous utility promoting user connectedness into an information network exploiting user connectivity can hardly be evaluated in isolation. The double paradox laid out in the previous sections did not simply emanate from the owners' decision to change objectives. Instead, the proliferation of Twitter as a platform has been a complex process in which technological adjustments are intricately intertwined with modifications in user base, content channeling, choices for revenue models, and changes in governance policies and ownership strategies. By tracking the process of interpretive flexibility in its first six years, I sketched how Twitter developed as a niche service in the social networking domain to one of the major online players. And yet Twitter's embeddedness in the larger ecosystem, which is partly responsible for its past growth, will also account for some of its future vulnerabilities. As of the spring of 2012, Twitter found itself at the crossroads of a maze of interdependent platforms where it needed to define its position vis-à-vis users as well as its various competitors.

Perhaps against all odds, Twitter is still an independent company, having conquered a dominant position in a niche of online sociality it has itself coded and branded. Microblogging has become virtually synonymous with tweeting. The platform's microsyntax of @ and # epitomize how following and trending—both as active and as passive verbs—are part of a quotidian discourse the basic grammar of which is understood even by nontwitterers. The brand is perceived as a generic practice, much like "googling." Twitter's early image as an echo chamber of serendipitous chatter, a town hall of public dialogue, and an amplifier of suppressed voices still lingers in the minds of people.[36] This image motivates other social media platforms and traditional media to mobilize Twitter as part of their armamentarium. One might well argue that Twitter's future success as an information network is conditional on the strong resonance of its earlier ambition to be a neutral utility; many users still regard the platform's utility function as its prime objective and hence accept the platform's claim to neutrality even if the exploitation and manipulation of tweets has gained wider recognition. In the face of the platform's refurbished ambitions, the question is how Twitter will live up to that new paradox-based image.

Twitter's strongest asset in the competition with other platforms is its ability to generate enormous amounts of "live" streams of short-lived online traffic that can be minutely tracked in real time. Neither Facebook nor Google+ nor YouTube is equipped to serve this function. Therefore, Twitter hopes to strategically position itself in the market of predictive analytics and real-time analytics. The algorithmic drive to analyze online behavior on the basis of past and live behavioral data bolsters the cultural logic of following and trending as practices that simultaneously comprise a passive reflection and active manipulation of social motion. Amazon's famous taste recommendation system is just one example of the predictive analytics that is growing more ingenious and powerful by the day; major offline and online companies hire engineers to evaluate their customer's data for individualized tracking and targeted advertising.[37] The new hot science of online data engineering interprets consumer data while concurrently steering consumers' desires. No competing platform has access to vast streams of "live" social data the way Twitter does, but developing the tools to analyze these data streams and translate them into profitable algorithms is another matter. With Google Analytics as its preferred partner, Twitter may well strengthen its position as a global player in the information-networking field, because "search" is a crucial factor in the successful deployment of predictive and real-time analytics. The alliance with Google also brings a vast potential for integrating online advertising services.

Besides playing a growing role in online consumer markets, trend mining and opinion mining are also deployed for nonmarket purposes, varying from political campaigns to promoting civilian grassroots causes. Twitter celebrities with large followings (Oprah, Beyoncé) are regularly mobilized to bring noble causes to the attention of their followers, whether poverty in Sudan or animal cruelty in Puerto Rico. Hashtag activism, as it is also called, embraces Twitter as a tool for instant propagation of social causes, and Twitter is a powerful weapon in the hands of grassroots groups and NGOs like Greenpeace to harness consumer awareness or organize boycotts. The flipside of low-threshold, Twitter-driven protests is that they become shorthand for easily garnered public support. Indeed, as some journalists observe, protests-by-the-click are now so common that hashtag activism fatigue threatens to blur all causes.[38] More troublesome with regard to these concerted efforts, though, is the mounting difficulty of distinguishing narcissistic self-promotion from truly engaged activism, and idealistic from commercial purposes. Activist's online choreographies seldom involve just one platform; the goal of most political and ideological causes is to go viral across online and offline media in order to accumulate massive attention.[39] These short outbursts of massive viral looping may illustrate how the algorithmic syntaxes of liking, friending, trending, following, favoriting, and other "social verbs" blend into a seamless composition, but that harmonized algorithmic grammar often masks a cacophony of push-and-pull forces.

And yet it is extremely important to identify the mutually reinforcing mechanisms and contriving alliances that inform the underlying rationale of social media's ecology. Twitter's partnering with Google is not just an incidental duet between two microsystems, but signals a system-wide trend of consolidating and confounding forces—a topic I will return to in the last chapter. The transformation of Twitter's corporate ambitions and strategies over time, far from being unique, is a recurring trope in the short histories of various competing platforms. The double paradox that evolved in Twitter's years of interpretive flexibility is peculiarly mirrored in other platforms' arrested development (as we will see in the case of Flickr) or successful transformation (as in the case of YouTube). The dynamics between hyperconnected influencers and followers as well as the power of predictive analytics have attracted attention to Twitter's potential as a predictor and producer of future social trends.[40]

Turning the analytical prism to Twitter's own future, though, it may be precarious for the company to predict what happens next. Since the meaning of microblogging has not stabilized yet and the ecosystem of connective media is still in great flux, predicting the future is like playing the stock market: you can monitor all elements meticulously and not be able to forecast turbulence, owing to the volatility of the system. In the waxing and waning culture of connectivity, Twitter's fate is dependent on its interoperability with other microsystems and also on the equilibrium between owners' ambitions to exploit tweets and users' motivation to keep tweeting. Twitter has not yet lived up to Jack Dorsey's aspiration for the platform to "fade into the background." People do not (yet) take Twitter for granted. A platform is not a phone. A tweet is not electricity. The period of interpretive flexibility is far from over; it may still be a long journey to attain the stage of stabilization.

CHAPTER 5

Flickr between Communities and Commerce

5.1. INTRODUCTION

> Before Twitter, Flickr was the only social network I needed. I was using it for everything: designs, posters, mock-ups, photographs, sets, experiments, even embarrassing updates from time to time. Then Facebook came along and promised to be the best at it. After some time I was disappointed by two facts: people joined Facebook because it was cool, not because they wanted to be part of a community. Second reason was that Flickr was acquired by Yahoo!—they didn't get the fact that Flickr was a network of small communities that could interact between each others [*sic*].[1]

As this blogger's post demonstrates, social media are not just about owners building relationships with users through platforms; users want a relationship with their site because they care about what a site does to their experience of online sociality. Facebook and Twitter, as examples of successful platforms, concentrated on becoming the largest social network and microblogging network, respectively. To achieve these goals, owners cajoled users to conform to their strategy, while balancing off their own interests with those of users, advertisers, third-party developers, shareholders and stakeholders. Users were not always happy with Facebook's and Twitter's strategic maneuvers, and, as we learned in the previous chapters, some users expressed concern about "their" site mismanaging "their" experience. The fact that the overwhelming majority of users comply with changes even if they don't like them may partly explain the success of these two platforms. Another explanation may be, as this blogger suggests, that Facebook and Twitter users are not interested in community building but in networking experiences that serve individualized user needs. As soon as big corporations propel a site's ambitions to become the biggest, they generally care more about generating large volumes of fast turnover traffic than about building sustainable communities. The blog post quoted above suggests that this is what happened when Flickr was taken over by Yahoo—a move that sealed Flickr's fate.

What explains success or failure in the volatile ecosystem of connective media? While some platforms have succeeded splendidly, others have flopped spectacularly, and yet others have waxed and waned in the public's sympathy. There are no impartial or objective definitions of success and failure, and the ultimate accomplishment for owners (e.g., a platform's IPO or a high-priced buyout) may be considered a disappointment to users who want their online experience to be free of commercial pressures. Success and failure are not entirely in the eyes of the beholder, however; definitions of what constitutes success and who has a stake in its outcome are part of a struggle over online sociality. In *Aramis; or, The Love of Technology* (1996), Bruno Latour investigates the demise of the Paris personal rapid transit system by arguing that technological systems fail not because any particular actor killed or neglected it, but because the totality of actors involved in the process fail to sustain it through negotiation and adaptation to a changing social environment. Swift swells and sustainable growth are at the heart of this discussion between various interdependent actors.

Flickr, founded in 2004 and still one of the best-known online photo-sharing sites, attracted millions of users before it experienced a substantial setback in popularity and user numbers.[2] Some will see Flickr as an example of a "failed" microsystem—a platform that did not survive the ecosystem's vagaries. However, with 51 million registered members, 80 million unique visitors per month, and over 6 billion pictures on its site, it still occupies a comfortable position in the global rankings. It is interesting to investigate why Flickr did not succeed amid big contenders like Facebook, Twitter, Google+, and YouTube. According to some, Flickr even lost the race with small challengers, such as the quickly surging start-up Instagram, which was bought up by Facebook in the spring of 2012. If you ask users—particularly avid bloggers and critical users—for the causes of their site's pitiful demise, many of them will have quite a different story to tell. They may refer to the thriving groups that survived in spite of a corporate owner making a halfhearted commitment to the platform's communities; or they may relate the story of a platform that learned from its users and built a better online experience than the "big winners" in the ecosystem.

This chapter seeks to explore how Flickr's wavering position between community and commerce, between success and failure, is negotiated in terms of coding technologies, user and content strategies, ownership structure, governance policies, and business models. Unlike Twitter, Flickr did not replace one kind of strategic ambition with another; instead, it moved back and forth between various different interpretations of online photo sharing and thus between various platform functions: from community site to social network platform, from photo news site to memory service and archival facility. Flickr's vacillating movements derive not only from diffident management and assertive users, but also from profound roots in a cultural economy characterized by clashing notions of collectiveness versus connectivity, of commons versus commerce. Rather than diagnosing Flickr as a failed system, I want to examine the site's evolution as symptom of a larger transformation toward a culture of connectivity.

5.2. FLICKR BETWEEN CONNECTEDNESS AND CONNECTIVITY

Technology

When Flickr started out as a platform in 2004—a time when neither Facebook nor Twitter had yet had a chance to code or brand online sociality—Flickr's interface design reflected the site's aim to be a social networking site with pictures at its core. You may also call Flickr a user-generated content (UGC) site with a strong networking component. Even in its earliest version, Flickr offered its users sophisticated tools to control their sociality: they could mark any photo as private, identify a few trusted viewers, open up the picture to a group of friends, or share it with anyone. Flickr's interface offered features for posting, favoriting, distributing, curating, exhibiting, and storing photographic objects online. Many of these activities already had an equivalent in the offline world, but the platform added a new social dimension to these creative activities by including buttons to comment on postings and click on favorite photos. Users signed up and communicated through their e-mail addresses. An important part of Flickr's social appeal was built into the "group" button, a default stimulating users to join groups to discuss their common interest in pictures.

Flickr defined itself in its earliest years in relation to competitors such as Photobucket (started in 2003) and Kodak Gallery (2001), and offered by far the most complete set of tools for photo aficionados wanting to move their social practice to the online world. In Flickr's original concept, photos were not a by-product of sociality; online picture sharing was the core of a creative and communicative function. After 2005, Flickr's strong community or group function certainly was built on, but the centrality of this focus was also diluted when the platform added a number of features aimed at integrating Flickr in the larger constellation of Yahoo. In 2007, much to the chagrin of its original users, all Flickr members were required to sign up with a Yahoo ID, rather than exchanging content via users' e-mail.[3] Other features served to render Flickr more compatible (and competitive) with big platforms. In April 2008, Flickr began to allow subscribers to upload videos limited to 90 seconds in length and 150MB in size.[4] The lure of the Facebook, YouTube, and Twitter coding architecture definitely shows in Flickr's capricious interface design between 2005 and 2010, when the site implemented, revised, deleted, and reinserted a number of interface features.

Early versions of Flickr imitated users' real-time photo-sharing activity in a multiuser chat room called FlickrLive, an online environment where photographs served to trigger live discussion. The chat room feature was shelved in 2005, only to return in 2011, reincarnated into a feature called Photo Session. Photo Session allows up to ten people to view a digital slide show together while talking through a chat window built into the product, either on Skype or on the phone. After being absent for several years, the talk feature was thus restored to its prominent position. "We want to help people make their photos available to the people who matter to them," reads a statement on the Flickr home page, underscoring the paradigm that pictures trigger social activity, not the other way around.[5] Markus Spiering, recently appointed head of product design with Flickr, commented on the introduction of Photo Session, saying: "This feature brings back the old feeling, sitting on a couch and looking at a photo album."[6]

The functions of exhibiting, collecting, and storing pictures online were an integral part of Flickr's interface. The site enabled users to tag favorite photos, make "sets" or collections of photos that fall under the same heading, and display them as slideshows or embed them in other websites. A feature called Flickr Gallery encourages members to curate and exhibit up to 18 public photos or videos in one place, as we can read on the home page: "It's an opportunity to celebrate the creativity of your fellow members in a truly unique way around a theme, an idea or just because."[7] The implementation of a so-called Photostream prompted users to constantly add new pictures to their pool rather than using the site as a photo album, thus boosting the site's traffic. According to ethnographer Nancy Van House (2007), photostreams helped define collections of online photos as "transitory, ephemeral, 'throwaway,' a stream, not an archive" (2719). The Photostream feature counterbalanced the site's storage and archival function, for which it became popular as users added a steadily growing number of photos. Flickr was keen to be perceived as a constantly evolving pictorial database, which never fossilizes into a stable archive.

To make this giant dynamic picture archive searchable, Flickr developed its own search functions. Features like "tagging" rendered the collection searchable for individual users and motivated them to contribute to a user community (Nov and Ye 2010). It was one of the first sites to implement tag clouds—a visual depiction of user-generated tags, which can be categorized alphabetically or by importance (indicated by font size or color). In addition, Flickr gradually included more automatically uploaded metadata in its software design, such as geotags and time stamps—location data transmitted by default from location-aware camera phones and digital cameras. Geotags enable a social dynamics based on geographical proximity called geosocial networking; users may choose interactions relative to location and in time, and Flickr's interface can be deployed to visualize users' interactions. Needless to say, both user-added tags and automatic tags added considerably to Flickr's commercial potential, especially in the area of app development and recommendation systems, as we will see shortly.

For several years, Flickr foregrounded coding features that accentuate newsiness and transience rather than historicity and retention—features commonly attributed to a visual archive. In 2008, around the time when Twitter began to surge worldwide, Flickr added an instant news photostream to its home page, containing continuously refreshed pictures of worldwide events. The design contained buttons to view "Interesting photos from the last 7 days" and "Most recent uploads," as well as an automated teller of "Uploads in the last minute," all intended to boost traffic and generate interest in current affairs. Through its interface design, users were prompted to check the site for its constant feeds and endless streams of new pictures taken by users all over the world, reflecting general media values surfacing through the news. Several years later, the news photostream disappeared from the home page. The site's current design contains a "Discover" button, a feature that lets the user "see what's going on in the world." After the latest interface overhaul, in February 2012, the Discover button urges users to go "tell a story with your photos." This explicit turn to storytelling, combined with an emphasis on larger pictures and less open space on the site, subtly hints at Facebook's Timeline.

Flickr's interface history shows an eclectic range of features with alternate degrees of prominence. Early interface design positioned the platform as a tool for building communities and groups. Later interface modifications tilted the service toward a news and information tool, or a general social network, or a personal memory tool. Features have come and gone, implemented at one moment, shelved at another, pushed to the fore, then de-emphasized or refurbished. However, despite Flickr's inconsistency in its choice of technological features over time, the site kept creative and social activity at its core, even when this function got temporarily back-benched by more fashionable features. Some changes were clearly motivated by Yahoo's need for Flickr to blend with the company's larger infrastructure or were sparked by the surging popularity of major competing sites such as Facebook, YouTube, and Twitter. In this respect, a more poignant question is how interfaces translate into user practices. What usages were inscribed in Flickr over the years, and how did users respond to the platform's seemingly inconsistent choices?

Users and Usage

It is important to realize that photo sharing, unlike microblogging, was not exactly a social practice that could be invented from scratch; online platforms built on age-old analog routines of photo creation, distribution, and sharing. Moreover, they built on private rituals, in rather intimate settings, such as family picture albums and photo exchanges, as well as professional and artistic practices, such as archival collections and photo galleries. Flickr never decided to focus on one type of usage—private or public, artistic or commercial—or one type of user base—amateurs or professionals—but instead catered to a heterogeneous pool of photo enthusiasts from the very onset. Although some argue that this eclectic user base caused Flickr's demise, it may also have been the profound incongruence between users' needs and owners' strategies that contributed to its slow decline. On the one hand, Flickr developed as a site for users interested in community building and intimate sharing, regarding photos as their prime contribution to an enhanced online experience. Flickr members wanted the owners to invest in user *connectedness* and were willing to pay for the privilege. On the other hand, Flickr developed as a platform for app designers, third parties, and advertisers who regarded the site's mass of generated photographic content as a unique resource waiting to be monetized. Corporate and commercial users wanted Flickr to invest primarily in *connectivity*, and regarded connectedness merely as a means to this end. Let me first focus on the former strand of users.

Flickr's original design in 2004 featured the simple motto "Share your photos"; behind this simple motto hid a sophisticated apparatus that connected users to each other via their content while giving them a fairly large amount of control. The site enabled users to upload their (self-made) photos, discuss images as expressions of group taste or shared interest, and use the platform as an online tool for distribution and storage. In this capacity, Flickr appealed to all users—hobbyists and professionals alike—who shared a love of photography as a means of artistic or personal expression.

Sharing photographs was presented as an intrinsically communal experience, a notion reflected in Flickr's default choice for group activity. As we can still read on its home page: "Groups are a fabulous way to share content and conversation, either privately or with the world. Believe us when we say there's probably a group for everyone, but if you can't find one you like, feel free to start your own."[8] Flickr groups are formed around relational or thematic principles: they may be centered on someone (John's pictures) or something (pictures of San Francisco, desert flowers, dogs, etc.). The comment function turned out to be an important instrument not only for developing community bonds but also for building shared aesthetic judgment. As the American photography theorist Susan Murray contended in 2008: "Flickr has become a collaborative experience: a shared display of memory, taste, history, signifiers of identity, collection, daily life and judgment" (Murray 2008: 149).

When Flickr started to help users move their personal pictures to an online environment, digital photography had already begun to shift people's memory practices in a communicative and public direction.[9] The platform was eager to combine photo sharing as a memory practice, cherished mostly by older users, with young adults' growing inclination to socialize in online groups.[10] Research based on Flickr's visual (meta)data repository demonstrates the site's capacity to forge connections between visual data and user data; in 2006, as Facebook gained clout among college-age users, Flickr started to emphasize its own networking potential, hoping to tap into a younger demographic.[11] When Facebook in 2007 expanded its SNS-function to include an unlimited number of pictures, Flickr responded not by increasing its own limits on upload and storage capacity, but by further pushing its communicative functions at the expense of its creative-artistic and memory potential (van Dijck 2011). Not surprisingly, Flickr lost its SNS edge to Facebook, while Facebook quickly added more features of a UGC site. Flickr may have underestimated the distinct demographics sustaining the functions of reminiscing and socializing.[12] It was not until 2011, with the implementation of Flickr Session, that Flickr firmly restored its emphasis on the memory function, changing its motto to "Share your *life in* photos" (emphasis added).

From its inception, Flickr appealed to users as photographers not just of private life and aesthetic objects but of the world at large, inviting pictures from global hot spots and encouraging eyewitnesses to post pictures of current events. Much in line with the platform's concentration on community formation, Flickr stimulated the formation of groups in response to natural disasters, such as wildfires, hurricanes, and earthquakes, or terrorist acts, such as metro bombings and plane hijackings. Unlike twitterers, Flickr groups used pictures to communicate their experiences in order to tell personal stories primed by visual evidence, rather than to create short-lived trends or viral looping. Whereas twitterers shared eyewitness reports for a limited period with the largest possible followings, Flickr users inhabited their platform as a place to swap stories about, for instance, people's traumatic experiences, and they held on to a story for a much longer period. Some researchers argued that Flickr reinforced feelings of belonging through shared experiences of current events through photographs, which consequently shape a collective perception of the world. For instance, in their content analysis of disaster-specific Flickr groups established in response to the London metro bombings in 2006 and the Virginia Tech shooting in 2007, Liu and colleagues (2008) characterize Flickr's photography as a "documentary practice" and describe the platform as an image aggregator as well as an experience aggregator.

In 2008, the site began to more prominently display the information-networking function on its home page, featuring a new motto: "Share your photos. Watch the world." Flickr chose to compete with Twitter to become a forum for eyewitness photography, especially in relation to events involving human tragedy and revolts. When the Iranian elections in 2009 led to an uprising, several groups published pictures of beatings and protests on Flickr, such as, for instance, the dramatic pictures of Neda Agha Soltan, who was killed during a protest demonstration in Iran in June 2009. But Flickr's role remained fairly marginal in comparison to Twitter and Facebook—platforms that became known in the public mind as tools for political organizing, even if it is disputable to what extent they lived up to that role. In contrast to Twitter's quickly waning waves of hashtag-themed news groups, Flickr user groups fed traditional news channels outside Iran with images and eyewitness stories. Harrowing images of Neda Agha Soltan were picked up by major Western news sources to serve as evidence for journalist's narratives.[13]

In spite of management's various attempts to make the site more competitive in the face of big contenders, Flickr users stubbornly held onto their site's original goal—a site made *by* communities *for* communities—or simply left to join another platform. Flickr's original user base had strong ties with blogger communities around the globe, and they cherished the spirit of collaboration and mutual exchange. User numbers dwindled, as many were bitter about their site's neglect of the community function. On the Flickr Central and Flickr Help Forum—pages where users post questions and commentaries—discussions revolved around the true community character of their site and the reluctance of users to cooperate with the platform's attempts to "go mainstream."[14] Through this site as well as through numerous blogs, users explicitly commented on how they appropriate the site for their needs, teaching each other what is good and what is bad about the platform.[15] Besides negative comments on Yahoo's pressuring of Flickr's management to implement features they do not like, there are also positive posts of loyal members who want to keep up the old community spirit:

> Lately I've been pleased to see some truly innovative community stuff that has been built as a layer on top of Flickr to regain some of the smallness and community that old school members used to enjoy. Flickr is Flickr and Flickr will always be the community that it is. Even as it grows and gets more mainstream there will still be hidden pockets around where the old style community takes place. And this won't change regardless of who is running the mother ship.[16]

Flickr users indeed sported a sharp notion of what social networking meant to a community-minded site like theirs. "Sharing" on Flickr signifies a different concept than "sharing" as defined by Facebook. "Favoriting" photos on Flickr does not resemble Facebook's Like button or Twitter's "trending" feature. And Flickr's role as a news and organizing tool is a far cry from Twitter's hashtag activism. The staple of Flickr's use was its members' love for photographs as propellers of group formation and community building; a critical mass of Flickr users refused to subscribe to the popularity principle or the quick-trend principle that conditioned most big sites' architectures. In sum, the online world according to assertive Flickr-users was about creating connectedness, a value firmly rooted in the participatory culture from which the site had emanated.

Content

Although the active user base may have been Flickr's most important asset, certainly at the early stage of its development, it hardly comprised a core value in the eyes of its corporate owner. When Yahoo bought Flickr in 2005, the company was clearly after the *content* users had generated and would generate over the following years, as well as the coding technologies Flickr had developed to make photos accessible. As a former Yahoo employee explains in one blogger's intriguing analysis of Flickr's demise:

> Because Flickr photos were tagged and labeled and categorized so efficiently by users, they were highly searchable. That is the reason we [Yahoo] bought Flickr—not the community. We didn't give a shit about that. The theory behind buying Flickr was not to increase social connections; it was to monetize the image index. It was totally not about social communities or social networking. It was certainly nothing to do with the users.[17]

Yahoo, in other words, was interested in connectivity rather than connectedness as it bought up the database that gradually accumulated 6 billion pictures—a database consisting not just of online photos, but photos that carry large amounts of metadata connecting content to users and personal profiling information to users' behavioral data. After all, the same code that facilitates group formation and personalized photo sharing also allows advertisers and third-party developers to monetize user-generated content.

Researchers had long cherished the bounty of Flickr's metadata as a gold mine for visual data analysis. They were interested in detecting patterns of use and developing predictive algorithms to steer users' aesthetic and thematic predilections—much the way Amazon deploys algorithms to whet its customers' appetite for other content.[18] Some APIs, for instance, measure the intensity of cross-linking between users in order to reveal patterns of individual and collective behavior (Mislove et al. 2008). A group of Swiss researchers found distinctive patterns of photo-to-group sharing practices, such as group loyalty, degree of active participation, and group affiliation (Negoescu and Gatica-Perez 2008). Information scientists and statisticians also analyzed behavioral data to find meaningful patterns of social activity triggered by picture sharing. Aggregated content and metadata offer insights into large-scale behavioral trends (who shares pictures with whom and how often?), as well as into relations between users and themed content (who shares pictures of dogs?), only to translate these insights into predictive algorithms (who is likely to buy dog food?). It did not take long for Flickr and third parties to design advertising schemes and consumer apps on the basis of the rich database. Flickr implemented algorithms connecting data derived from profiles, cross-referencing, and tagging on its site that resulted in selective placement of ads next to searched content.[19]

Flickr's rich reservoir of user-tagged photos and automatically tagged images was crucial to software engineers and information scientists specializing in visual algorithms who looked at the platform's connectivity as a potential resource. Tags can be searched alphabetically or by popularity, as can all words provided in the comment sections. Most search information comes from content tags or from profiling data added by members, thus enabling users to find images related to particular topics, such as people's names, places, or subject matter. The inclusion of geotags in Flickr's giant picture database triggered the development of a score of applications using Flickr's database to test visual search algorithms. Flickr's data allowed engineers to generate aggregate knowledge in the form of representative tags for specific areas in the world, combining information from visual content (what is shown in the picture) with location data (where was it shot) and user-added tags (Kennedy et al. 2007). The software they developed automatically identifies clusters of images of landmarks, such as the Golden Gate Bridge or the Eiffel Tower. Peculiarly, the researchers' ambitions to find connective patterns are often phrased in terms of *collectivity*; for instance, when they state the goal of their research to be the formation of "common knowledge" and "collective cultural heritage," they emphasize social ambitions rather than technical or commercial ones (van Dijck 2011).[20]

Flickr's coded and (geo)tagged visual database turned out to be a gold mine for commercial app developers. Based on Flickr's coded content, Microsoft built Photosynth, a now widely available software package that has the capability of pulling a wide variety of images of an object (e.g., the Arc de Triomphe or Notre Dame), analyze them for similarities, and then stitch them together into a smooth three-dimensional space. The resulting 3D image looks like an areal picture and can be viewed from multiple angles, with viewers endlessly zooming in and out, thus enabling detailed looks and bird's-eye views. Although the amalgam picture is clearly the result of clever visual algorithms, computer scientists involved in the development of this software affix much higher ambitions to their technological pursuit.[21] According to one of its developers, Photosynth's ability to suture together an endless number of pictures into one amalgam 3-D model is the result of a "cross-user experience," whereby data are culled from "collective memory" before they are stitched together.[22]

It may not be a coincidence that developers and researchers invoked the original connectedness paradigm to justify their exploitation of Flickr's connective resources. Flickr's content is obviously value-laden, and the meanings that developers bestow upon the platform's offshoots reflect a wider awareness of the social and cultural order in which the platform is embedded. Supporters of the connectivity approach did not just accidentally invoke the community-connectedness values subscribed to by Flickr's vocal user base; they were quite alert to the site's origin story. Flickr's operational management obviously wrestled to find a pristine balance between the users' strong demand for an affective relationship with their platform, and the site's corporate owners and external partners interested in mining photographic content as connective resources. Many users took notice of the effort to separate "Flickr" and the site's management from "Yahoo" as the brand's aloof corporate owner—an issue that prompts us to scrutinize the socioeconomic level of the microsystem.

5.3. FLICKR BETWEEN COMMONS AND COMMERCE

Ownership Structure

Flickr was developed by Ludicorp, a Vancouver-based company, and was a by-product of what was originally intended to become a multiplayer online game. The platform's independence did not last very long: when Yahoo acquired Ludicorp in March 2005 for a reported $30 million, the new owner gave up its own competing photo-sharing service called YahooPhoto. Still, Flickr had many competitors in the specific branch of online photo-sharing: Photobucket, Picasa, Snapfish, and Kodak Gallery, to name just a few.[23] Members of Flickr's active user base, which by then had grown to over one million, considered themselves the moral proprietors of the site, and they were extremely wary of a corporate takeover, not just this one but also the several attempts that followed. For a few years, Yahoo managed to maintain Flickr's start-uppy brand image emphasizing community value over corporate gain. Every major and minor change in the site's architecture or organization, such as the earlier described requirement to sign up with a Yahoo ID, triggered anxious responses from Flickr's longtime members— photo aficionados fearing that corporate ownership would affect their site's communal and artistic identity, pushing its members into the mainstream of social media.[24]

Most Flickr members loathed their involuntary "incorporation," yet the advantages of more and better features, as many acknowledged, were also a prerequisite for keeping the site cutting-edge and state of the art. In 2008, Yahoo entered negotiations with Microsoft. A possible merger brought tempting visions of advanced image search technologies and huge archives of stock photography being added to the site, and some users argued that Yahoo's teaming up with Microsoft would be advantageous.[25] Not surprisingly, though, the potential takeover was met with fierce resistance from a user-created group called "Microsoft, keep your evil grubby hands off our Flickr!"[26] More than a thousand longtime members joined the group, fueling a discussion about the upsides and downsides of corporate ownership. The fierce discussion illustrates the double bind that Yahoo ownership brought along: old-school Flickr users cherished community bonds, and while resenting corporate meddling with "their" site, they also welcomed the technical prowess that comes with incorporation. For owners, the loyal membership of their customers was a valuable asset and simultaneously a potential major impediment; in trying to build a profit-based enterprise, they risked a loss of business any time strategies changed and users threatened to quit the site. Yahoo eventually ignored its resisting old-school users and joined forces with Microsoft and AOL in 2011, forming a partnership that allows each of the allies to sell the other's display ad inventory.

As a matter of fact, Flickr had started to lose a substantial number of customers long before the Microsoft deal was closed, and traffic shrank accordingly.[27] Analysts identified lax ownership and volatile management as the culprits of the site's underperformance. Owner Yahoo was blamed for putting its ambition to build an empire of platforms above the interest of Flickr and its customers.[28] Detractors criticized the platform's management for diverting the site in too many directions, recalling Flickr's abandoned effort to implement photos of breaking news events on its home page. Business observers identified heavy competition from Facebook as the main cause of decline. Engineers pointed out that Flickr had missed the boat in mobile apps—a niche shrewdly picked up by Instagram, a free photo application that allows users to apply special filters and share their photos on a large number of SNS sites. In less than a year, Instagram, launched in 2010, had combined its popular style of Polaroid-like images with features such as the Like button and the #hashtag to render their technical idiom compatible with Facebook's and Twitter's grammar of instant short-lived trends and mass followings. When Facebook later took over Instagram, in April 2012, Flickr was painfully contrasted with the hip successful start-up as a flailing example.[29]

And yet Flickr's struggle with *corporate* ownership signified just half of the site's delicate balancing act. Over the years, Flickr also developed several initiatives to team up with partners from the *public* and *nonprofit* sector—initiatives that certainly met the approval of its longtime amateur users. In 2008, Flickr started the Commons, a project servicing heritage institutions, such as national archives and museums, wanting to engage users in identifying and interpreting historic photographic material.[30] The idea behind this global project was to facilitate community formation by having them engage with their own cultural heritage. During the first year of the project, dedicated Flickr users actively tagged and commented on history's forgotten treasures. In a relatively short period, the Library of Congress and a number of its counterparts in the Western world managed to draw a group of amateur historians into active heritage building.[31] The project was considered the perfect intermediary between the huge numbers of knowledgeable citizens who actively participate in Flickr communities, and archives eager to turn collective memory into cultural heritage collections.[32]

Even if the project did not become a spectacular success, Flickr Commons certainly placated the site's community-oriented users and strengthened the ties with its strong core of amateur photographers. In this respect, we also need to mention the site's overtures toward the professional photographer segment of its user base, for instance by forging a strategic alliance with Getty Images in 2009. Flickr Collection, as this initiative was called, offered a selection of Flickr photos to be distributed and sold through Getty Images—a stock photography service for professionals—thus enabling Flickr users to make money on their photographic content. Although many professionals welcomed the initiative, some were critical that Getty did not work as an agent for photographers but only for selected *photographs*; moreover, they were not happy with the fact that Getty Images represented their work on the condition of exclusivity, meaning that selected photographs could not also be sold through the photographer's own website.[33] A few professionals argued that Flickr would have done wiser to organize the Collection initiative through a Creative Commons license.

If we look at eight years of ownership turbulence, it is hard to escape the idea that Flickr management vacillated between the forces of the market, arguably cheered by Yahoo's determination to face competition with Facebook, Google and Twitter, and the dynamism of the user base, who pressed for a noncommercial, commons-based platform that represented the interests of amateurs and professional photographers. In a reconciliatory effort, Flickr tried to combine commerce with commons—in line with the theories of Yochai Benkler introduced in chapter 1. And while the hybrid ownership model had its supporters, many resented the platform's lack of clarity—an observation that gains more cogency when we look at the levels of governance and business models.

Governance

Flickr's contentious ownership battle, exemplifying the platform's desire to strengthen its community-oriented image vis-à-vis its corporate owner's aspirations to make Yahoo a dominant brand, is clearly reflected in the site's governance. Since Flickr members were forced to sign up through a Yahoo ID, Flickr's terms of service inevitably became coupled with Yahoo's. There is a distinct hierarchical order between Yahoo's ToS and Flickr's own ToS, which puts pressure on the platform's ambitions to fit in with the larger corporate regime. Yahoo's terms of service state very clearly that the company is entitled to transpose data from any of its platforms onto others and is licensed to sell or display "any advertising, attribution, links, promotional and/or distribution rights in connection with your User Content"; in addition, Yahoo reserves the right "to retain all revenue generated from any sales or licenses of such advertising, attribution, links, or promotional or distribution rights."[34] In compliance with its owner's ToS, Flickr may grant API licenses to third parties in order to create programs or services based on Flickr resources, but the site has the right to bar members from the site who use it for commercial purposes. As the home page states: "The Flickr API is available for non-commercial use by outside developers. Commercial use is possible by prior arrangement."[35] If members are caught selling products or services through their photostream, their account is promptly terminated.[36]

As mentioned, many members of Flickr's longtime user base are professional photographers or semiprofessionals making money out of their hobby. To them, the definition of what constitutes "commercial use" of their Flickr account is far from clear-cut. Subscribers whose pages were deleted after being caught engaging in commercial activities through the site publicly declaimed their puzzlement: what exactly is "commercial activity" in an environment that is so connected and interlinked that they can hardly separate one (social) activity from another (commercial) one?[37] Bloggers also lashed out at the hypocrisy of a corporate owner telling their resource-providers-cum-customers to refrain from monetizing their work while keeping the privilege to themselves. The arrangement between Flickr Collection and Getty Images precisely exposed this perceived unfairness: if photographs were singled out by the service for commercial distribution, they could no longer be sold through the photographers' own websites. Flickr's semiprofessional and amateur photographers critically questioned the double standards cemented in Yahoo's binding ToS as the company negotiated the deal with Getty.[38]

The implementation of Flickr Commons, illustrating another clash between commerce and commons, was also reflected in the struggle over rules regarding the permissibility of online content. What happens when artistic, aesthetic, or historical photographic content published on Flickr Commons is subjugated to the ToS of a general online information firm? Yahoo's terms of service stipulate, for instance, that you cannot post any photographic content that is "harmful, threatening, abusive, harassing, tortious, defamatory, vulgar, or obscene."[39] If Yahoo considers content to be in any way offensive or sexually explicit, it removes it from the Flickr site and deletes the specific user's pages. Not surprisingly, Flickr Commons user communities were confused by the dual governance regime applied to this new online space. When one participant in the heritage project came across pictures from the National Archive that were clearly not suitable for children's eyes, he or she wondered whether this meant they should not be posted on the site as part of the historical project. In a blogging response, this participant sharply articulated the governance dilemma:

> It is not clear to me how to tell the difference between an image that is not appropriate to be uploaded to Flickr and an image that is okay but needs to be marked with a safety level of "restricted." I am very interested to see how this category of "appropriate but restricted" evolves. For now, I am going to keep a watch on how the Flickr Commons grows and what range of content is included. The final answer for some of these images may be to only provide them via the institutions' web sites rather than via service providers such as Flickr.[40]

The rules concerning the exhibition of visual content in Flickr Commons are understandably a cause for puzzlement and concern. Can a corporately owned and operated platform install a "commons" space and assume that the norms and values pertaining to this space are respected by the owners' general governance regime? Just as users questioned the double standard of an owner disallowing members the right to monetize their own content while operating on a for-profit basis by selling members' data, they now questioned the sincerity of a declared "commons" domain running on a general commercial license. Is a declared Commons space subject to the same aesthetic and ethical criteria as a general social network service aimed at commercially serving a large general audience? Since Flickr Commons literally has to comply with its owner's governance rules, it can hardly be expected to create a public haven within a corporate sea.

Business Models

The same dilemma presents itself with regard to Flickr's business models. Like most SNS and UGC platforms, Flickr began without a plain business model in mind, offering its free services to enthusiastic users whose backgrounds varied from ordinary snapshot photographers to professionals. After selling Ludicorp to Yahoo, Flickr's founders expected the site to earn money in the long run from subscription fees by members, from ads (mostly from companies in the photo and printing industries), and from shared revenue made on users' photos.[41] Not all of these expectations were met, but over the years, Flickr developed several strategies to monetize the site under Yahoo's tutelage.

In 2006 Flickr, as one of the first platforms in the ecosystem of connective media, introduced the so-called "freemium" subscription model. This model, which combines free usage with paid membership, has since been gradually embraced in the online world (Teece 2010). Nonpaying Flickr users may store up to 300 MB of pictures a month and two videos; they can only view their last 200 uploads and they have to accept ads in their photo-sharing experience. If a free account has been inactive for three consecutive months, Flickr has the right to delete it. Flickr-Pro accounts, on the other hand, allow unlimited uploading, HD video playback, and ad-free browsing for a low yearly fee. The idea behind the freemium model is that heavy-use hobbyists and semiprofessionals become paying subscribers, while money is made on free users by means of targeted contextual advertising and the sale of metadata on searches.

At first sight, the combination of these schemes appears to promise Flicker-Pro members an ad-free experience, but, much to the frustration of some users, this is not the case. Although Pro members do not see targeted ads, their interaction with the site still confronts them with paid messages and "narrative advertising"—a tactic described in chapter 3. By 2009, companies like McDonald's, Visa, Ford, and, obviously, Nikon and Kodak were inviting Flickr-Pro users to "share their stories" by sending pictures and rejoice in a "communal experience" of the brand. Longtime Flickr fan Thomas Hawk sharply articulates his criticism of this conspicuous business strategy:

> [W]hy is Yahoo/Flickr promising you an ad free Pro account when you pay up with an annual fee and then turning around and advertising at you? . . . [T]he point is, why are they pumping all these adverts out at paid members when they promise you an ad free experience on Flickr if you pay and upgrade to Pro. . . . My own opinion is that paid members ought to be exempt from having these adverts directed at them. Either that or Flickr ought to drop the "ad-free browsing and sharing" claim from their own advert above.[42]

Flickr-Pro members are not opposed to their site's need to monetize content in general, but they expect clarity and consistency from their platform; it can at least explain how its business model works. Besides making money on subscription fees and selling targeted, personalized advertisements, Flickr charges app developers for using its API. As mentioned above, commercial exploitation of Flickr's database is strictly regulated in its ToS and is not always clear to members. Just as the deal with Getty Images raised questions about the site's governance policies, Flickr's partnership with preferred partners Microsoft and AOL also triggered concern about how user data were traded and resold. In all these cases, users demanded they be informed about the fine points of Flickr business models.

If the question of *how* Flickr monetizes the site is key to its users, the question of *how much* the platform adds to Yahoo's yearly revenue is clearly of interest to investors and business analysts.[43] Flickr has probably been profitable for Yahoo since 2009, but the company does not publicly share figures on its sites' specific gains. Flickr is likely not as profitable as Yahoo wants it to be, as many changes did not translate into big boosts in traffic volume and user numbers, with Facebook and Instagram dwarfing Flickr's development. Over the years, business strategies vacillated between Yahoo's seamless-integration policies and Flickr management's orientation toward user communities. Projects like Flickr Commons cannot even be considered business models, although the project might have aimed indirectly at gaining new members, attracting more traffic, and generally boosting the site's community image. The double strategy of commerce and commons, however, confused many and convinced few.

5.4. FLICKR BETWEEN PARTICIPATORY AND CONNECTIVE CULTURE

Over the eight years of its existence, Flickr's hybrid nature is manifest on virtually all levels of the platform. Its alternating mix of interface features divulges competition with major SNS and UGC platforms. A fluctuating blend of artistic, creative, memory, and information-news functions signals various endeavors to cater to user communities' need for connectedness and to satisfy owners' need for exploiting connectivity. If Flickr is viewed as a socioeconomic organization, the site oscillates between establishing itself as a corporate player in competition with the ecosystem's Big Players and branding itself as a community service in cooperation with major nonprofit institutions such as museums and archives. Attempts to combine two classic paradigms—commerce and commons—in one platform result in bifurcated governance regimes and nebulous revenue models, which predictably frustrate the site's loyal users and its investors.[44] We can safely assume that the platform's instability and inconsistency caused a decline in user numbers. But does this mean Flickr can be labeled a "failure"? The answer depends on whom you ask.

Many outside observers, former users, business analysts, and investors will confirm Flickr's failing status. After all, compared to many other players in the ecosystem of connective media, the once promising and thriving photo-sharing site did not live up to its expectations. In an intensely competitive market, various social media sites succeeded in occupying particular niche markets while Flickr tried to be a little bit of everything. The site's pendulum, swinging between commercial and commons objectives, caused many users to switch loyalties, either turning to competing platforms like Picasa (owned by Google) and Instagram (now owned by Facebook), or to nonprofit sites like WikiCommons.[45] Instead of "flickering" becoming an alternative to "tweeting," the verb became at best a synonym for the platform's wavering. In the eyes of many, Yahoo was consumed by bigger fish.

At the same time, there are still many original and new Flickr users who do not agree with this assessment. If most of these users do not care about how big their platform is or what position it conquered in the global rankings, they do care about the site's functionality. They may (still) judge Flickr by their old standards of community orientation and assess its merit according to the satisfaction they derive from their online experience. Some users articulate very precisely why they prefer Flickr to general SNSs or popular photo-sharing services like Instagram, and behind these evaluations lay distinct ideological motives:

> On Instagram, everything is public. Audiences appear and disappear almost as quickly as images on the stream. That is not the case on Flickr, where users have granular settings for changing photos to public, visible to friends, visible to family or completely private. Communities are more deliberate. Following is not an option, but joining is. . . . What Instagram lacks, Flickr fulfills: A possibility for adjusting privacy settings so that every photo uploaded doesn't appear out there, for the entire Web to see. On Flickr, there is no such thing as social media celebrity. The public nature of Instagram makes the idea of celebrity not only normal, but encouraged.[46]

To this and other users, Flickr positively presents itself as a platform that is not entirely driven by short-lived trends, celebrities, and big followings, but is a platform that cares about privacy settings; a platform that values communities over quickly vanishing audiences of friends; in sum, a platform that shies away, when possible, from the popularity principles and frictionless sharing mechanisms explained in the previous chapters—principles that dominate the seamless Facebook-Instagram, Twitter, and Google universe. Perhaps ironically, what explains fiasco to some users defines accomplishment to others.

As Bruno Latour (1996) showed in his narrative on the demise of the Paris rapid transit system, failure is more interesting than success for the purpose of demonstrating social and cultural patterns of normalization. The acceptance or rejection of a particular (micro)system is the result of many convoluting factors and interreliant actors. Depending on whose definition you accept, Flickr may be called a half-baked market failure or a triumph of user engagement. Flickr's ambiguity, though, is less instructive as a provisional outcome of a struggle for the survival of one microsystem than as a *symptom* of the changing cultural climate in which the platform evolved.

If we look at Flickr as part of the ecosystem, the site initially began operating in 2004 under the aegis of participatory culture, embracing a "new" economy accommodating users and owners alike, while simultaneously harboring community collectivism and commercial utilization. The premise of collectivism, which buttressed a large number of online platforms at the time, was rooted in the conviction that Web 2.0 technologies afforded a new kind of mediated sociality that smoothly merged community needs with market forces. Between 2006 and 2010, the ecosystem gravitated toward a culture of connectivity, a culture in which a handful of explosively growing platforms set technical and normative standards for online social practices. It was extremely hard *not* to adapt to this new environment and be immune from the larger economic and cultural trends that defined the conditions for operating in that ecosystem.

If we look at Flickr's short history, it is interesting to notice how both owners and users adopted a wide-ranging armamentarium of Internet utensils to fortify their positions. Flickr management, aware of the value users added to the site, tried to reconcile two opposing demands and, as a result, found itself in a contentious double bind. The original concept of collectivism and community-based collaboration, however well intended and deployed with integrity, ill suited a gradually corporate-based, profit-oriented ecosystem. Flickr's waxing and waning success—or, for that matter, failure—played out in a global context of competing market and nonprofit forces; but rather than a product of this competition, the platform's hybrid state reflects a *process* of negotiation over the very *meaning* of "public" and "corporate." Evidently, people's expectations of corporate and public spaces differ, as did their expectations of Flickr's ability to reconcile different needs. Whereas public institutions are supposed to guard community needs and values, corporate spaces are likely to put commercial values ahead of public values. In the evolving ecosystem, the larger issue at stake is how commercial online space affects general norms and values formerly considered public, and, more urgently, whether a nonprofit or public platform can fully function as such in an ecosystem that is overwhelmingly corporate and where platforms are intensely interrelated. I will return to these questions in chapters 7 and 8.

On the other hand, Flickr adepts who resented seeing "their" site being incorporated in this culture of connectivity helped steer the platform, often against the wish of its reigning powers. As the rules of the game changed, they insistently tried to influence the conditions for play through blogs and comment pages. Indeed, the site lost many users, up to 20 percent by some accounts, and their resignation was a clear sign of discontentment. But a large number of dedicated users remained, even if they were adamant in their commentaries and persistent in their criticism. Perhaps more than other sites, Flickr had a vocal and active user base, not of "followers" or "friends" but of loyal detractors. These users were less interested in trends or short-lived engagement than in long-term commitment to their creativity-sharing social communities. Maybe against all odds, they managed to get their site where they feel it belongs: not as part of the top five of most successful social media brands that dominate the fiercely competitive ecosystem, but as a niche player that adheres to different values and norms. In the spring of 2012, several Flickr adepts concluded, even if cautiously, that Flickr's owners, after making many mistakes, may have come to understand the real value of their brand.[47] And in a volatile market where users appear increasingly to care about the quality of their experience and control over their data and demand insight into the mechanisms that push their sociality, Flickr's reputation may just recapture value.

As I have tried to show in this chapter, the cat-and-mouse game between platform users and owners is not a duet following a predictable choreography; it is rather a struggle to define the conditions for online sociality that are cemented in online techno-material and socioeconomic dimensions. Once we begin to comprehend the interrelated forces between microsystems, we may start to understand the principles underpinning the cultural, technical, economic, and political conditions on which the ecosystem of connective media evolved and is still evolving. In the next chapter, I will consider another UGC site for visual content: YouTube. Although YouTube's starting position much resembled Flickr's, Google's strategies pushed the platform in a radically different direction than Yahoo did Flickr. Comparing these processes will further expose the ecosystem's volatilities and contingencies and will deepen our understanding of the fabric that holds it together.

CHAPTER 6

YouTube: The Intimate Connection between Television and Video Sharing

6.1. INTRODUCTION

After YouTube was conceived in a Silicon Valley garage in 2005, the site was nurtured as a platform for sharing self-made amateur videos, an "alternative" to watching television. It was alternative at all levels: a different technology, a shift in user routines, a new type of content, and a radical overhaul of the traditional broadcast industry, including its business models. Starting in 2006, YouTube's adoptive parent, Google, appeared to foster the platform's youthful, rebellious image as it helped YouTube grow up in a media landscape historically dominated by television. The years 2005 to 2007 were a formative stage in consolidating the site's unconventional character. YouTube promised to revolutionize the experience of lean-back TV into lean-forward interactive engagement and pitted user-generated content (UGC) against professionally generated content (PGC). Admittedly, the site's technology may not have been as revolutionary as broadcast television was in the early 1950s, but the speed at which online video-sharing was propelled into audiovisual culture was truly unprecedented.

Between 2008 and 2012, YouTube's teenage spirit seemed to yield to a complacent, rationalized adult temperament. Rather than fighting the television industry, Google stepped up its efforts to collaborate with the companies its abrasive child had initially antagonized, and it settled many pending court cases concerning intellectual property and copyright laws. When YouTube started to look more like television, the broadcast industry, in turn, had to rethink its conventional viewing model and reconsider its core business. Clearly, the traditional broadcast industry needed Google as much as Google needed its former rivals to succeed in the ecosystem of connective media. Eventually, in late 2011, Google announced YouTube's marriage with its former foe, television, by radically changing the site's interface; enthusiastic users symbolically helped consummate the matrimony. Within the short time span of eight years, YouTube became the third most popular Internet site in the world, boasting four billion videos and uploading more content per month than all three major U.S. television networks combined have done in sixty years.[1]

Such is the short success story of YouTube, told as a fairy tale where children are kindled by loving stepparents, where adversaries are turned into collaborators, and where happy viewers/users applaud all plot structures played out by the owners. Looking more critically into YouTube's origin story, though, we find a variety of angles, some of which challenge the linear plot of bliss and indulgence. For one thing, YouTube did not really invent video sharing as a sociotechnical practice, and neither did it revolutionize broadcast technology. Contrary to public image, Google pushed professional content at an early stage, and its innovative online strategies soon merged with conventional broadcast tactics; and, last but not least, YouTube's users were anything but complacent dudes. Anytime they found themselves brushed away or shortchanged, they started to beat the drum to restore the platform's "alternative" function as a user-generated content provider. YouTubers may not have been as successful in channeling their platform back to its original state as their Flickr counterparts, but their story deserves to be told.

In addition, the legend of YouTube-Google's success remains incomplete if the story of one microsystem is severed from the larger milieu through which it progressed. Google's growing dominance in the world of networked sociality not only put a stamp on YouTube's maturing identity; the platform also irrevocably redefined the very conditions for audiovisual production and consumption, dragging television production into the ecosystem of connective media. Broadcast and television, rather than being replaced by online viewing systems, are quickly becoming part of social media's logic; the growing interdependence between television and video-sharing platforms, and the frictionless exchangeability of YouTube, Facebook, and Twitter's features, simultaneously reflect and construct the emergent culture of connectivity. The implications of conventional content industries integrating with search engines, measurement, and advertising systems become poignantly visible at the level of the ecosystem, by comparing their various underlying mechanisms. A fairy tale is not history; it becomes history, though, if we fail to account for its fairytale-ness.

6.2. OUT OF THE BOX: VIDEO SHARING CHALLENGES TELEVISION

Technology

In the public mind, YouTube is still often mistaken for one of the file-sharing platforms that became popular in the early 2000s, such as Napster, Gnutella, Freenet, and Grokster. And yet YouTube never pioneered a new technology the way Napster did when introducing peer-to-peer technology for the exchange of music files. Even though YouTube operated in a digital networked environment, the platform for watching audiovisual content did not challenge TV's technological basis; in fact, the new platform and the old tube had a number of technical features in common, such as centralized distribution and the option of content being retrievable on demand. Among YouTube's real novelties were the site's introduction of *streamed* content, *uploading* video, and *social networking* abilities—techniques that, in the context of audiovisual production, would turn out to have a substantial impact on the old broadcast model. YouTube's manifestation as a video-sharing site first and a repository and social networking site second helped proliferate it as a serious rival to broadcasting, a threat that had presented itself with the growth of the Internet in the 1990s.[2]

Articulating its technological difference with broadcasting was an important element in the establishment of YouTube's image as an alternative to television. Whereas broadcasting was regulated by a central agency controlling the supply and deliverance of signals, YouTube purportedly offered a space where reception and production of signals occurred from numerous individual terminals in the network. The platform presented itself as a hybrid of broadcasting and of home video, also called homecasting (van Dijck 2007b). However, YouTube was similar to television in that it operated from a central server holding and distributing all content. Broadcasting had already adjusted its mass-sending model in the 1990s, well before the popularization of Web 2.0 channels; the advent of "narrowcasting" engendered the proliferation of hundreds of cable outlets, leading to the fragmentation of audiences and socially splintered mediascapes (Smith-Shomade 2004). The conversion from analogue to digital television, in the early years of the new millennium, added the possibility of personal viewing schedules and content targeted at specific consumer profiles of preferred lifestyles and cultural tastes.[3] Homecasting, in other words, only gradually differed from broadcasting, as the technical conditions for both systems were progressively overlapping.

The absence of a central content producer on YouTube and the potential for two-way signaling made it appear as if there was no "organizational force" responsible for the regulation and distribution of content, which was a profound misreading of the technology. Indeed, YouTube did not have a programmed flow—a continuous stream of programs and commercials planned to glue the viewer to the screen (Williams 1974). YouTube's owners do not decide what viewers get to see at what time by means of a programmed flow, but that does not mean its content flows unmediated; instead, it is heavily steered by search engines and ranking algorithms. YouTube's interface design and its underlying algorithms select and filter content, guiding users in finding and watching certain videos out of the millions of uploads, for instance through buttons for "most popular" videos. The site controls video traffic not by means of programming schedules but by means of an information management system that steers user navigation and selects content to promote. Even though users feel they have control over which content to watch, their choices are heavily directed by referral systems, search functions, and ranking mechanisms (e.g., PageRank). In other words, ranking and popularity principles rule YouTube's platform architecture.

An early misconception was that YouTube popularized the technical possibility of downloading, akin to Napster promoting the (illegal) downloading of music files. However, YouTube never facilitated downloading, but pioneered the technology of *streaming* video from the very beginning. Streaming implies that viewers do not "own" the content they retrieve from YouTube, but they are granted access to view content. Such a misconception may be understandable in the light of the analog technique of videotaping: since the emergence of the VHS in the early 1980s, television had already become familiar with time-shifting technologies. The concept of "owning" content through taping or downloading was not at all new, while the concept of "lending access to" only gradually gained ground as a different technology with a different practical use. As we will see later on, this concept had a major impact on the television industry's viewing model.

A feature that really set YouTube apart from broadcasting in the early stages of the site's proliferation was the novelty of having users *upload* self-produced or preproduced audiovisual content via personal computers from their home to anybody's home—that is, networked private spaces. The dimension of uploading immediately caught fire and grabbed the audience's imagination. Homecasting's semantic kinship to home video and its ostensible predilection for amateur content greatly boosted YouTube's "alternative" character.[4] Families, political activists, and garage bands were equally capable of streaming their messages across the Internet, be it person-to-person or worldwide. In the earliest stages, YouTube and its rivaling platforms GoogleVideo, Myspace, Revver, and Metacafe did not produce any content of their own; they merely accommodated the distribution and storage of content produced by their users.[5] Significantly, YouTube's initial logo was "Your Digital Video Repository," denoting the platform's original function as a container or an archive for home videos (Gehl 2009). The motto changed into "Broadcast Yourself" soon after Google purchased the site in 2006; the motto referred not only to the site's capacity to globally distribute homemade personal content ("broadcast your Self"), but also to the platform's ability to redistribute professional content (PGC) already broadcast on television ("you can broadcast it yourself").

A second unique feature pitting broadcasting against homecasting was YouTube's function as a platform for *social networking*. Homecasting's potential for two-way communication via the Internet sharply contrasted with the one-way distribution involved in broadcasting and narrowcasting. Emphasizing its SNS qualities on top of its UGC ambitions, the early YouTube promoted video content as a means for community formation and group activity.[6] If we look at YouTube's interface in 2008, we can still observe the centrality of the user on its interface: buttons for commenting on each other's videos and for communities were visibly present on the home page. Interface features promoting connectivity gradually complemented or replaced features encouraging creativity: the inclusion of thumbnail videos and prominent buttons for ranking "most viewed" and "top favorited" videos enhanced consumer routines. Several architectural modifications distracted attention from group and social functions in favor of watching and ranking videos, or, as some have argued, watching databases (Lovink 2008; Kessler and Schaefer 2009). As Burgess and Green (2009: 64) pointed out, the technology of streaming video and the de facto ban on downloading content were never particularly conducive to YouTube's original intention to stimulate video production, but rather stimulated consumption.

YouTube's gradual moves toward prioritizing television features over social networking and group interaction culminated in a complete interface overhaul. The presentation of the new YouTube interface on December 11, 2011, might as well have been a wedding announcement: the site's home page definitely took over the look and feel of television. For one thing, the site was organized by means of *channels* rather than presenting itself as a collection of videos. Channels for entertainment, sports, music, news, politics, and so on, direct the user's navigation as if the home page interface were a remote control giving access to 500 narrowcast channels provided by cable. The top one-third of the home page, upon opening, is taken up by a moving ad—the first time I clicked it was a commercial for the local cable provider. Comments addressed by users can no longer be found on the first page, but are relegated behind the visible interface. Also invisible became the friending function and the subscribers and subscription function that added people to your channel—all features that accentuated the user as participant. And, not unimportantly, the former logo "Broadcast Yourself" disappeared from the site's banner. From now on, the user was definitely to be treated as a viewer. But how did users experience these changes over the years?

Users and Usage

"Video sharing" was launched in 2005 as shorthand for the multiple online social activities triggered by YouTube. The term covers watching and uploading of content, but also refers to quoting, favoriting, commenting on, responding to, archiving, editing, and mashing up videos. In its early stage, YouTube formed a network for sharing creative practices, aesthetic values, political arguments, and cultural products. Much as Flickr did for photo sharing, YouTube's sociality revolved primarily around video as the main vehicle for communication, building taste communities and exchanging discoveries centered on video (Burgess and Green 2009: 58). User activities were associated with cultural citizenship and participatory culture—amateurs taking charge of a new medium that they appropriated to their own needs of production and distribution (Lange 2008). Information scientists described YouTube's social networking function as a "small world phenomenon": groups of enthusiasts or theme groups tended to be strongly connected (e.g., anime fans, groups of amateur singer-songwriters), even if the large majority of YouTube videos never received a single comment or rating.[7] This original group of YouTubers, as they were called, was the generation of mostly active "produsing" amateurs that earned *Time* magazine's "person of the year" accolade in 2006—an image that was easily ascribed to all users.[8]

And yet a significant shift from active user agency to passive consumer behavior was already noticeable in 2007 when user numbers started to soar. Increasingly, users came to YouTube contents by means of referrals—either from other Internet platforms (blogs, friends, news sites) or from automated referral systems on the YouTube home page; viewers who never uploaded a single video or never commented on a posted video became the majority of the site's users. By 2008 researchers had already observed that users were far more willing to watch videos than to log in to rate and make comments (Cheng, Dale, and Liu 2008). As the social practice of "video sharing" increasingly came to mean video watching, the persistent classification of YouTube users as active participants called for demystification, just as the myth of the coach potato—the passive television consumer—had been dismantled in the late 1980s (Ang 1991).

In early 2012, YouTube claimed to have 800 million unique monthly visitors, up from one million in 2005.[9] How many of those users can be considered active contributors of content or so-called uploaders? Recent research shows that less than 20 percent of YouTube visitors actively provide content, and that 20 percent of these active uploaders contribute 73 percent of the videos (Ding et al. 2011). In other words, 4 percent of YouTube's users provide almost three-quarter of the site's content, and these active uploaders are not quite demographically representative in terms of gender and age.[10] More interesting than these statistics on the quantity and demographics of uploaders, though, is the observation by Ding and his co-researchers that "some uploaders are more popular than others, with more users viewing their uploaded videos" (Ding et al. 2011: 363). The unequal distribution of views among uploaders, as the researchers suggest, is hardly a matter of fair competition among users, but of YouTube tweaking its engine to benefit some heavyweight users:

> Our conjecture is that uploader popularity has been tuned by YouTube intentionally by YouTube's recommendation system. On the other hand, among all uploaders, the most popular 20 percent of the uploaders attract 97.0 percent of views, which does not follow the 80–20 rule. Thus YouTube's recommendation system seems to be also biased to the very popular uploaders. (Ding et al. 2011: 363–64).

The site's algorithms thus explicitly undercut the impression that most YouTubers are active "produsers" and that all uploaders are treated equally.

In addition, the idea that YouTube is a site dominated by *amateur* producers and performers was also soon ready for deconstruction. With YouTube's explosive growth in 2007 came the mounting influence of professional producers of audiovisual content. As researchers Rotman and Preece (2010: 325) argue, original YouTubers started to refer to themselves as "us," whereas "them" designated the commercial YouTube channels deployed by media corporations. It became increasingly difficult to distinguish content in terms of professional and amateur producers, as YouTube's uploaders gradually professionalized (Jakobsson 2010). After 2007, YouTube rolled out its Partnership Program in an attempt to upgrade the quality of videos and increase its volume of professionally produced content.[11] I will return to this program in the next section.

Along similar lines, YouTube was idealized as a platform that propelled amateur performers to a mass audience, feeding the myth that

YouTube was an unmediated gateway to the professional media world of stars and fame. Magic stories of teenage singers recording an act with their webcam in their bedrooms, then uploading the video to YouTube only to be "discovered" by many fans the next day, were nursed by mainstream media and loathed by critics.[12] As much as cultural critics like Andrew Keen (2008) disparaged the upsurge of amateurs at the expense of professionals in the growing years of Web 2.0, ordinary users never really rivaled mainstream pros. Instead, as media theorist John Thompson (2005) predicted, professional and amateur usage—PGC and UGC— became increasingly interlocked. A performer's way to fame was not only engineered through YouTube's popularity mechanisms, but was also filtered by mainstream media using YouTube as a test pool for aspiring professionals (Mitchem 2009). YouTube started to organize competitions such as Next Up, which selects amateur performers who may become "the new pros" by helping them produce their next clip.[13] In that respect, YouTube fitted in nicely with the trend of star-discovery contest formats that television had rebooted since the new millennium, including *American Idol*, *Looking for* (a musical star), and *The World's Next Top Model*. The idea of amateur producers gaining a worldwide television audience had equally strong roots in popular programs such as *America's Funniest Home Videos* that have been distributed and franchised to many countries since the 1980s (Moran 2002). The worlds of amateur and professional performers and producers not only have a long history of convergence; conventional media have also provided constant models for ordinary people to shape their individual expressive needs, exemplified, for instance, by the many videos of teenagers imitating their pop idols on television.[14]

YouTube's hierarchical ordering of users into producers and consumers, stars and fans—inscribed in its interface features and underlying algorithms—increasingly gravitated toward viewer-based principles and away from community-oriented social networking. Most of YouTube's massive user base adjusted to the gradually changing user experience. And yet the assumption that all YouTube users turned into gullible consumers would be another myth in need of deconstruction. Quite a few (original) YouTubers vocally opposed the smooth convergence of new and old media into one seamless virtual space over the years. Some of them stood up to protest the marriage that they felt left them disenfranchised when their stepparent entered a ménage à trois with television. After Google had introduced its revamped interface with much fanfare in 2011, a wave of complaints and protests flooded the media, also filling YouTube's own online space. Users posted numerous verbal and audiovisual messages, all aimed at demanding back their rights as users and coproducers of "their" site. As one protest-video articulated its discontents:

> Face it: This is NOT only about an ugly design & unwanted changes for 98 percent of its users. This is about the DEATH of YouTube as you know it. IT'S GONE. It became a totally DIFFERENT site. . . . Join the BOYCOTT YOUTUBE days. When views are dropping, so will YouTube's INCOME. They will be FORCED to listen to the community & make ADJUSTMENTS to the layout. The new YT does not want YOU anymore. The OLD YOUTUBE LAYOUT will disappear FOREVER in just a few months. YOUTUBE will be a TOTALLY different site from then on.[15]

A large number of variations and mix-ups of this video appeared within weeks, some videos explicitly demonstrating how to return to the "old YT layout" or asking users to sign up for a boycott to not watch YouTube on Sundays.[16] The protests received little attention in the mainstream media in the weeks that followed and slowly faded away. The perceived paradox of a video-sharing site metamorphosing into an online channel for TV triggered both enthusiasm and disapproval; the distinctiveness of YouTube as an alternative to television was no longer defendable, particularly when we look at the site's content.

Content and Cultural Form

In its early years, YouTube featured a wide variety of UGC forms, ranging from original creations and transformative derivatives to copied, remixed, and "ripped" videos; not surprisingly, the site was immediately accused of promoting "stolen" content. Articulating these accusations implied the confirmation of a hierarchy between protected professional content and recyclable amateur content. YouTube's original adepts were adamant in defining the site's idiosyncratic cultural form in contrast to television. Broadcasting's conventional products, *programs* and *formats*, are tradable goods produced for, and distributed among, regional, national, and international markets.[17] Contrasting programs and formats, which are end products protected by laws regulating intellectual property and copyrights, YouTube proposed several features that would warrant the distinct status of video fragments or "snippets" as an autonomous cultural form.

In line with this argument, snippets, unlike traditional TV programs, are of limited length, ranging from several seconds to ten minutes, with the bulk of postings averaging between three and six minutes.[18] Snippets may be fragments or may imitate the begin-middle-end form of a polished audiovisual production (Burgess and Green 2009: 49). Although most snippets are onetime contributions, they may be accessed serially, for instance, when the same uploader posts a line of thematically connected videos. Another feature of snippets would be their status as *resources* rather than as products; they are meant for recycling in addition to storing, collecting, and sharing. Snippets, in this vision, are posted on video-sharing sites to be reused, reproduced, commented upon, or tinkered with. Their function as input for social traffic and group communication or as resource for creative remixes is thus touted as typical of YouTube's content (Lessig 2008).

Asserting its status apart from the broadcast industry, YouTube had to claim its own cultural form in order to break away from the legal-economic order governing the media landscape dominated by broadcast companies—a move I will return to in the next section. Several scholars defended YouTube's distinct cultural form, warranting their claim by pointing to its informal way of addressing the audience and its haphazard editing (Peters and Seiers 2009; Muller 2009; Lange 2007). The argument that snippets required a typical kind of authorship or craftsmanship was grounded in the practice of erstwhile video-sharers who commented on each other's style and technical skills; these "quality discourses" were part of the formation of so-called taste communities among original contributors (Paolillo 2008).

However, the distinct nature of YouTube content vis-à-vis television content has been subject to debate since the site's launch. As YouTube's user base started to soar in 2007 and user-generated content was outnumbered by professionally produced content, it proved increasingly difficult to uphold the claim to a snippet's distinct cultural form. Some researchers observed that at least two-thirds of all snippets on YouTube consisted of fragments from professional broadcast and mass media sources: "In practice, there is a great deal of slippage between the categories of traditional media and user-created content" (Burgess and Green 2009: 47). Others pointed out that typical UGC was hardly present among the site's most popular and most viewed items (Kruitbosch and Nack 2008). And as researchers Ding and colleagues found in 2011, over 63 percent of the most popular uploaders do not contribute user-*generated* content (UGC) but user-*copied* content (UCC) to the site—user-copied meaning that the videos are not created by uploaders themselves.[19] These research outcomes certainly warrant the conclusion that YouTube has gradually shifted toward being a site for recycling PGC.

Indeed, if we look at much of YouTube's current content, it is hard to tell any distinction between typical YouTube content and broadcast content because of mutual imitation. Mass media channels such as MTV and ABC have programs that imitate the "amateurish" aesthetics and style typical of

YouTube clips—an aesthetics that befits a marketing strategy promoting the new upcoming star. It is now quite common for musicians or performers, supported by major labels, to grow a following on YouTube first before they break through in mass media. All major music industries exploit their own channel on YouTube, and the flow between music videos on YouTube and major TV channels has become virtually seamless. The relation between UGC and PGC is one of mutual imitation, and the success of UGC platforms as mediators between anonymous users and stars can hardly be conceived apart from "old" media conglomerates' power to select, promote, and remunerate artistic content.

In sum, YouTube's early proliferation as an alternative channel to television was bolstered by technological, social, and cultural arguments. Despite the initial adversarial rhetoric, there has always been a tight interlocking between broadcasting and homecasting, between watching television and video sharing, and between programs and snippets. Nevertheless, the bipolar logic appears to have been crucial to the cultivation of YouTube's image as an alternative medium for amateur producers and performers. The same logic has certainly helped smooth the incorporation of "televisual" and commercial mechanisms into YouTube. The net result was that, after 2008, ostensibly opposite parties (television and YouTube) gradually became attuned to each other's strategies—a change that transpires most poignantly when we dissect the rapidly changing organizational structure of the platform.

6.3. BOXED IN: CHANNELING TELEVISION INTO THE CONNECTIVE FLOW

Ownership

When its wealthy stepparent adopted the 18-month-old toddler in 2006, Google's moves with YouTube received close scrutiny from media moguls dominating the television branch. Not unexpectedly, Google was bombarded with court cases over copyright infringement and intellectual property violations. Hollywood did not know whether to see YouTube-Google as a friend or a foe. Should it go after the new player and use its own historical prowess in electronic media distribution to impose its rules on this newcomer? Or should it side with it in creating new business and marketing models that would help homecasting channels to create buzz for television programs or movies?[20] The stakes on both sides were undeniably high: the power to mediate online creativity and render it "social." In networked platform logic, content cannot stand by itself; it needs to be buzzed and connected to audiences, preferably to viewers who spend considerable amounts of time on a platform. Bringing specific people to specific content and thus creating high-yield audience attention for advertisers was in fact YouTube's unique selling point. The broadcast industries lacked precisely what Google owned: search engines turned out to be crucial in connecting audiences to content. And Google lacked precisely what the television industry could offer in quantity: attractive PGC.

Mindful of these complementary needs, YouTube began to play the entertainment industry by brokering attractive search deals to broadcast companies; on both sides, interest grew in deals for the mutual use of content, which would prevent or settle expensive legal battles.[21] Established broadcast organizations renegotiated their relationship with the new kids on the block, not because they liked this development per se, but because it was crystal clear that the valuable combination of UGC and PGC attracted the interest of advertisers. And even if they were still engaged in a few turf battles over copyright and IP rights, YouTube and the broadcast industries realized that collaboration was more lucrative than court fights. In pursuit of viewers' attention, YouTube tried to become more like television, while television increasingly adopted features from YouTube. Since 2008 video sharing and broadcasting technologies have been rapidly converging, not only in terms of hardware and software, but also in terms of audience and content strategies.

As far as hardware and software are concerned, users increasingly watch video content away from their computers, so Google began facilitating viewing on small mobile screens (tablets, smart phones) as well as on big TV screens. In 2010, the company introduced Google TV; incorporating web functions in television systems, the distinction between a home page and a TV screen further dissolved. The simultaneous introduction of YouTube Leanback—a service that allows you to watch YouTube videos on a full home screen—promised a friendlier, more social user interface to accommodate users' switching behavior. The idea is that users watch TV and YouTube as part of the same routine. This fluidity also shows in audience and content strategies. One of YouTube's problems is that watching videos commonly results in limited attention spans; YouTube at best creates a staccato flow of snippets that is easily abandoned by users, in contrast to the programmed flow of television stations.[22] Because professionally produced content is likely to keep viewers glued to the screen much longer than video content, Google started to close deals with content providers and major broadcast producers to fill their channels. Every major television station (public as well as commercial) now has its own "channel" on

YouTube to promote broadcast content and lure viewers. Besides, professional web-content providers, such as Blip.TV and Channel Awesome, also started creating professional streaming video content both for YouTube and for their own emerging channels. And in March 2011, YouTube acquired start-up Next New Networks, a platform for the development and packaging of original web video programming, or "webisodes," for online audiences.[23]

Perhaps more remarkable than YouTube's steady alliance with the broadcast industry is the industry's assimilation of YouTube's logic. Broadcast and cable companies particularly borrowed the site's streaming on-demand function and integrated it into their own services. After 2008, YouTube found itself in direct competition with services like Netflix, Amazon, Apple's iTunes, and Hulu, all offering ad-supported subscription services for on demand retrieval of broadcasting content.[24] Initially, large broadcast companies such as Time Warner and Disney rejected on-demand models, but they slowly came to see the advantage of a more engaged viewership. As the surge of tablet computers and mobile devices drove up the demand for streaming content after 2010, broadcast companies pushed for subscription-based content models to serve multiple devices. The introduction of streamed "long-form content" posed a new challenge to YouTube, which responded by making deals with content industries to serve as the broadcast's referral service, in exchange for licensing the streaming of television shows and movies.

Obviously, the attention economy got increasingly caught in a cross-platform paradigm: the interest of consumers needs to be caught as eyeballs migrate from television to tablet to mobile phone to laptop. As a result, the experience formerly known as YouTubing began to dissipate into even more directions. While YouTube began to behave more like broadcasters, broadcasters adopted viewer models emanating from video-sharing sites.[25] The fact that Google is now fully immersed in the production of mass audiovisual content divulges the company's goal, to win over the living room. For news and entertainment industries wanting to obtain a substantial piece of the television advertising market, people's living rooms are strategic turf. And although YouTube still has to yield dominance to broadcasters in this domain, as far as the cross-platform paradigm is concerned the site's owner has one tremendous asset over its rivals in broadcasting: Google can integrate platforms for UGC, television, search, advertising, social networking (SNS), and trade and marketing sites (TMSs) into all-encompassing business models, thus expanding the reach of advertisers across platforms. This integrative mission is clearly reflected in the platform's governance.

Before its takeover by Google, volunteer users monitored YouTube for polluted content, as they helped run the site with a community-based philosophy. In 2006, the new owner vowed in a press statement to respect YouTube's integrity as a community platform; the pledge also confirmed the site's status separate from Google' conglomerate of platforms (Wasko and Erickson 2009: 372). YouTube would keep its own terms of service, thus guaranteeing its users their distinct identity, the ownership of its content, and privacy over its data within the limits of the platform itself. As we have seen in the previous chapter, autonomous platform ToS did not always serve the broader interests of the parent company, and in the case of Flickr-Yahoo, the struggle over the platform's user terms led to confusion and strife. YouTube's history shows a rather different evolution in the site's governance regime, which was quickly integrated with its owners'.

Between 2006 and 2007, Google kept its promise to protect its stepchild's vulnerable position as a video-sharing site from predators in the television branch. Snippets and short videos posted on the original YouTube site were issued under a Creative Commons license. During the first couple of years, YouTube's alternative community image aided Google in challenging the legal-economic paradigm of mass media entertainment dominated by publishing and broadcast firms. Lawyers on both sides contested the definition of UGC versus PGC, a fight that ostensibly pitted the Davids of individual users (represented by "their" platform, YouTube) against the Goliaths of the broadcast industry. Viacom and Disney waged court battles against YouTube to protect their intellectual property as the only possible *type* of property in the audiovisual content market by articulating the stakes of this debate in industrial-legal terms (Lessig 2008). The hybrid status of UGC challenged the governing legal-economic order in which terms like "programs" and "snippets" represented two seemingly incommensurate legal schemes. Whereas programs and formats are copyrighted and owned by corporations, Google's lawyers made the case that they cannot hold a *distributor* responsible for copyright infringement—especially a distributor who explicitly warns its users to respect copyright laws. YouTube's terms of service contained explicit warnings against the illegal copying of broadcast content, but at the same time it stated that the company is "not responsible for the accuracy, usefulness, safety or intellectual property rights of or relating to such content."[26] In other words, YouTube positioned itself as a connector of users and UGC, while implicitly inducing the appropriation of content produced under an adverse regulatory (PGC) regime. When Google gradually began to make peace with the broadcast industry, the company stepped up its efforts to weed out copyright infringement from its users' content. It also began to conform to the television industry's definitions by producing its own content that in turn needed protection from the very legal regime it had previously contested. Lawyers backed out as Google's admonishments of YouTubers to behave as "professional" adults started to pay off, and when negotiations resulted in Google's compromise: crediting PGC with more referrals and interlinking and reserving a Creative Commons license purely for noncopyrighted content.[27]

Apart from Google's efforts to attune its governance strategies to those of conventional media companies, it also moved toward a smooth integration of its own platforms, ostensibly to provide a more seamless online experience and to avoid situations in which a platform's ToS differed from Google's regime. With the rapid expansion of Google's conglomerate into a wide range of online niches—Google+, Gmail, Search, Maps, Chrome, Streetview, Play, and so on—the company needed to bring all separate platforms' policies under one all-encompassing Google ToS license, a move that was announced in early 2012.[28] Critics and government regulators almost immediately voiced their concern over the company's attempt to not just streamline a user's online experience, but completely control it: the project enabled Google to combine and merge all behavioral and profiling user data from all Google platforms. Regulators argued that such integration violated the privacy rights of consumers because all user data culled from one online context could be smartly combined with data collected in a very different online situation. Once again, quite a few YouTubers reacted very critically to this new policy; they spawned a number of videos arguing that the new uniform terms of service were "evil" or "freaked them out."[29]

And yet Google's move toward full integration of its ToS could not have come as a big surprise to those users who had kept track of the company's strategic movements. With platforms sprawling into all possible niches of online commerce, publishing, and networking, the company was facing mounting charges of antitrust violations. Aware of these legal challenges, Google seems to define itself more and more as a publisher rather than as a connector, which is a remarkable move away from its earlier stance.[30] This streamlining strategy is nowhere more visible than in the company's business models.

Business Models

Looking at the shift in business models, we can discern how Google gradually stepped up its monetizing strategies to achieve the Holy Grail: maximizing the ability to distribute *personalized* commercial messages to *mass* audiences. YouTube, which did not make any profits for the first years, was instrumental in Google's multiplatform strategy. In 2006, Google's takeover of AdWords and DoubleClick—a conquest that raised far less attention than Google's takeover of YouTube in the same year—marked the beginning of a period of experimentation in combining advertising, search, and streamed video content. Exploiting connectivity as a resource, Google developed several strategies to capitalize on streaming video's viral marketing potential. Branded video channels create a home for companies to feature their own videos—comparable to fan pages on Facebook. Another form of monetization on YouTube is called Promoted Videos, where ads show up in the right-hand column alongside contextually relevant videos that are based on search results (much like Promoted Tweets, explained in chapter 4). Advertisers pay per click on the promoted video ad. A third type, Invideo advertising, lets companies run ads in the video stream or use pop-ups at the bottom of videos.

YouTube's interface illustrates the power of combining UGC and PGC with *search* and *advertising*, all held in one hand. As Wasko and Erickson (2009) observe, Google's search engines give preference to Google platforms and its certified partners. But there is more than that. Rankings such as "Most Viewed" or "Most Popular" are prone to manipulation, as we have seen; if precious digital space is auctioned off to the highest bidder, as is Google's general model for its search engine, the intimate intertwining of video content with online ad systems and search engines raises concerns about power concentration. Attention measurement has become automated in a cost-per-click business model, introduced by AdWords. Google later refined this model by including a click's performance: the more successful a particular ad's links to a particular keyword, the more prominent it will be in later appearances on the search results page. Compared to the methods used by ratings firms such as Nielsen for measuring viewing behavior of television audiences, online audience measurement is far more precise in determining an ad's performance (Bermejo 2009).

However, the integration of content, search, and advertisement raises critical questions about their inseparable entanglement. Audience measurement, which still to a large extent defines the value of television advertisements, "seems to have lost part of its relevance in the world of online advertising, to the point of being totally irrelevant for understanding the economics of search engine advertising" (Bermejo 2009: 149). Attention is no longer the product of (semi-)independent ratings firms that measure how many eyeballs a program attracts every minute; instead, attention is measured by the very systems that also produce and distribute content, organize and rank a video's display, connect ads to content, and attune the algorithms that connect content to advertisers. The vertical integration of services is not unlike combining the functions of banker, regulator, ratings agency, and consumer advocate in one and the same hand.

Compounding the potential of power concentration is the gradual integration of user-generated content (YouTube, Google Music) and advertising (AdWords, DoubleClick) with other kinds of online services: search (Google Search), social networking (Google+), trade and pay services (Google Shopping and Google Wallet). Google's construction of a chain of integrated platforms seems similar to Facebook and Yahoo's partnership strategies—explained in chapters 3 and 5—and yet there is an important difference: Google *owns* all platforms and engineers data across platforms. Content sites, ads, search, shopping service, and payment system are all programmed to keep user traffic within the Google stream. When a user uploads a recording of a popular Eminem song, instead of taking down the recording—as it used to in the early days because of copyright violations— YouTube now runs pop-up ads to let customers buy the ringtone or the song through its own pay service, Google Wallet; YouTube may help boost the song's ranking and audience attention; and finally, Google shares the revenue with the copyright owner while also taking part of the pay system's revenue share. The exploitation of combined services across platforms is still in its infancy, and the implications of this expansion in terms of power distribution may be momentous—a subject I will return to in the last chapter.

Symbolizing its cross-platform strategy was a 2011 TV advertising campaign to promote Google's browser, Chrome.[31] For a company that has typically shied away from offline advertising, it is remarkable to launch a prime-time campaign for such an invisible piece of technology as a browser. However, a browser is an essential instrument in connecting people to Google services: from content platforms like YouTube to search engines, and from messages via Gmail to photos on Picasa. The flow of programmed content formerly sustained by a television station is symbolically replaced by a flow of platform-mediated content whose navigation is sustained by an Internet browser. Whereas YouTube users, over the years, adapted to personalized advertising messages and professional contents that permeated their UGC platform, television audiences increasingly accepted browsers and search modalities in their experience of watching TV.

Google's successful business models also comprised partnerships with users. Popular uploaders who work with YouTube through the Partnership Program are remunerated through the splitting of ad revenue; YouTube, in turn, boosts the popularity of partnered videos through its systems.[32] YouTubers seemed to like the scheme because it allows a few successful "produsers" to make a living of their videos. But some were more critical, wondering whether this business model stimulates the creativity of individual users or whether it is aimed at commercializing content. Some uploaders who were invited to participate in the scheme objected that YouTube cajoled them into a "partnership" that straightjacketed their original product with the platform's model, which clearly valued advertising profits over creativity.[33] As one YouTuber articulates his objection in a video clip:

> YouTubers put videos up because they want recognition for their work, they want to share something funny . . . or they want their 15 minutes. Now every time you watch a video you must ask yourself: "Is this self-expression or marketization?" It can't be both and the line is beginning to blur. AdSense culture is not what made YOU Time magazine's person of the year, is it?[34]

Obviously, users were not always pleased with the transformation of their site into part of a global information-networking-broadcasting-production-advertising conglomerate. Unlike in the case of Flickr, though, their protests, so far, have not made a dent in YouTube's image or, for that matter, Google's revenue. Resistant voices decrying commercialization are minor drops in the big flow of everyday users choosing convenience over apprehension. And with major broadcast companies now siding with Google, chances are even less than before that mainstream media will pick up protests.

6.4. YOUTUBE AS THE GATEWAY TO CONNECTIVE CULTURE

In a short time span of eight years, after successive years of fighting, conciliation, courtship, and heavy petting, the former antagonists YouTube and television finally got married, despite disgruntled reactions by some "alternative" users. As we can read on the official Google blog, the latest interface overhaul transformed YouTube into "your gateway to a vast entertainment universe."[35] A far cry from its original design, YouTube is no longer an *alternative* to television, but a full-fledged player in the media entertainment industry. The customer is ushered into an integrated television-UGC-SNS platform by rhetoric that would have been unimaginable back in 2006:

> To help you get more into YouTube, we're making it easier to find and follow great Channels when you arrive. On the left side of the homepage you can create your own, personal, customizable YouTube Channel line-up. Sign-in, or create a YouTube account. Then you can browse recommended Channels; customize your homepage's feed; even link your YouTube account to Google+ and Facebook to see what your friends are sharing.

Apparently, the new interface ushers YouTube users into a seamless experience, an experience that merges old media—television and music video clips—with the ecosystem of connective media. One Google account gets you access to an entertainment universe conditioned by the business and governance models underpinning the company's integrated platforms. Television and online video-sharing have not completely merged, nor has one replaced the other; they coexist and intermingle in an expanded connective media space. However, the big entertainment companies that, during the twentieth century, controlled the programmed flow and consolidated their power through mergers, takeovers, and legal bartering over copyright and IP are no longer sole gatekeepers of the entertainment universe. In 2012, technological toll keepers like Google guard access to the twenty-first-century entertainment universe, steering the creativity of users, the eyeballs of consumers, and the wallets of advertisers in the same direction.

On the one hand, media theorists have embraced this trend, arguing that the ultimate convergence of PC and TV portends a technological fluidity of systems that lets audiovisual content flow across multiple channels, resulting in "ever more complex relations between top-down corporate media and bottom-up participatory culture" (Jenkins 2006: 243). Along similar lines, Mark Deuze (2009) predicted that the convergence between users and producers, amateurs and professionals, media makers and consumers would some day lead to the integration of various media industries in one and the same global production network. Proponents of the convergence theory consider online platforms the perfect space in which to harmonize users' and corporate interests. On the other hand, political economists contend that platforms like YouTube epitomize the new concentration of capital and power. Vertically integrated industries—combining content producers *and* search industries *and* advertising agencies *and* information aggregators—are typically the focus of political economists theorizing the macroeconomics of media industries, most of whom have updated their approach to include the new digital industries (Schiller 2007; Mosco 2004, 2009). From their perspective, theorists like Jenkins and Deuze are academic cybertarians who "maintain that the new media provide a popular apparatus that subverts patriarchy, capitalism and other forms of oppression" (Miller 2009: 425).

Convergence theory and political economy represent disparate academic prisms through which the meanings and ideological implications of a phenomenon like YouTube-Google have been assessed. Whereas, in my view, the convergence angle lacks a critical interrogation of social media platforms' corporate structure and business models, political economy approaches tend to gloss over the shaping role of technology; they also undervalue the role of users, content, and cultural form. Lacking in both approaches is an analytical mode that integrates a techno-cultural viewpoint with a socioeconomic perspective. That is one of the reasons that I sympathize with theorists such as Siva Vaidhyanathan (2011: 37), who in his book *The Googlization of Everything* regards YouTube not as a product constructed by a powerful company, but as the "central battlefield in the struggle to define the terms and norms of digital communication." Google watchers and state regulators are closely monitoring every move of a company that has gained unprecedented power over all kinds of private and public data. And yet Google's strategy of connecting platforms to create a cross-platform flow should not just be scrutinized as the pursuit of a single powerful company. The influence of "googlization" goes way beyond Google's platforms and the political economy of its conglomerate strategy.

What is most striking about sites like YouTube is their normalization into everyday life—people's ubiquitous acceptance of connective media penetrating all aspects of sociality and creativity. Millions of users across the world have incorporated YouTube and video sharing in their quotidian habits and routines, and despite the vocal opposition of some users and creative video-protests of YouTube enthusiasts, Google never really had to adapt its strategies to pacify the loyal disciples of its former rebellious self.[36] This gleeful acceptance of YouTube's evolution by an overwhelming majority of users points to a deeper cultural logic that affords media platforms the power to shape sociality and creativity. This logic stems, first, from a seamless integration of most dominant platforms' architectural designs and principles; and, second, from the communal neoliberal ideology that undergirds their smooth concatenation.

As far as the integration of platforms is concerned, Google's "seamless cross-platform experience" perfectly meshes with what Facebook calls "frictionless sharing" and also blends in with Twitter's ubiquitous implementation of following and trending functions. Friending, liking, following, trending, and favoriting are all subject to their respective site's engineering mechanisms of filtering, selecting, and promoting certain users and content over others. The commercial incentive underlying all systems is the idea of bringing personalized ads to mass audiences. Pushing some users to be influential and others to be susceptible, cross-platform compatibility ensures the mutual enhancement of each microsystem's individual effects, illustrated, for instance, by sudden short-lived viral explosions across platforms. But the conjoined effects of the online connective ecosystem would not be half as effective if they had not also progressively aligned with the mechanisms of "old" media such as television. YouTube, particularly, has made serious inroads on television's mass audience appeal.

The platform recently started testing the broadcast of live events such as concerts and baseball games, experimenting with the use of live Twitter streams to boost user traffic and lengthen attention spans. It is no coincidence that television and other offline mass media (newspapers, publishing industry) are now easily mixing the online mechanisms of Twitter, Facebook, and YouTube into their own offline and online strategies. Tweets, snippets, and webisodes are the perfect complement to sound bites, trailers, and TV series.

However, the seamless amalgamation of online platforms and mass media into one and the same connective economy cannot be simply accounted for by shared technical and economic conditions. Both developments took place over a much longer period in history than just the last ten years; in fact, the larger cultural trends of personalization, mass customization, commercialization, and the blending of public and private space started years, if not decades, before YouTube's enfolding success. Twitter's and YouTube's push for celebrities to create large followings and for popular musicians to monetize personal fame has firm roots in television culture of the 1980s and 1990s; Facebook's and YouTube's filtering and ranking principles built on mass media's role in cultivating promising and potentially lucrative reputations. If we look at most platforms' metamorphoses, it is easy to understand why YouTube's alternative image, which thrived on a cultural mood of participation and community building, could never hold up in the face of the powerful commercial incentives propelling the site forward into the mainstream. The neoliberal ideology of technology pushing economic needs is not always conducive to the ideal of creating a sustainable environment that nourishes community-based platforms. Commercial owners favor—over the need for sustainable communities— quick turnovers, short-lived trends, celebrities attracting mass audiences, attention-grabbing experiences, influential power-users, and a large pool of aspiring professionals. And yet it is remarkable how often the participatory ideal of connectedness is invoked to warrant the need for commercial exploitation of connectivity. Google is still most eager to praise YouTube as a site for activists and creative people; it direly needs the image of being a site for friends recommending videos to friends, even if its interface no longer foregrounds taste communities.

It is only against the backdrop of such cultural and ideological continuities that we can understand the amazingly swift and radical way in which the logic of connectivity infected the entire media landscape. In less than a decade, YouTube has become naturalized as the nexus of amateur videos, personalized ads, commercial audiovisual content, and mass audience appeal. To achieve this goal, Google wielded technologies, governance, and business models to shape new forms of sociality and connectivity and, in the process, establish a new paradigm for communication traffic. Indeed, YouTube and its owner, Google, will gain more control over users' online video-sharing experience by giving amateur videographers less exposure, funneling viewers toward fewer choices, and shepherding them toward TV-like channels.

The case of YouTube is used in this chapter to connect the technology and its users with its organizational framework and reveal how this evolving microsystem is part of a larger ecosystem of connective media, which, in turn, arises from the matrix of culture. This mutual shaping of technology and culture, of microsystems and ecosystem, is at the core of this historical reconstruction. The story of YouTube's rebellion from, courtship of, and marriage to television, even if it strikes you as a fairy tale that ends with its customers living happily ever after, should leave users with a number of philosophical questions regarding the control over content and the vertical integration of platforms in the hands of one owner. These questions concern the powers of citizens versus corporate agents, users versus owners, and old versus new media. I will pick up on these reflections more extensively in the last chapter. First, we need to look more closely at the one platform in the ecosystem of connective media that by all popular accounts rises above commercial ambitions, to give the resource of connectivity back to the crowds: Wikipedia.

CHAPTER 7

Wikipedia and the Neutrality Principle

7.1. INTRODUCTION

> Wikipedia is an online encyclopedia. It incorporates elements of general and
> specialized encyclopedias, almanacs, and gazettes. Wikipedia is *not* a soapbox,
> an advertising platform, a vanity press, an experiment in anarchy or democracy,
> an indiscriminate collection of information, or a web directory. It is *not* a dic-
> tionary, newspaper, or a collection of source documents; that kind of content
> should be contributed instead to the Wikimedia sister projects.[1]

This 2012 definition of what Wikipedia is, and especially what it is *not*,
forms the first of five principles on which the platform is founded. A far cry
from its original description in 2001 as "the free encyclopedia that anyone
can edit," Wikipedia has shifted from being a collaborative project experimenting with the online production of encyclopedic knowledge, to being a
professionally run, volunteer-based, nonprofit organization whose goal is
the online production of an encyclopedia. During the intermittent decade,
Wikipedia has become the world's sixth-largest platform; with nearly 15
million registered users and contributors, it is unprecedented in scale and
scope, covering almost 3.7 million articles on different subjects and still
growing.[2] The platform's success has stunned a global community of Internet specialists, policymakers, and business people alike. In 2011, the online
encyclopedia was nominated for the UNESCO World Heritage List, underscoring its status as a global cultural phenomenon.[3] To many, Wikipedia is
one of the few examples of what Yochai Benkler (2006: 5) has called "nonmarket peer-production" in an otherwise overwhelmingly corporate digital
environment.

So how did Wikipedia evolve as a unique peer-produced microsystem, and what makes it different from commercially run platforms? The online project is still regarded as the epitome of crowdsourcing: made by users, for users. Thousands of volunteers have contributed millions of entries and edits. But rather than being an open and serendipitous stream, content contribution to Wikipedia has gradually become a process strictly managed by humans and machines. A complex procedure of negotiation based on five basic principles, of which neutrality is the most important one, this process necessarily results in consensus. In contrast to its commercial counterparts, Wikipedia shapes online sociality not by implementing buttons for liking, friending, following, and trending—functions anchored in the popularity principle—but by constructing a platform for "knowing" that is moored in the neutrality principle. This ideology is mirrored in Wikipedia's nonprofit organization. Once cheered for its anarchic structure—the embodiment of a free and open (source) information society—the platform's nonprofit status was consolidated through the establishment of the Wikimedia Foundation, to guarantee a steady flow of funding and continue large-scale operating power without impacting the encyclopedia's content or editorial decisions.

Over the first ten years of its existence, many have acclaimed Wikipedia's laudable goals and successful nonprofit organization, but some also criticized its gradual institutionalization. As Wikipedia's short history in this chapter divulges, the platform's active user base of volunteers and amateurs has been cheered for its generous contributions and slammed for its lack of expertise. Wikipedia's technological architecture was praised for its transparency, but its interface has been denounced for obliterating nuances and silencing dissent. The encyclopedia's content has been subject to heated debates about accuracy, yet it survived several tests comparing its quality to established encyclopedias. Wikipedia's governance structure and policies have been praised as the reinvention of democracy in a Web 2.0 environment but have also been interpreted as indicators of autocracy and bureaucracy. In sum, what defines the encyclopedia's success for some people embodies disenchantment for others.

Wikipedia's status as the biggest nonmarket, peer-produced platform in the ecosystem of connective media raises important questions about its viability and independence in an online environment that is dominated by commercial mechanisms and principles, even if they are often cached in the rhetoric of commonality and public values. For instance, how does Wikipedia's consensual apparatus relate to the ideology of sharing, as professed by Facebook and others? How does the platform's ideology of neutrality compare to the logic of popularity ingrained in Google's ranking mechanisms? And how can Wikipedia hold up its nonprofit status in a network of media conglomerates that are overwhelmingly driven by the profit motive? To answer these questions, we will have to gauge Wikipedia's efficacy in the context of a normative culture of connectivity.

7.2. THE TECHNO-CULTURAL CONSTRUCTION OF CONSENSUS

Users and Usage

From the very onset of the project in 2001, Wikipedia has been primarily described in terms of the masses of people involved in its production. The ideal-turned-platitude "wisdom of crowds" (Surowiecki 2004) kept haunting the project long after it had taken the road of systematized professionalization. Over the years, the wiki platform has been heralded as an example of "many minds collaborating" (Sunstein 2006) "distributed collaboration" (Shirky 2008), "mass collaboration" (Tapscott and Williams 2006), "crowdsourcing," and "collaborative knowledge," to name just a few such qualifications.[4] Wikipedia enthusiasts used these terms to praise the project's democratizing potential as well as its ethos of community and collaboration, and of course, to underline its laudable goal: providing a source of knowledge free for everyone to read and write.[5] But summarizing these ideals in the single "wisdom of crowds" epithet is reductive and fallacious; even the platform's founders repudiated the notion of crowds producing Wikipedia. If we pay closer attention to the platform's history, we can notice an interesting curve reflecting shifts in usage and user engagement.

What characterized Wikipedia's users in the first and second stage of development? Were they many or few, experts or amateurs, active contributors or passive readers of encyclopedic entries? During the first five years of the platform's existence, content production was largely dependent on the work of a small group of dedicated volunteers. Although they soon formed a thriving community, the notion of a massive collective of contributors simply did not apply. Until 2006, Wikipedia was largely written and maintained by a core of dedicated editors—2 percent doing 73 percent of all edits.[6] Wikipedia is not alone in this respect: the same disproportionate contributions of small groups of users vis-à-vis common users can be found in the early stages of virtually all UGC platforms, as well as in the open-source movement (Ghosh and Prakash 2000).[7] It would be a mistake, though, to dismiss the idea of Wikipedia's many contributors as a complete myth; actually, the real wisdom of Wikipedia can be found not in its crowds but in its crowd *management*.

Starting in 2006, the online encyclopedia showed a distinct decline of "elite" users while at the same time the number of edits made by novice users surged. Various researchers noted this dramatic shift in workload, but instead of endorsing the wisdom-of-crowds cliché, Kittur and colleagues (2007) researched "the rise of the bourgeoisie": a marked growth in the population of low-edit users. After a period of hegemony by a small group of high-powered, dedicated volunteers, the "pioneers were dwarfed by the influx of settlers" (Kittur et al. 2007, n.p.). In response, the early adopters selected and refined their technological managerial systems to discipline the growing majority of novice users, who soon became the primary contributors as the number of elite users relatively decreased. Kittur and his colleagues observe a similar development in other Web 2.0 platforms, and explain this shift by describing Wikipedia in terms of a dynamic social system that evolves as a result of the gradual development, implementation, and distribution of a content management system. They suggest that what happened to Wikipedia may be a common phenomenon in the evolution of online collaborative knowledge systems.

Alongside the question whether few or many produce Wikipedia, a parallel debate revolved around whether experts or amateurs should produce online encyclopedias. The idea of thousands of lay contributors runs counter to the professional expert approach, an approach vehemently defended by the publishing industries as well as by a few cultural theorists.[8] Interestingly, Wikipedia originally intended to be an expert-generated encyclopedia. Starting under the name Nupedia, a small team of selected academics was invited to write entries with the aim of creating a "free online encyclopedia of high quality" made available with an open-content license (Shirky 2008: 109). Founder Jimmy Wales and his staff employee Larry Sanger put into place a protocol based on academic peer-review and grounded in the principles of openness and objectivism.[9] This expert approach failed, though, partly because of the slowness of scholars invited to serve as editors. To speed up the process, Sanger suggested a "wiki" as a collective place where scholars and interested laypeople from all over the globe could help with drafting and editing articles. The ensuing success of Wikipedia and the commitment of the Wikipedians took the founders by surprise. They made a great effort to keep Wikipedia organized while at the same time providing space for some of the disorderliness—edit wars, inaccuracies, mistakes, fights—that collaborative editing brings along (Niederer and van Dijck 2010). Early 2002, however, Sanger turned away from Wikipedia toward an expert-written encyclopedic model, while Wales chose to further pursue the wiki model.[10]

Alongside the debates on amateurs versus experts, the issue of specialists versus generalists surfaced occasionally. Did Wikipedia need specialists to contribute entries on one specific area, or were generalists who could write about different areas more valuable to the site? As it turned out, researchers proved that the site needs both types of input. Whereas specialists boost the site's quality level, generalists are crucial to the connective fabric of the encyclopedia, as they tend to make more links *between* domains (Halatchliyski et al. 2010).

In fact, the key to understanding Wikipedia's "crowd management" is probably the site's ability to accommodate a large *variety* of users: frequent *and* occasional contributors, passive readers *and* active authors-editors, generalists *and* specialists. Wikipedia's success as an online encyclopedia may be largely attributed to its capacity to handle enormous user diversity and align the various contributions toward one communal product. In the early days, Wikipedians were commonly viewed as a single community, but since its explosive growth after 2006, that community has gradually progressed into an organized hierarchy of different user categories who are all effectively marshaled into executing well-defined tasks. Less frequent contributors and "newcomers" are tactically welcomed and encouraged to improve their edits by experienced contributors using socializing tactics (Choi et al. 2010). Even passive users may be considered indispensable participants rather than free riders because reading is a gateway activity through which newcomers learn about Wikipedia and because large numbers of readers legitimize and raise the encyclopedia's status (Antin and Cheshire 2010). It is precisely the socialization of many different *types* of users into a single regime that accounts for Wikipedia's ability to mobilize and manage crowds.

Successful user socialization thus heavily depends on a techno-managerial system, which facilitates and channels the collaboration of experienced content suppliers, occasional contributors, and (passive) readers at various levels. Starting in 2006, journalists and Wikipedia observers noticed that the platform had begun implementing a strict organization to manage its crowds and open-editing policies.[11] Indeed, a sociotechnical system of sophisticated protocols distributing permission levels to types of users imposes a strict order on decision making over what entries to include or exclude, what edits to allow or block. If we look more closely at Wikipedia's user hierarchy, we can distinguish various user categories with incremental permission levels.[12] Starting with the lowest user group on the ladder, we have, in ascending order, blocked users, unregistered users, new users, and registered (or autoconfirmed) users. One step higher on the ladder, we find bots, administrators, bureaucrats, and stewards; developers and system administrators take the highest positions. The pecking order in granting permission to execute tasks is defined by hierarchy: blocked users have the least permission, for they can only edit their own talk page. Unregistered or anonymous users obviously have less authority than registered users, who in turn are at a lower level of power than bots; bots are just below administrators ("admins"). Productive workers who have proven to deliver solid edits are identified and granted administrator's status (Burke and Kraut 2008). System administrators (or developers) have the highest permission power in the Wikipedia universe, including server access. This is a small user group of only ten people who "manage and maintain the Wikimedia Foundation Servers."[13]

While this hierarchical system of distributing user power and functions was developed, a number of original Wikipedia supporters started to complain about the implementation of what they considered a cumbersome bureaucracy (Kildall and Stern 2011). Users were no longer given the freedom to edit, they contended; instead, contributions were straightjacketed into a rank-an-file techno-bureaucratic system grounded in Wikipedia's normative patrol of content. Critics such as Nicolas Carr objected that Wikipedia was no longer an egalitarian collective or an expression of collective intelligence, calling for the burial of that "Wikipedia myth" (Carr 2011: 195). I will return to this criticism later in this section, but first I need to say a few things about the platform's dependence on technological agents in the production of consensus.

Technology

What is particularly surprising in Wikipedia's user dynamics is the significant role that nonhuman actors or bots play in the content management system, not only in terms of quantity but also in their qualitative ranking as autonomous agents. Human editors would never be able to keep up with the massive amount of authoring and editorial activities going on at the online encyclopedia if software robots did not assist them. Bots are pieces of software or scripts designed to "make automated edits without the necessity of human decision-making."[14] They can be recognized by a username that contains the word "bot," such as SieBot, TxiKiBot, 3RRBot, and Rambot. In contrast to most proprietary algorithms, for example, Edge-Rank or PageRank, Wikipedia's algorithmic tools are the result of open-access engineering; once approved and deployed by Wikipedians, bots obtain their own user page. They also form their own user group with a certain level of access and administrative rights—a level made visible by flags on a user account page. One year after Wikipedia was founded, bots were first introduced as useful helpers for repetitive administrative tasks.[15]

Since 2002, the number of bots has grown exponentially. In 2006, the number had grown to 151, and in 2008 there were 457 active bots.[16] As of 2010, over 16 percent of all edits in Wikipedia were made by bots, a number that is still growing (Geiger and Ribes 2010: 119).[17]

In general, there are two types of bots: editing or *coauthoring bots* and nonediting or *administrative bots*. Each of the bots has a very specific approach to Wikipedia content, related to its often-narrow task. Administrative bots are most well known among Wikipedia users: they are deployed to perform policing tasks, such as blocking spam and detecting vandalism. Vandalism combat bots come into action when suspicious edits are made, such as a large amount of deleted content in an article or a more than usual change in content (Shachaf and Hara 2010). Spell-checking bots check language and make corrections in Wikipedia articles. Ban enforcements bots can block a user from Wikipedia, and thus take away his or her editing rights, which is something a registered user is not entitled to do. Nonediting bots are also data miners used to extract information from Wikipedia and find copyright violation identifiers; the latter compare text in new entries to what is already available on the Web about that specific topic, and they report this to a page for human editors to review. Most bots are created to perform repetitive tasks and thus make many edits.

Most vandal-banning strategies can be considered joint human-bot ventures. Researchers Geiger and Ribes (2010) demonstrated in an experiment where they tracked instances of Wikipedia vandalism how humans and bots distribute the work between them; each actor makes separate judgments as they become mutually attuned to each other's tasks. Identification algorithms automatically register obvious signs of vandalism, for instance, a significant removal of content or repeated content reversals during a single day, upon which they alert human editors. Popular tools like Huggle, Twinkle, and Lupin feature algorithms programmed to execute very specific tasks, such as rolling back multiple edits by a single user or signaling a problematic user, so that human editors can decide whether to delete or reverse an edit. Detection algorithms systematically discriminate against anonymous and newly registered users, as they are lowest in the hierarchy. Vandal fighting in Wikipedia is a process of distributed cognition, made possible by a "complex network of interactions between humans, encyclopedia articles, software systems and databases" (Geiger and Ribes 2010: 118).

The category of coauthoring bots seems to be much less known to Wikipedia users and researchers. One of the first editing bots to become productive was Rambot, a piece of software created by Derek Ramsey.[18] Rambot pulls content from public databases and feeds it into Wikipedia, creating or editing articles on specific content, either one by one or as a batch. Since its inception in 2002, Rambot has created approximately 30,000 articles on U.S. cities and counties on Wikipedia, using data from the *CIA World Factbook* and the U.S. census. In the course of time, bot-generated articles on American cities and counties were corrected and complemented by human editors, following a strict format: history, geography, demographics, and so on. The articles appear strikingly tidy and informative and they are remarkably uniform. To date, it still is Rambot's main task to create and edit articles about U.S. counties and cities, while human editors check and complement the facts provided by this software robot.

While not every bot is an author, all bots can be classified as "content agents," as they all actively engage with Wikipedia content. The most active Wikipedians are in fact bots; a closer look at various user groups reveal that bots create a large number of revisions with high quality.[19] Adler and colleagues (2008) discovered that the two largest contributors in their edit-longevity-survival-test were bots. Wikipedians rely heavily on these notification systems and feeds for the upkeep of articles. Describing Wikipedians in bipolar categories of humans and nonhumans doesn't do justice to what is in fact a hybrid category: that of the many active users assisted by administrative and monitoring tools, also referred to as "software-assisted human editors." One might also argue that bots are Wikipedians' full-fledged coauthors of many entries, justifying their recognition as "human-assisted automatic editors."

Bots and humans occupy distinct positions on the hierarchical ladder of users, but it is neither human users nor automated bots *alone* that create and maintain Wikipedia's encyclopedic project. It is an integral system of human-bot interaction that helps produce and maintain a kind of modulated sociality, which is unprecedented in scale: Wikipedia's engineered social order structures collaboration of thousands of active contributors, hundreds of bots, and millions of readers who are also potential contributors. As Nathaniel Tkacz (2011) rightly observes: "Bots now police not only the encyclopedic nature of content contributed to articles, but also *the sociality of users* who participate in the community" (79, emphasis added). And that is exactly what some users hold against the techno-managerial system: it may enhance Wikipedia's vigilance, but it also imposes a uniform regime of delegated tasks aimed at perfect execution. Such regimented protocols, critics contend, preclude dissent and nonconsensual behavior. Much like Facebook's thwarting of individual attempts to protest or hack its protocols, Wikipedia's users worry about their site becoming a semiautomated, impermeable operational system that prohibits discord and favors consensus at the expense of a variety of opinions.

Indeed, the operational apparatus that enforces consensus on its users cannot be seen apart from a set of principles on which the construction of encyclopedic content is grounded. As demonstrated in previous chapters, any algorithmic activity incorporates epistemic assumptions about how content *ought* to be constructed. Wikipedia's content management system is firmly anchored in techno-human protocols, but on what principles of content production do these protocols operate, and how do these principles scaffold the consensual process?

Content

As pointed out in this chapter's introduction, the production of Wikipedia content is based on five core principles; these principles serve as guidelines for contributors, instruct the algorithmic logic of bots, and anchor the encyclopedia's quality standards.[20] Three of these rules are relevant to this discussion. First, the rule of verifiability means that readers have to be able to retrace Wikipedia content to reliable sources; therefore, referring to published articles and verifiable resources is necessary to have the article (or edits) accepted. A second related rule is called "No Original Research." Wikipedia simply does not accept new or unpublished research or original thought; again, reliability on Wikipedia means citing proven, published sources. Third, articles have to be written from a "Neutral Point of View" (NPoV); to avoid bias, entries have to be based on facts and facts about opinions, but not on opinions. All contributors, whether single anonymous users, bots, or administrators, are required to comply with these rules, and noncompliance is punished by removal of edits. These standards are maintained through the mechanics of Wikipedia's content management system and enforced through the regime of socialized-user control.

During the first five years of Wikipedia's existence, the first two principles figured in many debates, played out in academia as well as in the press, on the accuracy and reliability of encyclopedic content. The accuracy debates revolved around the question of the alleged quality and corruptibility of sources; the reliability debate concentrated mainly on the lack of trust due to the absence of verifiable authorship. With so many anonymous and amateur contributors, inaccuracy and sloppiness were likely. Researchers entered the quality-of-content debate by testing Wikipedia's robustness in terms of content vandalism.[21] In December 2005, the first academic research that systematically compared the accuracy of Wikipedia to *Encyclopedia Britannica* entries was published in *Nature* (Giles 2005). Investigators checked 42 science articles in both publications without knowing their source and found Wikipedia and Britannica to be almost equally accurate. Not surprisingly, the news was trumpeted on the BBC News as "Wikipedia Survives Research Test."[22] With this outcome, Wikipedia was recognized as a reliable encyclopedia, at least in terms of accuracy. Many such accuracy tests followed; peer-reviewed studies performed between 2006 and 2011 again proved the reliability of sources as a thermometer of exactitude in diverse disciplinary fields.[23]

The second debate concentrated on the reliability and questionable integrity of *anonymous* sources. How can an entry be objective if the encyclopedia accepts copyedits from anonymous contributors who might have a vested interest in its outcome? Critics like Keen (2008) and Denning and colleagues (2005) fiercely objected to the distribution of editing rights to all users. In response to these objections, various technological remedies have countered the weakness of anonymous authorship. First, Wikipedia's content management system, as we have seen above, allots very limited power to anonymous contributors, whose edits can be overruled by anyone who has a higher level of permission (which is anyone except for blocked users). Since anonymous users are very low in the Wikipedia pecking order, their edit longevity is likely to be short when they break the ground principles. Besides, there is an increasing availability of "counter-tools" that allow for checking the identity of contributors, or at least their location of origin. Starting at the most basic level, on the History page of each Wikipedia entry we can find the time stamp and IP address for every anonymous edit made. Third-party apps, like the WikiScanner, make it possible to geolocate anonymous edits by looking up the IP addresses in an IP-to-Geo database, a listing of IP addresses and the companies and institutions they belong to, and track a potential interest.[24] With the introduction of WikiTrust, in the fall of 2009, the reliability of newly edited parts of Wikipedia articles was coded in colors, indicating an author's reputation based on the lifespan of his or her other contributions. Instead of turning to experts to check all articles, Wikipedia further enhanced the robustness of its sociotechnical system to enforce its principles.

Of all five principles, the Neutral Point of View (NPoV) caused most discussion among Wikipedia adepts; it was regarded as the principle that most rigorously coerced users into consensus formation and hence squelched discussion and diversity of opinion. Perhaps ironically, it was also precisely this principle and the apparatus built on it that initially drew praise as one of Wikipedia's greatest innovations. Historian Roy Rosenzweig (2006), for instance, stated that Wikipedia's value lies precisely in the dynamics of its continuous editing process, where a regulated system of consensus-editing bares *how* history is written: "Although

Wikipedia as a product is problematic as a sole source of information, the process of creating Wikipedia fosters an appreciation of the very skills that historians try to teach" (138). Rosenzweig points to some of the platform's most important interface features, such as the built-in History page, a feature that lets you check the edit history of each entry, or the Recent Changes pages, which allow users to see how an entry has been modified.

Whereas Rosenzweig lauds this aspect of Wikipedia's interface, others object that the diversity of opinion and discussion should not be relegated to pages *behind* the visible interface because it requires extra clicks as well as technical or interpretative ingenuity from the reader. Instead, civil debate and discussion should be included in the entry's main page. Some detractors reject the NPoV rule as ideologically suspect to begin with, particularly if strictly enforced by and extensive operational apparatus. As British historian Daniel O'Sullivan (2011) observes: "In contrast to a world of increasing homogeneity in which difference is subsumed under the rule of dominant opinion and standardized knowledge, Wikipedia has the potential to proliferate voices and dissent—and yet the increasingly bureaucratic 'policing' of its content, as for example with NPOV, means it is in danger of merely mirroring the typical knowledge economies of the West" (48). In other words, hiding discussion behind the visible user interface stimulates homogenization while discouraging alternative interpretations and discord.

Actual contributors to Wikipedia have complained not only about the rules' conspicuous ideological portent, but also about the cumbersome policing apparatus these rules bring along. In a humorous article on his attempts to contribute edits to the online encyclopedia's entry on the American Haymarket trial in 1886, Timothy Messer-Kruse, a professor in American labor history, expresses his frustration about the system that forces him to oblige to Wikipedia's consensual disciplinary system:

> My improvement lasted five minutes before a Wiki-cop scolded me, "I hope you will familiarize yourself with some of Wikipedia's policies, such as verifiability and undue weight. If all historians save one say that the sky was green in 1888, our policies require that we write 'Most historians write that the sky was green, but one says the sky was blue.' . . . As individual editors, we're not in the business of weighing claims, just reporting what reliable sources write." I guess this gives me a glimmer of hope that someday, perhaps before another century goes by, enough of my fellow scholars will adopt my views that I can change that Wikipedia entry. Until then I will have to continue to shout that the sky was blue.[25]

The NPoV rule is thus a guiding principle for building a functional apparatus, but that apparatus simultaneously shapes the meaning of neutrality as the "average opinion" or "shared interpretation." In 2006, American talk show host Stephen Colbert launched the term "wikiality" to indicate the encyclopedia's circular logic of creating a reality that we can all agree on: "If you claim something to be true and enough people agree with you, it becomes true."[26] Viewed in this light, the neutrality principle shows at least some likeness to the popularity principle employed by Google and Facebook. Some Wikipedians have countered this criticism saying that the NPoV principle may at times be untenable, especially in those situations when a disinterested position is impossible, but in general, it works as a functional guideline for processing content.[27]

Consensus, as may be concluded from these debates, has become a sociotechnical construct—sociality regimented in a technocratic system that yields formatted content. Sociologist Christian Pentzold (2011: 718) articulates this very precisely in his ethnographic study of Wikipedia users when he observes that contributors do "not only have to learn to use the software tools, but they also have to acquire the appropriate beliefs, values, common understandings and practices." The consensual apparatus that Wikipedia has become, however, cannot be regarded separately from the socioeconomic structure through which it evolved. Therefore, we now turn to Wikipedia's ownership structure, business model, and governance, in order to see how the norms for consensus formation are sustained by the platform's organization.

7.3. A CONSENSUAL APPARATUS BETWEEN DEMOCRACY AND BUREAUCRACY

Ownership Structure

It is important to recall that Wikipedia is the only nonprofit, nonmarket platform in the top ten of ranked Internet sites, a list that is topped by Google, Facebook, and YouTube respectively. However, few people realize that Wikipedia started out in 2001 as part of the Bomis Company, a for-profit enterprise founded by Jimmy Wales. The original founders' skirmishes over "Nupedia" and over the best context in which to build an open-access and open-licensing platform made Wales realize that a "wiki" model could only flourish in a nonprofit organization. When the Wikimedia Foundation was established two years later, it first operated as a fundraising body run by volunteers. Wales, as the platform's founder, was still very much the driving force behind the project, yet despite his charisma

Wikipedians did not always appreciate his personal involvement with every part of the operation. The Wikimedia Foundation, directed by a board of trustees and operating under U.S. law, raised funds to cover the online encyclopedia's operational expenses, such as servers and equipment.[28]

Meanwhile, ownership of the Wikipedia platform—that is, its content and trademark—remained with the Wikipedia community, which was also represented in the foundation's board. As noted in the previous section, the community grew exponentially after 2005, which is why the platform developed a substantial governance apparatus with its own rules and norms to manage the large numbers of volunteers. Between 2006 and 2009, the foundation simultaneously metamorphosed from a volunteer-based nonprofit organization to a global organization run by paid employees, with a centralized American headquarters and decentralized national chapters (Fuster Morell 2011). All national Wikipedias are governed and overseen by the Wikimedia Foundation. The online encyclopedia is just one of many wiki projects overseen by the foundation; other projects include Wiki-quotes, Wikiversity, Wikinews, and Wiktionary.

Wikipedia's management decision to build and sustain its platform in the nonprofit realm was completely apt and logical; and yet the ultimate structure it developed also divulges signs of awkwardness, as the encyclopedia's "nonmarket peer production" is not free from corporatized features. Predictably, a number of early adepts were disappointed in the managerial structure the platform eventually developed. The resulting structure, reflected in the Wikimedia Foundation on the one hand and the Wikipedia project on the other, may be considered the online equivalent of the American public broadcast concept, represented by the Corporation for Public Broadcasting and the Public Broadcasting System. By dividing the Wikimedia Foundation from the encyclopedic project, it strictly adhered to a separation of fund-raising and editorial activities, but the inequity between the two entities felt awkward to some people. Internet researcher Mayo Fuster Morell voiced some Wikipedians' disenchantment with the platform's hybrid organizational structure, which harbors two different democratic logics:

> The Wikimedia Foundation adapted a traditional, representational democratic logic, while the community remains an innovative, elaborate, organizational model. The foundation is based on a contractual relationship with the staff, while the community relies on voluntary self-involvement. The foundation runs according to an obligatory hierarchy and a representational board, while the community relies on openness to participation, a volunteer hierarchy, and (mainly but not always) consensus decision-making. The foundation bases its

power from a centralized base of coordination and long-term planning in San Francisco, while the community is decentralized and serendipitous. (Fuster Morell 2011: 333)

The gradually evolving professional structure of the project reminded some early Wikipedia adepts of the traditional editorial, and even corporate, structure of mainstream publishers or public broadcasters. However acute these observations, the dissatisfaction of assorted Wikipedians with the platform's ultimate organization may have lain less with its managerial decisions concerning ownership *structure* than with its governance model, which was hailed as democratic by some and decried as pure bureaucracy by others.

Governance

Wikipedia's elaborate governance system has been likened in recent years to both public state organizations and private businesses, yet neither model really applies. Some studies described Wikipedia's governance using qualifiers such as "anarchy" and "monarchy," while others have pointed to the project's democratic, statelike organization that has taken on the characteristics of a bureaucracy. According to the "wisdom of crowd" paradigm, Wikipedia should have taken the form of anarchy where everyone, regardless of qualifications, is allowed to participate, and where there is no top-down control. Others asserted that Wikipedia is essentially run by an autocrat, Jimmy Wales—the "uncrowned king" who patrols his domain with the help of a "selected army of volunteer sheriffs" (O'Neil 2011: 312). Both claims can be dismissed as hyperbole.

Arguments that Wikipedia has turned into a democratic bureaucracy seem to hold more weight, though. Indeed, the process of consensus formation among editors and contributors resulted in an extensive apparatus of committees and ruling boards, the apex of which is the Mediation Committee, the highest body of arbitrators for handling serious conflicts about content.[29] An extensive Mediation Policy guides the committee in handling disputes over content, differences in opinion with regard to neutrality versus interested positions.[30] In addition, Wikipedia also installed an Arbitration Committee, acting as a final binding decision-maker, which for instance examines disagreements over serious misconduct, banned users, and vandalism—disputes the community has been unable to resolve itself.[31] Both policies are extensive documents prescribing precise steps in processes that are conspicuously similar to legal procedures, including appeal boards and clerks.

For some, legalistic governance procedures are precisely what turned Wikipedia into a bureaucratic monster. Perhaps not entirely serious, but certainly revealing an undertone of criticism, is Nicolas Carr's description of the intricacies of Wikipedia's hierarchy and the breadth and complexity of its rules as follows:

> Maybe it should call itself "the encyclopedia that anyone can edit on the condition that said person meets the requirements laid out in Wikipedia Code 234.56, subsections A34–A58, A65, B7 (codicil 5674), and follows the procedures specified in Wikipedia Statutes 31-1007 as well as Secret Wikipedia Scroll SC72 (Wikipedia Decoder Ring required)." (Carr 2011: 200)

Aggravating Wikipedia's dense bureaucracy is the total absence of democratic elections or a perspicuous representation of users, according to some critics. Social scientist Mathieu O'Neil, for instance, argues that the semi-legal system of regulations and bylaws was not democratically formed, and that Wikipedia defies any democratic potential as long as it lacks a constitution and clearly defined voting procedures (O'Neil 2011: 321).

To be sure, the platform's choice for this elaborate governance structure has pertinent advocates and strong defenders. According to longtime Wikipedian and researcher Konieczny (2010), the project is neither anarchy nor monarchy, nor can it be called a democracy or bureaucracy, although it certainly mixes features of all four. Since Wikipedia's eclectic model of governance does not fit one established model, Konieczny proposes to apply the concept "adhocracy" to the online encyclopedia's organization. First coined by Alvin Toffler in his book *Future Shock* (1970) as an antonym to "bureaucracy," the term refers to the thousands of ad hoc, multidisciplinary teams forming temporary alliances to create and maintain content according to narrowly defined tasks. With nearly 15 million registered volunteers worldwide and over 1,500 administrators to marshal its contents, Wikipedia has certainly tested a new model of public governance in digital space; there are teams to write specific entries, but also teams for content review and editing, teams to review requests for administratorship, and teams to select featured articles for the home page. Projects are highly decentralized and leadership is based on "requests from respected editors" (Konieczny 2010: 277). In an adhocracy, leadership and policies "emerge" instead of being consciously decided upon (Mintzberg 2007). All these features of adhocracy apply to Wikipedia's governance philosophy and are highly relevant to the success of the site.

Needless to say, adhocracy is ultimately dependent on an extensive sociotechnical apparatus to sustain the scale and scope of Wikipedia's decentralized leadership and to guarantee the ultimate cohesion of encyclopedic content produced by multidisciplinary teams. As Gilles Deleuze (1990, 1992) has pointed out in his acute revision of Foucault's disciplinary institutions, a "society of control" deploys technology as an intricate part of its social mechanisms. Like any large public system, Wikipedia works through disciplinary control by means of an extensive hierarchy composed of distinct roles, such as administrators, system operators ("sys-ops") and developers; the system, as explained in the previous section, exerts control through reward and punishment, by raising a dedicated user's authority level, and by blocking contributor's rights of those who deviate from the rules (Burke and Kraut 2008). But that system of normative control could never work on such a large scale if it were not for an extensive set of tools: bots, algorithms, interface features, and a content management system.

Wikipedia's consensual apparatus is indeed a techno-cultural construct that is cemented in a matching socioeconomic model of governance and ownership—a complex and refined system that has been fine-tuned over the years. The platform's operation and governance is firmly anchored in an ideology of objectivism and neutrality—values that are coded into mechanisms and protocols for consensus and branded by the Wikipedia seal of "factual" approval. Some resent its outcome because the platform does not reflect the messiness of democracy, complaining that Wikipedia has straightjacketed egalitarian processes in an enforced hierarchical regime of sociotechnical control. Others laud the result because the project mobilizes an unprecedented number of users, while consensus formation has turned into and orderly and transparent process for everyone to check and see, even if that means clicking behind the visible interfaces. Whatever view one takes, Wikipedia still distinctly distinguishes itself from other market-based platforms in the way the project is funded.

Business Model

In 2003, Wikipedia distanced itself from the profit model under which it was started; since then, the encyclopedic project has never allowed advertising or commercial promotion to support its site. The Wikimedia Foundation accepts donations from private and corporate parties; donations have no purported impact on Wikipedia content because independence and neutrality are the online encyclopedia's trademarks. As we have seen in previous chapters, when large companies in the first part of the decade bought up UGC communities, such as YouTube, they were quick to align the site's original purpose with the company's monetizing schemes. The social and intellectual activity of encyclopedic knowledge production has a strong allegiance to a nonmarket public sphere, a sphere that, according to Yochai Benkler (2006), "enables many more individuals to communicate their . . . viewpoints to many others, and to do so in a way that cannot be controlled by media owners and is not as easily corruptible by money as were the mass media" (11). It is unlikely that volunteers would have kept contributing their knowledge and skills if corporate owners had exploited the site for monetary gain. Research has shown that users' strongest motivation for contributing to Wikipedia is their internal drive to share knowledge with others (Yang and Lai 2010).

In other words, the nonprofit, nonmarket business model that Wikipedia has chosen is inimically interwoven with the volunteer-based peer-production system the platform so successfully implemented. Even if not all users are valued equally and some have more powers than others in the Wiki-universe, no users can financially profit from the encyclopedia; the only gain they receive is recognition. The friction in this respect might be located in the fact that employees of the foundation are paid, while unpaid volunteers carry out all encyclopedic projects. If we recall YouTube and Flickr's monetizing schemes tested out in a "commons" environment, the clarity of Wikipedia's model certainly distinguishes itself from the mixed or unclear user remuneration models for-profit sites experimented with.

However, not everyone takes the inextricable intertwining of a peer-production model with nonmarket funding schemes for granted. For one thing, many commercial enterprises have mistaken the kernel of Wikipedia's success—its ability to harness the expertise and input of millions of users—as a business strategy that can be isolated and transposed to a for-profit environment. Looking at Wikipedia's success, economists started to propagate peer production as a kind of overarching humanist principle of organization that effaces the distinction between market and nonmarket schemes. Tapscott and Williams, authors of *Wikinomics* (2006), for instance, praise the convergence of commerce and commons and introduce a new kind of management-speak favoring buzzwords like "co-creation" and "prosumption." Social networks, according to leading business scholars, were changing the rules of the create-and-capture-value game, as more and more firms are "using them as platforms to reach out to customers and exploit their lock-in effects" (Wirtz, Schilke, and Ullrich 2010: 282). In other words, one element of Wikipedia is uncritically transferred to the commercial domain, where it is expected to translate into profitable customer value—an expectation that is problematic on more than one account (van Dijck and Nieborg 2009).

Unlike Google and Facebook, Wikipedia firmly grounds itself in a nonmarket space; the site does not exploit proprietary algorithms; its governance model, albeit complex, at least is transparent for its users; and the platform's operation suits its nonprofit objective. Notwithstanding some misgivings, one could argue that the Wikipedia model proves the perennial viability of a nonmarket peer-production model amid a market-driven environment. And yet it is disputable whether Wikipedia has truly managed to occupy a privileged space independent from the main corporate players and the norms and principles undergirding the ecosystem of connective media.

7.4. A NONMARKET SPACE IN THE ECOSYSTEM?

At first sight, Wikipedia has managed to carve out a separate space for itself in the Web 2.0 universe, having procured a nonprofit realm and having adopted a set of rules that prohibits commercial, controversial, one-sided, or overtly self-promotional content. Following the footsteps of traditional professional journalism or, for that matter, institutional knowledge production, the online project succeeded in translating the ideology of neutrality and objectivism into a system for protocolled consensus that mobilizes millions of active users and attracts a huge readership. But how separate or "sovereign" is this space? Can a nonprofit enclave of neutrality exist when it is woven into the corporate fabric of connective media? And how does the ideology of neutrality and objectivity relate to the sharing logic and popularity rankings fostered by Facebook and Google? In short, how does Wikipedia hold up in a culture of connectivity where the default is on frictionless sharing and data mining?

Wikipedia's nonprofit status represents a minority in the entire ecosystem of connective media; few small platforms with a nonprofit objective appear in the top 500 ranked platforms. Far from being threatening to corporate players in the same realm, Wikipedia may actually benefit from its lonesome-at-the-top position because it is hardly competing for the same user resources, advertiser dollars, or surfer's attention. If anything, the presence of one respected nonmarket peer-producer actually boosts the functionality and image of corporate platforms such as Facebook, YouTube, Flickr, Twitter, and others. Wikipedia's users generate content that purportedly has more than entertainment or socializing value, hence uplifting the status of *all* social media content. Amid a sea of goofy videos, pointless babble tweets, endless updates, and nippy snapshots, Wikipedia's encyclopedic content at least has the dignified status of being verified, impartial, and durable.

In contrast to ephemeral messages and trending topics, online encyclopedic entries are built to last, and yet they are as dynamic and flexible as the Web itself. One of the platform's unique properties is that content grows in value as time passes, and that an entry's truth is validated by an elaborate system guaranteeing verification and accuracy. Therefore, having a page on Wikipedia has more gravity in the world of mass self-communication than having a profile on Facebook. In more than one way, Wikipedia has become an online trademark for reliability, quality, authoritative content, and convenience, due to the extensive editorial protocols for consensus formation, staked in the ideology of neutrality. The brand has almost achieved the status of judge and jury of content validation; if listed among other search results, links to Wikipedia entries are perceived as neutral and impartial. The platform's nonprofit status is undoubtedly vital to the brand's independent image, but its rigid system for peer production and governance protocols is at least as crucial.

And yet the platform's peer-production model cannot be equated with its nonprofit structure. Of course, on the level of the microsystem the site functions as a nonprofit model, anchored in an independent foundation that raises the necessary funds. However, in the context of the wider ecosystem of connective media, Wikipedia's nonmarket status—an important part of its trademark—may be harder to maintain, as the space in which the platform operates is increasingly interpenetrated by other (commercial) platforms, notably Facebook and Google, resulting in these platforms mutually enhancing each other's ideology and operating logic. Two examples may illustrate this development.

In the summer of 2010, Facebook announced its collaboration with Wikipedia by including so-called "community pages" on the social network site.[32] Community pages are pages that link fields a user has filled out on his or her Facebook profile to Wikipedia articles about that same topic, as well as to posts from other Facebook members interested in that topic. For instance, if you fill in the term "cooking" or "lizards" on your Timeline, Facebook will link you to Wikipedia's page on this topic and simultaneously connect you to other members who are interested in the same topic. As Facebook points out: "Community pages are based on the concept of 'shared knowledge' that underlies Wikipedia." Facebook has licensed Wikipedia content under a Creative Commons license. Hence, Facebook's notion of "sharing information" and Wikipedia's definition of "sharing knowledge" are not only semantically equated but also literally integrated. The connection is mutually beneficial: if there is no lemma on Wikipedia to connect you to, Facebook will send you an invitation to suggest a Wikipedia article. The ideology of sharing and the ideology of neutrality seem perfectly aligned to serve the same purpose, even though they are pursued in entirely different—commercial versus nonprofit—contexts.

Another seamless fit appears to be Google's search rankings and Wikipedia's consensual apparatus. Wikipedia appears to be highly dependent on large corporate platforms in the ecosystem for boosting its traffic volume, and these platforms' algorithms and business models are intrinsically commercial. Since 2006, Wikipedia pages have ranked extremely high in the Google Web searches. In 2007 and 2008 researchers found that as much as 96 percent of all Wikipedia pages ranked in the top ten results of Google searches; the online encyclopedia also draws over 60 percent of all its traffic from Google.[33] Indeed, this could well be the result of Wikipedia's popularity as a source for information seekers; it could also represent Wikipedia's reputation for usefulness as measured on the Google scale. But an almost perfect score in Google's top rankings without more aid than just PageRank's algorithmic judgment seems too good to be true. More likely, Google boosts Wikipedia traffic because it benefits the search engine in more than one way.

As media theorist Siva Vaidhyanathan (2011) observes, Google likes to link to Wikipedia articles because they have already worked out norms and processes for neutralizing controversial content and contentious topics, a quality that aids Google's search engine value. In turn, he argues, "Google serves Wikipedia well because the editing standards for inclusion in Wikipedia depend on an entry's relevance; and relevance, circularly, depends on how prominently Google presents that subject" (Vaidhyanathan 2011: 63). Wikipedia's neutrality and consensus apparatus thus perfectly complements the popularity-ranking logic underpinning Google Search, where the most popular results allegedly rank highest. Google's ranking algorithms have often been questioned in terms of their impartiality, as distinct from the company's advertising interests (Batelle 2005). As we have seen in the previous chapter, ad space is awarded to the highest bidder, and the popularity principle is intimately intertwined with the profit principle. But platforms mutually profit from the alliance. Google's reliability as a search engine indisputably benefits from being associated with Wikipedia's neutral and impartial content, boosting the search engine's image. Mutatis mutandis, Wikipedia profits from increased traffic volumes. In the wider universe of platformed sociality, Google's popularity principle and Wikipedia's neutrality principle are complementary and mutually enhancing.

What we learn from the interconnectedness between Wikipedia and its commercial counterparts playing in the same Ivy League of connective media is that their algorithmic and operational logics, while distinctly separate, also perfectly mesh. The Wikipedian definition of "knowing" or rather "building online knowledge" is the largest possible consensus about facts we can agree on. Wikipedia neutralizes its content by distinguishing two layers: a visible layer of consensus backed up by an invisible yet accessible layer of discussion and a heterogeneous interpretation on the History and edit pages. This division of layers is mirrored on the organizational level by separating foundation from platform. Fund-raising and editorial activities are strictly divided in the organizational management and production of encyclopedic content. But how strong is this division of interests? In 2010, the coziness between Google and Wikipedia was underlined by Google's gift of $2 million to the Wikimedia Foundation. As one British journalist subtly remarked, Google's donation to the nonprofit foundation is "not a grant, it's an investment in making sure it can keep dominating search."[34] Of course, a donation does not mean that Google influences Wikipedia's editorial decisions, but it can hardly be denied that frictionless partnership strategies are pursued at every level of the ecosystem.

So what does Wikipedia imply for the possibility of carving out a nonprofit space in an ecosystem dominated by corporations? If we recall Flickr's half-baked attempts to create a nonmarket niche within the microcosm of its own platform economy, described in chapter 5, the uncomfortable fit between commons and commerce could well be explained by Flickr Commons's subordination to Yahoo's general for-profit objectives. This is not true for Wikipedia, which rigorously pursues a nonmarket model on the level of its microsystem. And yet this consistency is undermined not at the platform level, but at the cross-platform level—the space where platforms operate in a highly interdependent ecosystem of connective media. Is it possible at this level to secure a space *away* from market principles and establish a truly nonprofit realm? And how does this inevitable partnership of profit and nonprofit platforms reflect (and enhance) a wider culture in which these coalitions become the norm?

Connections between profit and nonprofit organizations in the ecosystem of connective media are modeled after American private-corporate partnerships, such as museum foundations and nongovernmental organizations. In contrast to some other parts of the world, Western culture has decreasing *public* space in which social and creative activity can take place; corporate and nonprofit organizations fill this zone. In more than one respect, online sociality mirrors offline sociality—a realm where the boundaries between for-profit, nonprofit, and public space are porous, but an implicit hierarchy dominated by market forces inevitably defines the conditions for development. Not surprisingly, as I concluded in chapter 4, the global space of interconnected media has encouraged digital companies to commercialize social areas that governments and states have neglected or have left underfunded: education, art projects, health care, archives, and knowledge institutions. There are no niches of online sociality that are purely nonprofit or public, simply for the reason that they can hardly flourish without support of the infrastructure "made social" by Google, Facebook, Twitter, and other companies. Wikipedia's success as a nonprofit online encyclopedia is highly dependent on its frictionless compatibility with mainstream big players; if its mechanisms, principles, and ideology did not mesh with theirs, Wikipedia's position in the ecosystem would likely dwindle.

All this hardly detracts from Wikipedia's laudable goal and much-appreciated result. The platform's history shows ample symptoms of a connective culture—a culture that is at once inescapable and yet abstruse—where the norms for online sociality and the meanings of profit, nonprofit, and public are still being negotiated. Since this process is ongoing, it is important to uncover the underlying structures and stress the big picture. The previous five chapters have related the critical histories of five individual platforms, explored their distinct positions vis-à-vis each other and laid out the various fibers the online fabric is made of. In the next chapter, we will turn the spotlight on the ecosystem as such and investigate how the larger constellation of connected platforms informs and shapes sociality, creativity, and knowledge.

CHAPTER 8

The Ecosystem of Connective Media: Lock In, Fence Off, Opt Out?

8.1. INTRODUCTION

Remember the Alvins, introduced in the first chapter? Sandra Alvin, a free-lance publicist who depends for her income on platforms like Facebook and Twitter, made a disturbing discovery. When she checked her popularity index on Klout—part of her regular routine to gauge her online reputation—she found that a Klout page had been created for her 12-year-old son Nick, a minor who is not yet allowed on Facebook. Nick had no confessions to make, so Sandra concluded that his addiction to CityVille must have automatically assigned him a place in the ranked universe of social media. Adding to both parents' annoyance was 16-year-old Zara's announcement that a major cloth-ing and apparel firm had sent personalized promoted stories to all her Face-book friends' Walls, stating how much she "liked" a particular pair of jeans. As much as Sandra rejoiced in the professional benefits and personal pleasures of social media, she loathed the targeting of minors for marketing purposes.

All these events made Pete Alvin rethink the quality of his online experi-ence; an early adopter of social media, he had become increasingly averse to the commercialization of content and what he felt to be an invasion of pri-vacy. He decided to quit Facebook, a move already impelled by the announce-ment of the site's latest interface changes: a Timeline feature he did not want, and which he disliked even more when he received uncalled-for per-sonalized ads. It took him several weeks to find out how to really quit Face-book—pushing the "quit" button apparently was not enough to disconnect him from the site. What troubled him most, though, were the negative reactions from his friends, relatives, and club members who complained they now had to send him separate e-mails to garner his attention. Contrary to his wife, Pete felt locked in by omnipresent connective media, both technically and socially; paradoxically, he felt caught in the trap of a normative online sociality he had himself helped create over the years.

The micro-behaviors of a family like the Alvins reveal the complex tensions that underpin the normalization of connective media in everyday life—a process of gleeful appropriation as well as critical resistance. These tensions play out on the various abstract levels introduced in this book: not just at the techno-cultural and socioeconomic levels of separate microsystems, but also at the level of the ecosystem and the culture that sustains it. The process described in the previous chapters is one of transformation, whereby all actors are constantly exposed to new options and challenges that also redefine them as they unfold. Juxtaposing the histories of microsystems prompts reflection on the changing nature of the ecosystem and online sociality, including, among other things, the role of algorithms in the steering of desires, the power of users to control their data, the apparent tension between community-based connectedness and commercialized connectivity, and the meaning of "public" and "nonprofit" in an ecology that is dominated by corporate forces.

For Pete, the spirit of community formation and democratic empowerment, which motivated him to be an early adopter, has become co-opted by the logic of connectivity imbued in the commercial drives and coercive formats of many platforms. Pete's position with regard to social media not only differs from his wife's but also from his children's; while he personally experienced the transition from a participatory culture to a culture of connectivity, the younger Alvins accept the ecosystem as a condition upon which their social lives unfold. It just *is*. The normalization of social media means they take them for granted as an infrastructure. But what are the implications of a platformed sociality that is conditioned by a corporate sector, wherein partnerships and competition define the coded ground layer upon which a myriad of apps is built? And what are the cultural and ideological underpinnings of this ecosystem that make it seamlessly connected? It is time to reassemble the histories of microsystems and explore how the interlinked ecosystem sustains online sociality.

8.2. LOCK IN: THE ALGORITHMIC BASIS OF SOCIALITY

Technology

When Google introduced its networking service Google+ in June 2011, the company trusted its interface's accent on distinctive "circles" of friends to lure away a substantial number of Facebook members. In response to

Google+, Facebook promptly offered Katango, an iPhone app that automatically organizes your Facebook friends into groups: algorithms compute who is a family member, who went to college or high school with you, or who is on your basketball team. Katango is incompatible with Google+. Plug-ins and apps are continuously invented to interconnect platforms and align their operability, even if they are incompatible. For instance, an app called Yoono helps you sync input from all your social networks—Facebook, Twitter, Flickr, YouTube, and instant messaging services—so you won't have to keep up with them individually, warranting the highest possible presence on multiple platforms.[1] Maximum presence is important if you want to rank high on the Klout scores or if a company wants high visibility. Thousands of apps connect major platforms and fill the gaps between them, securing interoperability and making online life "manageable" for users.

Major players in the ecosystem like to present themselves as conduits for data traffic. However, as I have argued in chapter 4, the world of connective media is anything but a neutral infrastructure. The fast-moving world of apps and social plug-ins discloses an intriguing fusion of competition and collaboration: whereas some platforms try to "lock in" apps and users by making their features and services incompatible with their competitors', others opt for ubiquitous presence of all features on all platforms, while complementary apps try to bridge the gaps. In the course of the past decade, the strengths and weaknesses of the ecosystem as a whole have played out particularly in the interstices between platforms. Microsystems have developed in conjunction, reacting constantly to each other's strategic interface modifications. Because of the ubiquitous presence of Like and Share buttons, Facebook has overwhelmingly won in the department of social networking, forcing others to penetrate a different niche, or, as in the case of Google+, to compete head-on. Twitter's algorithmic functions of "following" and "trending" secured its top position as a microblogging platform, and its omnipresence in all kinds of media guarantees its dominance in this sector. Meanwhile, YouTube's inimical connection to Google's search and advertising algorithms procures a chain of interlocking platforms, while each of their functions (search, video sharing, browsing, etc.) is absorbed by other platforms. Any platform dominating a particular niche of social activity is eager to have its buttons ubiquitously implemented on other platforms—a mutually beneficial arrangement because it boosts traffic for all parties involved—while the platform's owners also want to lure and lock users into their chain of platforms.

Algorithms undergirding all kinds of online social acts are becoming increasingly compatible and thus interchangeable. Twitter's microsyntax of

and @ fits Facebook's grammar of likes and pokes, and matches YouTube's vocabulary of favoriting and ranking. Code could be considered the new Esperanto of online sociality—a universal currency that makes social, cultural, political, and economic discourses interchangeable. Or, as philosopher David Berry eloquently explains:

> Code becomes the unavoidable boundary around which no detour exists in order to participate fully in modern life. It is ubiquitous. Formatted by code, harmonised with the language of machines, our life history, tastes, preferences and personal details become profiles, mailing lists, data and ultimately markets. (Berry and Pawlik 2008: 58)

Channeling users from social networking to commercial activity is increasingly shaped as a fluent movement of buttons: from Google+ to YouTube to the Google Music Store to Google Wallet takes four clicks, leading you from a friend's recommendation to watching the clip to purchasing the download. A user is thus lured and "locked" into the algorithmic flow programmed by Google. But even if that user chooses to escape the convenience of the Google flow and clicks to iTunes instead, Google still has an interest in interlinking because in a connective system all platforms profit from boosted user traffic. Algorithms that promote interlinking are not just securing a "frictionless online experience," but also making that experience manipulable and salable.

In barely ten years, algorithms have come to punctuate everyday social acts. EdgeRank, PageRank, GraphRank, and their many equivalents computationally convert past behaviors into future performance. Contacting a friend you have not seen since high school may be a thoroughly human act, but if performed online, a People You May Know algorithm typically prompts this deed. A teenager who never considered following her favorite singer may be pushed by cross-linked microsystems connecting viral videos via YouTube, Twitter, and Facebook. Technological pressure from multiple platforms to select the most popular and most connected person or idea, is, in turn, reinforced by peer pressure in real life. Peer pressure has become a hybrid social and technological force; connections between people inform automated connections and vice versa. Some hail this development as "augmented humanity"—technologies enhancing human social action—while people critical of the "technological unconscious" regard this coded layer as a black-boxed influencer of sociality.[2] Obviously, these evaluations of the same phenomenon derive from different ideological views.

Although each algorithm is a slightly different inscription of sociality and each interface shows distinct variances—a Like is not a Retweet—the technologies structuring platforms all operate from similar social norms and cultural logics. The algorithm underpinning the Like button, for instance, measures people's desire for things or affinity to ideas. Not coincidentally, Facebook chose a "like" feature rather than a "difficult but interesting" button or an "important" button. "Likes" are not just thermometers of desire but also generators of potential consumer trends. When people see what others like, they want it more—another consequence of peer pressure—and knowing what people want is the basis of constructing needs, as most marketers learn their first week on the job. A similar logic underpins Twitter's following function: the more people follow someone, the trendier he or she becomes; the more people Retweet a quote, the more impact it has in the twitterverse. YouTube's video-ranking mechanism, too, derives from the same driving principle; videos that are "favorited" gain a better ranking position and thus more visibility. Most platforms are compatible because they are staked in the same values or principles: popularity, hierarchical ranking, neutrality, quick growth, large traffic volumes, and fast turnovers. Moreover, social activities are inextricably bound up with economic pursuits in a culture of automated "personal" recommendations.

Users and Usage

In the short history of social media, individual microsystems evolved along with their user dynamics. In the early part of this century's first decade, the Web 2.0 promise of connecting and activating users abundantly resonated through social platforms. Most early adopters welcomed these platforms' contribution to sharing online creativity, community-based social activities, and egalitarian interaction—ideals rooted in liberal democratic paradigms. Over time, users' motives for participation changed as platforms became bigger and were increasingly run by large corporations. But the division of users into monolithic groups either holding up a community ideal or favoring a commercial objective turns out to be deceptive. For one thing, platform owners surreptitiously preempted the rhetoric of collaboration and gradually endowed concepts like sharing and friending with a different meaning. More importantly, active users well aware of the profit-driven motives of platforms still decided to use them; in the case of Flickr, for instance, many users who were persistently critical of the site's modifications remained faithful members.

Users obviously gained a range of benefits from mainstream platforms as they developed into a global system. Facebook's potential for global networking and Twitter's ability to create a large following arguably expanded the effectiveness of grassroots communication. YouTube's and Flickr's capabilities of sharing one's creative products with a group of like-minded enthusiasts are unprecedented in scale and scope. And an online encyclopedia with large numbers of people contributing entries and edits would have been unmanageable and unimaginable without the connective infrastructure that evolved. Users helped build platforms and thus co-developed the conditions for online socialization. At the same time, these platforms brought along privacy transgressions and monetization tactics users did not like. As much as users feel empowered by social media, many also feel they have less control over their once informal sociality. What is more, these ambiguous reactions might even come from the same person, which is why they deserve closer inspection.

The early expectation that Web 2.0 technology was going to usher in a platformed sociality conditioned by user equality and equal access turned out to be utopian. As we have noticed in the previous chapters, all platforms treat some users as more equal than others owing to the hierarchical system inscribed in their interface designs. Facebook, Twitter, Flickr, YouTube, and Wikipedia all reward users who have proven to be successful or reliable contributors of content. Gradually, the stratified star system of old media was complemented by an equally stratified ecosystem of connective media, where some users got pushed to the top. YouTube's professionalized contributors or skilled and drilled Wikipedians wield more influence in their respective microsystems than amateurs and onetime contributors. Online sociality needs influencers as much as followers, personalities as much as admirers, creators as much as consumers, professionals as much as amateurs, editors as much as readers. That is why twitterers with large followings are singled out to distribute promoted tweets and why teenagers with many friends on Facebook receive special offers from companies to endorse their products. Popularity rankings filter out people who are less "valuable" than others. A far cry from the egalitarian principle once ascribed to social media, platforms discipline their users into particular roles and modes of behavior.

The potential empowerment through social media thus presented itself as a double-edged sword. For some, user participation in social media has become a thoroughly commercial or consumptive act (Terranova 2004; Fuchs 2011b). Others have pointed to the fact that users may enjoy their roles as follower, consumer, and viewer, even if they are aware of the commercial mechanisms involved. Moreover, manipulating data streams is not the sole privilege of managers; users, too, can play the system to "crowdsource" opinions and rally support. Platforms endow their users with instruments to influence data streams through clicking, tagging, liking, trending, or pushing some topics to go viral. Indeed, users massively peruse the dashboard of buttons to cajole public opinion and steer trends. Although both owners and users can manipulate social media's filtering apparatus, it is important to distinguish their difference in power.

One way to clarify nuances in user empowerment is through implicit and explicit users. While implicit users may be "locked in" by microsystems and their programmed flow, actual users may actively try to modify or resist the roles inscribed in coding technologies. As we have seen in the previous chapters, individual users and user groups staged vocal protests when they were confronted with changes in a site's interface or ToS. Angry and wary members of Facebook, YouTube, and Flickr responded by writing critical blogs, circulating petitions, and posting protest videos. Concerned Wikipedia users openly criticized the disciplinary procedures of "their" site. Indeed, these protests and criticisms are typically directed toward single platforms and are commonly triggered by a site owner's specific actions, such as Facebook slipping new clauses into its ToS or YouTube changing its interface. But a growing number of users are critical of connective media's underlying mechanisms and start to look for fitting responses; they may ultimately switch to platforms that allow more user control over data or to sites that are more transparent in terms of their business models or privacy policies, even though of switching costs can be high.[3]

Over the course of ten years, users have negotiated their relationship vis-à-vis platforms through appropriation and protest, a process that has left no actor unaffected. If we think of Facebook's Beacon debacle or Flickr's move to insert a Commons space, these were not simply examples of clashes or compromises between owners and users; platforms altered their strategies as a result of these maneuvers, and the very notion of online sociality and community changed accordingly. The process of negotiation also involved a redefinition of norms and values, such as connectedness and community. This subtle cat-and-mouse game certainly yields winners and losers; but, as argued in chapter 5, the meaning of success or failure is not etched in stone either. The current dominance of some platforms in the ecosystem is precarious: after all, just as users have massively left Myspace or Flickr, they may get tired of Facebook or YouTube. Gullible followers may become critical dissenters who raise their voices through individual blogs and watchdog NGOs, or they may choose other forms of engagement.

Content

If we look back upon the past decade of the evolving ecosystem, it is instructive to recall the early promise that Web 2.0 platforms would liberate content. The production of music, films, videos, art, and texts would no longer be limited to professionals, as the tools for creative production would be yielded to amateurs and citizens. Content would be released of cultural constraints—restrictive cultural forms and formats—and economic restrictions, as it was to be distributed free of charge. "Making content social" was supposed to mean that users generate and circulate digital content so as to enhance informational diversity. However, over the past decade, users and platform owners have appreciated the value of online content differently. Whereas the first regarded it as something to be created and shared, the latter increasingly defined it as something to be managed and exploited. Whereas users cared mostly about the *quality* and form of content, platform owners were preoccupied by data *quantities* and traffic volume. Let me explain each of these contrasting views more precisely.

Connective media have indisputably given rise to a number of new (and arguably liberating) cultural forms: the tweet, the video snippet, the blog entry, the webisode, and the mash-up, to name just a few. Online platforms spawned a lot of creativity, allowing users to invent new forms that suited their expressive and communicative needs. They also encouraged the creation of page designs and an impressive number of tools and apps. In recent years, though, we have noticed the tendency on the side of major platforms like Facebook and YouTube to revert to strict formats: preformatted entries and home page layouts that force users to submit uniform content. YouTube's interface design features categories that predigest content, and Facebook regiments a narrative structure on each user page—a presentation mode it also imposes on brands and advertisers. Users who felt their creativity was seriously hampered by these coercive formats turned to specialized or alternative sites (such as Indymedia, SoundCloud, or EngageMedia), only to resort to mainstream SNS or UGC sites for their essential connective function.[4]

As stated above, the majority of large, mainstream platforms gauge content in terms of quantity, often measured by its potential to draw massive numbers of users. Content serves as bait to lure users who are eager to discuss and share pieces of music, videos, pictures, ideas, and texts with others. Viewers are prompted to actively rate and rank content, but are also passively tracked for what content they like by means of cookies. Tweets, snippets, and small talk coalesce into an infinite stream of data where they converge with metadata into a big flow of traffic filling the freeways of connective media. Big Data flowing through the arteries are the ecosystem's lifeblood, determining its vitality. Some theorists have argued that social media's data streams tend to clog in "filter bubbles." Users are "locked in" by the content streams filtered through few large platforms, so they end up seeing the same information, buying the same products, and watching the same clips.[5] Content has no value in and of itself: it is the combination of content, metadata, and behavioral and profiling data that makes the resource of connectivity interesting for data analysts and marketers.

Data culled from social media sites—including "affective traffic" coming from "like" and "favorite" buttons—provide the rudimentary resource for data mining. As explained in chapter 4, two specific methods—predictive analytics and real-time analytics—are utilized to process these resources into valuable assets. Predictive analytics allows statisticians to extract information from all data to capture relationships between variables from past occurrences and the likeliness of users will exhibit such behavior in the future. Facebook and Google are particularly interested in predictive algorithms to improve the effectiveness of ads and in advancing the exploitation of their enormous quantities of data. Google Analytics, an integral part of the Google dynasty, has now teamed up with Twitter to explore the potential of real-time sentiments and trends. Catching real-time trends in geographical areas, such as colds or flus across the American northeastern states, allows advertisers to attune their placement strategies of promoted tweets for cough medicine or other pharmaceutical remedies.

The philosophy of data mining through these platforms relies not simply on the idea that online behavior reflects offline social conduct, but on peculiarly hybrid assumptions about online content, explained in chapter 4 as the paradox of "affective economics" (Andrejevic 2011). Analysts often treat content and user data as unmediated, spontaneous utterances from an actual public—results that they can aggregate and interpret; at the same time, the perennial stream of data can be interceded in by owners, advertisers, and, if they make a concerted effort, users, all of whom try to exert influence on online sociality. Users' definition of content as people's "spontaneous" creative and communicative online expressions is thus peculiarly aligned with the platform owner's vision of content as something that needs to be managed and manipulated. Such a philosophy conspicuously parallels the conflation of connectedness and connectivity in the shaping of online sociality: people making connections and constructing communities is a necessary pretext for manipulating and monetizing social data.

In sum, *content* and content *management* have become virtual synonyms in the ecosystem of connective media. Even when the aim of platforms is not to exploit content for monetary gain, as in the case of Wikipedia, content can only be made functional or valuable if it is managed through systems operating on the dual premise of "authentic" yet manipulated processing. Twitter is increasingly considered a polling platform by political trend watchers who continuously want to measure the real-time sentiments and preferences of electorates; at the same time, though, a variety of interested parties utilize Twitter an instrument for promotion and manipulation. Users need platforms to voice their opinions and creative expressions, while platforms need users to funnel their expressions in presorted formats. Content is spontaneous yet controlled, unmediated yet manipulated. The interoperability of microsystems is dependent not only on the compatibility of algorithms and formats, but also on a shared processing logic.

8.3. FENCE OFF: VERTICAL INTEGRATION AND INTEROPERABILITY

Ownership Structure

In June 2011, Facebook announced a deal with Skype, allowing their users to connect in real time with their friends. One month earlier, Microsoft, which owns a small stake in Facebook, purchased Skype for a reported $8.5 billion, but the software company hastened to state that Skype would keep supporting all platforms and devices—not only the ones operated or owned by Microsoft.[6] In April 2012, a month before its IPO on Nasdaq, Facebook took over Instagram to secure its expansion in mobile image sharing. Over the past few years, Facebook has closed partnerships with Zynga, Netflix, Spotify, Rhapsody, and Ticketmaster, thus creating a chain of vertically integrated services, both offline and online. Google further ventured into different divisions while simultaneously strengthening its integration of platforms. In 2010 and 2011, the search giant started the trade and marketing sites Google Wallet (a pay service) and Google Offers (day sales), complemented by Google Shopping and a Google Delivery service. With Google+, Play, YouTube, DoubleClick, AdWords, Picasa, Chrome, Cloud, Maps, Scholar, and a host of other services, the imperium has branched out into practically every type of platform, caching virtually every kind of social, informational, creative, and commercial niche.

The result of these various moves is a gradual development of a few major platform *chains*—microsystems vertically integrated by means of ownership, shareholder, and partnership constructions—that are now dominating the ecosystem of connective media: Google, Facebook, Apple, and Amazon.[7] The first chain of microsystems, apart from integrating the aforementioned Google platforms, also developed partnerships with Twitter (see chapter 4), Wikipedia (see chapter 7), and Android (operating system for mobile). The second chain ties Facebook to Microsoft, Instagram, Flickr (see chapter 5), and Motorola (mobile hardware). While the Google chain developed its kingdom from online search and Facebook from social networking, both are trying to control the ecosystem's entries, luring users into their web of platforms.[8] As we saw in chapter 6, Google wants to be your "gateway" to the online universe; Mark Zuckerberg, in one of his IPO pitches, presented Facebook as a "passport" to the Internet, where every app is going to be tied in with Facebook.[9] A legitimate question arises: do platform owners fence off competition by branching out into multiple services and engaging in vertical partnerships, forming "walled gardens" to channel online sociality?

This question begs for a techno-economic as well as a political-economic answer. To start with the former: Google, Facebook, and Apple operate from fundamentally different techno-economic principles. Google wants the "social" layer on the Web to remain open so its engines can crawl any type of content regardless of where and in which context it is generated. Facebook does not let Google's engines index its content, except for its public pages. Contrary to the twitterverse, which is fully accessible to Google's crawlers, Facebook fences off access to its pages, as it wants to be an identity provider to other services. By the same token, Apple's content created through its mobile devices (iPhone and iPad) is part of a cultivated garden, and hence impenetrable by Google's search functions; since iTunes is available through the Web, this part can be accessed by Google, but the real data value is generated by Apple's mobile devices. Not surprisingly, Google often presents itself as the natural extension of the neutral Web because the company has a vested interest in openness for its crawlers and for its advertisers, who want to reach customers. With a growing territory of social media land now being walled off by Facebook and Apple, Google gets access to fewer resources for mining purposes.[10]

The political-economic view on vertical integration becomes more interesting in light of these techno-economic conditions. If we look at each platform's ownership maneuvers over the years, we can see a pattern of vertical integration emerge. Of all major platforms discussed, no platform has stayed the same since its inception: Facebook and Google have each allied with (or branched out to incorporate) social network services, play and game services, marketing services, and the more general services (search, browsers), as well as software and hardware. Tracking these movements over the years, one might argue these platforms have blurred the boundaries between search, social networking, entertainment, and commerce. Some claim that the "social" Web has created a "nirvana of interoperability."[11]

A vital question to ask is *for whom* these nirvanas of interoperability are most profitable. As argued in chapter 3, "frictionless sharing" can be mutually beneficial to all platforms working on the same premises.

Partnerships like the one between Facebook and Zynga are lucrative for both parties: by hooking up to Facebook, Zynga taps into a large reservoir of potential gamers, while Facebook profits from its revenues. Partnerships between moguls Facebook and Apple are based on win-win agreements, not only because their services are largely complementary, but also because they work from the same premise of routing user traffic through their own backyards. Rivals Apple and Google are uneasy partners. Not coincidentally, Apple has displaced the YouTube button from a prominent position on its mobile hardware (iPhone, iPad), so it now has to be downloaded from the app store. And, as explained in the previous chapters, Google's partnership with Twitter is advantageous for parties whose resources and analytic instruments are complementary and whose philosophies with regard to open data crawling match. With Facebook and Google as rivaling farmers and Apple as the third constant gardener, the process of cultivating online sociality is basically in the hands of three—or, if you count in Amazon, four—big players who share some *operational* principles (popularity and neutrality principle, quick turnover, short-lived trends, etc.), while they differ on some *ideological* premises (open versus closed).

But the nirvana of interoperability is not equally welcoming to all platforms wanting to secure a place in the ecosystem. There is no doubt that the nonprofit and certainly the public sector are seriously underserved in the walled Garden of Eden. Indeed, the distinction between for-profit, nonprofit, and public domains has further eroded as the ecosystem got built; perhaps more accurately, building the connective ecosystem substantially contributed to the erosion process already under way in the offline world. Wikipedia and Flickr Commons represent the tiny part of nonprofit land that may be mined under a different license, but their domains are intimately interlocked in the vertical chains. Wikipedia benefits from maximum connectedness to Google, while Google gains from harvesting Wikipedia's metadata—connectivity being a worthless commodity for the nonprofit encyclopedia. Flickr Commons was a daring attempt to carve out a community-oriented nonprofit plot inside the Yahoo estate but led to confusion and inconsistent governance policies. Despite the overpowering incorporation of the social media layer by for-profit companies, we can still find platforms that are loyal to community models, albeit in the niches of the ecosystem. The footprints of early communitarian ideals are visible in many corners of platformed sociality where small platforms have procured their spaces; among the moguls, these footprints too often serve merely as strategic and effectual reminders of the original settler's utopian spirit.

The ecosystem of connective media does not have a separate space for nonprofit or public platforms, fenced off from commercial space. Sociality, creativity, and knowledge are all plaited into the fabric of the ecosystem, where all coding activities and the exploitation of connectivity take place in the same corporately dominated ecosystem. Not coincidentally, network corporations have been eager to "adopt" services that used to belong squarely in the public sphere—think of Google Books and Google Scholar, not to mention Google LibraryLink. Over the past three decades, an increasing number of public services—in America even more so than in Europe—has been outsourced to the corporate sector: power supply, museums, prison systems, education, waste management, and so on. The incorporation of sociality, creativity, and knowledge therefore, continues an offline trend rooted in neoliberalist ideals of free markets and deregulation. At stake in the conquest of this new online space is what constitutes the *meaning* of public, private, and corporate in a seamless nirvana of interoperability.

So to call a platform "social" or liken it to a "utility" is part of the battle to define the corporate in terms of the public and the nonprofit. A utility, in the context of Google or Facebook, no longer means "public" and "neutral," but "ubiquitous" and "inescapable." Not coincidentally, Google and Twitter like to present themselves as guardians of net neutrality and the open Internet. They are obviously not Internet providers, but they emphasize the values of openness and connectedness because these are vital to their indispensability. Facebook's calling for "transparency" and "connectedness" apparently applies to users only, as the company has itself been reluctant, at least up to its IPO, to release any concrete plans for data mining. Yet in spite of their professed community values and democratic rhetoric, corporations like Google and Facebook are adverse to regulators who favor a neutral or public network governed through harmonizing global-local policies for data traffic in order to secure the ecosystem's interoperability (Schewick 2011; Cowhey and Aronson 2009). Connective media's giants warn against "over-regulation of the technology sector," which they fear will hamper innovation and entrepreneurial investment, and call for "openness" to be regulated by the market itself (Schmidt and Cohen 2010: 80). Arguing against this neoliberal view are concerned citizens represented by NGOs, who want to hold their governments accountable for information infrastructures, and who want democratically elected authorities to defend their lawful privacy and maintain control over their information. This brings us to the question of governance: who regulates the territory of connective media?

The issue of expansive platforms constituting walled gardens—locking in users, fencing off competitors, and incorporating nonmarket space—is, ultimately, a question of control over users' data and content. In the previous five chapters, we have seen how individual platforms regulate user privacy, data ownership, and copyright issues in their terms of use—sets of rules that are prone to frequent modification and have no mandate beyond the particular platform, or, as in Google's case, across its multiple platforms. What happens *between* platforms is part of a political bonanza played out between globally operating companies and government regulators distributed over many countries and different continents. A few big companies having too much control over people's private data has become a serious concern for government agencies and user advocacy groups, all of whom try to defend *public* and *private* interests against *corporate* dominance. But what exactly needs to be regulated in the new realm of online sociality where interoperability is the common creed and the freedom to switch services is said to be only "one click away"?[12] What needs to be governed if users choose the convenience of platform services at the expense of their own control over private data? Most importantly, who controls collective, aggregated data processed by commercial firms?

Few government agencies at a national or regional level defend the public interest against corporate dominance or control. The European Commission and the American Federal Trade Commission (FTC) have investigated Google's dominance in the search engine and browser market from an antitrust perspective. Legal experts have warned repeatedly that a few platform chains are rapidly monopolizing access to, and control of, data.[13] Indeed, search engines are a crucial instrument for access to distributed data—an instrument that Google's competitors lack or, if they have one, that pales in comparison. As stated above, Facebook's and Apple's strategies are different in terms of fencing off chunks of the ecosystem, and yet, all three companies are closed shops when it comes to their algorithms. For regulators, it would be extremely helpful to know *how* algorithms enable and constrain interoperability. The key to regulation seems to lie in technological secrets that are beyond any regulator's power. In that respect, antitrust legislation may yield to "trust regulation" in the realm of social media: how can citizens *trust* companies who profess to do no evil and make the world more transparent if they do not themselves comply with self-professed norms of openness and transparency with regards to their algorithms and, by implication, their business models? Antitrust laws that worked for "old" media do not always apply in the same way to connective media; whereas formerly *companies* were inspected for monopolizing markets, the level of *interoperating platforms* deserves more scrutiny from legislators now that new techno-industrial definitions of vertical integration emerge every day.

A similar expansive focus may be required from legislative bodies and advocacy groups defending *private* interest against corporate control in the realm of social media. Between 2000 and 2008, platform owners dismissed privacy as an irrelevant concern, arguing that users access their service free of charge and have other services to choose from. As argued in chapter 3, Facebook's CEO explicitly declared privacy to be "an evolving norm" and kept emphasizing the value of "sharing" over "protecting." So far, European and American regulators have negotiated specific privacy policies with individual corporate owners—Facebook most prominently among them—testing their interpretation of data use against the law. Beyond an impressive number of privacy violations taken on especially by European courts and regulatory agencies, there are at least three more general problems with individual platform's privacy policies that need to be taken seriously: terms of service are often hard for users to understand; owners can unilaterally change them; and resetting default privacy settings, instead of being "one click away," often requires considerable technical ingenuity. All problems are currently being addressed, but still mostly at the level of microsystems instead of the ecosystem as a whole.

Besides all due emphasis on *individual* private data and privacy policies of *individual* platforms, there has been another gray area of privacy legislation that has largely escaped the attention of legislators: connective data vis-à-vis collective privacy.[14] As observed, platforms are increasingly keen on exploiting aggregated data, while their terms of service contain no or at best vague rules about who has access to aggregated and "anonymized" data or whether platforms might sell this information. Data generated by many users and aggregated by Twitter Trending Topics, Google Trends, Google Analytics, or Facebook Memology are becoming a valuable crop—grown by users, harvested by platform owners, then processed, repackaged, and resold mostly to advertising or marketing companies.[15] Real-time and real-life data, as explained above, are rapidly becoming information commodities. Whereas before the advent of Web 2.0, public agencies used to gather and interpret social data, for instance about unemployment, epidemics, or economic recovery trends, these days Facebook and Google, through their refined social profiling systems, are way ahead of the government and universities in collecting and interpreting those kinds of data. In the current situation, connective media companies have an unfair competitive edge over (public) researchers when it comes to the availability and accessibility of Big Data for the assessment and interpretation of social and other trends, which is key to the production of knowledge. It is imaginable that scientists in the future will be dependent on commercial processing firms for obtaining access to social data.

If regulators take their concern over privacy and data protection seriously, they also need to pay attention to *collective* privacy: connective data are used to engineer individual as well as collective profiles of users, which in turn shape the production of sociality, creativity, and knowledge, even if subtly and unintentionally. Jonathan Poritz (2007) points to the large unmapped legal and moral territory where collective privacy is as of yet undertheorized and goes mostly unregulated. Since collective privacy is even harder to define—and therefore harder to protect—than individual privacy, Poritz calls for vigilance in tracking how social media platforms exploit instruments for aggregation and interpretation of data to which they have exclusive access. His concern stresses the urgent need for legislators to look at the ways in which media companies monopolize collective data and sell them back to users or public organizations, a development that is hard to miss.

Business Models

The balancing act between obtaining user data and selling them is even more discernable in the ways in which connective media companies have been monetizing their new services. From the very onset, the most central business principle for the emerging ecosystem has been the notion of "free."[16] The word has meant quite different things: content generated gratis by users, content distributed free of charge by platforms, and content untainted by mainstream media, commerce, or government interests. Early adopters of social media were particularly charmed by the concept of mutual gifting—services in exchange for user-generated content—and this concept made them averse to paying fees in whatever form. When collectives were replaced by corporate and nonprofit platforms, the mutual gifting idea kept lingering, but "free" also came to mean something else: "paid for" not in actual money but in users' attention as well as their profiling and behavioral data. Attention was the most conventional resource to be monetized in the form of selling screen space for advertising and product promotion; refined demographic clusters of user data offered great potential for mass customization.

The monetization of data connectivity gave a new twist to all conventional business models while also enabling novel ones. Advertisements previously catapulted indiscriminately toward mass audiences could now be delivered as personalized messages straight into a user's personal social space. The technique of automatically issuing customer recommendations through online friends gave rise to a novel category of "frustomers." And the ability of some tools, still under construction, to track and interfere in real-time trends and the use of predictive analytics for customer recommendations meant a big challenge to marketing departments. Customization seems to have become less the art of soliciting customers' needs than the science of engineering their desires. Indeed, the "free" content advocated by early Web 2.0 enthusiasts comes at a price, albeit a price that is not equally valued by all users. Many online users welcome personalized ads and customized services as the ultimate convenience, whereas others repudiate them as a blatant invasion of privacy and a "locking in" to services they do not appreciate. Depending on what ideological position you take on this issue, the original proposition of "free" is either a blessing or a curse.

And yet it is very hard to reverse this business principle on which the ecosystem was founded, now that most users have gotten used to "free" content. It has also irrevocably affected conventional media business models, such as membership fees or paid facilities. In recent years, a number of platforms began testing the option of charging fees for content (the *Wall Street Journal*) or charging premium services in addition to free use; this "freemium" model—described in chapter 5—often coupled payment for extra services onto promises of ad-free deliverance. Many platform owners are interested less in paid memberships than in "free" customers; in exchange for free services, they require the use of their data—a deal that is arguably more profitable than the collection of fees. In that sense, a user is simultaneously a resource provider, a product, and a customer. Buying into the "free" deal, users barter away privacy for convenience and facilities. Users who are fully aware of the price they pay may also adjust their norms to the conditions of free content. A recent study on the monetization of privacy tested how much people were willing to pay for services they could also obtain in exchange for private information; the results showed that approximately one-third of the experimental subjects were ready to pay more if the service provider promised not to use their data for marketing purposes.[17]

However, even if a substantial number of users prefer this option, it is doubtful whether they will be given the choice. For one thing, many platforms refuse to offer such option; while some offer freemium models in exchange for ad-free services, this does not mean they do not track or exploit user data for other purposes. Digital tech and advertising companies—most prominently Google and Facebook—are adamant in defending their business models against legislative moves, both in the United States and Europe, to introduce "do not track" options in the law. Other companies, notably Apple, Microsoft, and Twitter, take a different stance and have begun to offer their customers the possibility of not being tracked, turning the option into a competitive edge.[18] But the biggest problem that haunts those customers wary of bartering their privacy for online services is probably the opacity of business models that are typically partly hidden in the (proprietary) algorithms companies deploy. More often than not, we do not know *how* connectivity is exploited. Business models are the stakes in a dispute between owners and users over the monetization of content and online services: who provides what to whom at what price? Most big platform owners refuse to give users full disclosure about their techno-economic mode of operation. With products turning into services wrapped in algorithms that are constantly tweaked, it is virtually impossible to know what you buy for what price.

Those who tout the nirvana of interoperability have a vested interest in erasing boundaries and rendering its operational logic invisible: distinctions between automated algorithms (bots) and human users; distinctions between consumers and friends; distinctions between user content and promoted narratives; and boundaries between for-profit, nonprofit, and public organizations. User empowerment is dependent on knowledge of how mechanisms operate and from what premise, as well as on the skills to change them. So users find themselves in a double bind. On the one hand, they are considered agents in the production process who can quit any time, hence depriving a platform not only of a customer but also of a (data) provider. On the other hand, they are consumers who have too little knowledge of platforms' operational and economic logic to understand how they are "locked in" by the walled gardens of online social space. As some activists argue, the ecosystem of connective media calls for a new user rights movement that centers on user—not consumer—empowerment.[19]

One could argue that the ecosystem could be optimized if users were offered ways to "opt out" of the system or if they could at least switch platforms without paying the switching costs in terms of losing one's entire online personal networked data; or, at the very least, if those concerned about their personal privacy and control over their data were offered a simple way to adjust the default settings so as to prohibit platforms from tracking their data. However, when it comes to the possibility of opting out, we are confronted not only with techno-economic hurdles, but also with social norms and the ideological imperatives and cultural logics that scaffold them.

8.4. OPT OUT? CONNECTIVITY AS IDEOLOGY

Back to Pete Alvin, who tried to quit Facebook because he was irritated by the site's new interface. His failure to find a quick exit certainly was not owing to his lack of technological skills: an experienced user of online platforms, he is literate enough to push the right buttons. In this respect— finding it difficult to exit despite technological literacy—Pete is far from alone. Researchers at Carnegie Mellon University tested the skills of users in controlling their settings on social media platforms and found that *all* experimental subjects had problems customizing their privacy settings, even if they used special tools made available for this purpose. As the report, aptly titled *Why Johnny Can't Opt Out*, concludes: "None of the nine tools we tested empowered study participants to effectively control tracking and behavioral advertising according to their personal preferences" (Leon et al. 2011: 18). The problems with opting out are not restricted to Facebook but are endemic to the space of connective media, to such an extent that the current approach to self-regulation of opt-out mechanisms, according to the researchers, is fundamentally flawed. Apparently, it is easier to encode sociality into algorithms than to decode algorithms back into social actions.

The political counterpart of the question why Johnny can't opt out is why Pete Alvin can't opt in: why are platforms not legally required to offer opt-in instead of opt-out defaults when it comes to privacy settings and information shared with third parties? The simple answer is that such an option would impede commercial exploits. Legislators have negotiated hard to reach deals on this issue with platform owners. Facebook came under fire again, in the fall of 2011, for implementing a facial recognition tool that allowed users to tag faces and identify photos from their friends as an opt-out feature for its European users. In November 2011, the FTC reached an agreement with Facebook to make all its *new* privacy control settings opt-in. This sounds like a victory for the regulators, but it is really just another chapter in the stretched-out negotiation over information control. Corporations do everything to make their default accepted as the norm, as norms define habits and users do not usually question what is "normal."

As Pete Alvin experienced, opting out is hampered not only by built-in technical or commercial hurdles, but particularly by social impediments. The pressure of peers, friends, and colleagues to stay in the realm of online connectivity turned out to be immense. Apart from the automated "miss you" messages that Pete received from unwitting Facebook contacts, he was surprised by how many of his actual friends bugged him about his decision to leave the comfort zone of platformed sociality. Discussing the pros and cons of online platforms, Pete's arguments were met with various degrees of ignorance, resistance, and indifference. After having explained his reasons for quitting Facebook and discussing the larger implications of online connectivity for privacy and public interests with several people, Pete realized it was tough to dispute a norm that had become so pervasive among users they could hardly see his problem. Why not share everything? Why care about (targeted) advertising in their social space if using this space was free? Why not simply appreciate personalized advertising, even if uncalled for, as an extra service? Why worry about protecting private data if you have nothing to hide and if many people around you voluntarily disclose a lot more intimate personal details than you do? Many values that Pete had once taken for granted—privacy, a public space untainted by commercial interests, the right to know who controlled a certain social space—were no longer self-evident among his peers. He seemed the exception, opposing the norm.

Even within his own family, Pete felt the pressure of normative values, particularly the values of belonging and being popular. His wife Sandra, for one thing, was constantly worried about upping her Klout score: to interrupt her social networking activities on various platforms, even for a few days, would result in a substantial decrease of her rating, and this might hurt her business success, she feared. Both teenagers Nick and Zara were unable to resist the pressure of their peers and claimed they had to keep playing CityVille and frequenting Facebook if they wanted to be invited to parties or belong to the "cool" at school. For many of the plugged-in, opting out is not an option: it would mean opting out of sociality altogether, since online activities are completely intertwined with offline social life. Pete's worries, far from being a nostalgic longing—he refused to think of "real" offline sociality as an idealized state of the past—were morally if not politically motivated. The space he previously considered to be "his own" was now to a large part controlled by technological and commercial forces, causing a disconcerting feeling of disempowerment, in contrast to the empowerment he had felt when first joining a platform back in 2002. What happened to sociality? How come these norms and standards had altered so drastically and yet so unobtrusively?

It is one thing to disassemble individual platforms as sociotechnical constructions, following human and nonhuman actors in their pursuit of shaping social activities with these tools. It is quite another thing, though, to "reassemble the social," as Bruno Latour (2005) advises: to link microsystems onto the ecosystem in order to understand the normative structure underpinning platformed sociality. The power of norms, in the area of sociality, is much more influential than the power of law and order; Foucault's work on disciplining citizens and normalization, invoked in the first chapter, is still quite relevant when trying to account for this phenomenon. In less than a decade, the norms for online sociality have dramatically changed from emphasizing connectedness to aligning connectedness with connectivity and using these terms interchangeably. There is a remarkable predilection among social media enthusiasts for borrowing concepts from the public domain to tout the qualities of online platforms: common good, community, utility, sharing, "you," user participation, consensus, and, last but not least, the term "social media" itself. "Social" has become an umbrella term that hides more than it reveals, which is why I prefer the term "connective media."

Opting out of connective media is hardly an option. The norm is stronger than the law; if not, it would be too hard for any regime to control its citizens. That is why Facebook, Google, and other major competitors constantly wield the rhetoric of openness and transparency. Characterizing privacy as an evolving norm, Facebook's Mark Zuckerberg really pushed sharing as the gold standard. In one of his television appearances, he responded to a critical question asked by PBS interviewer Charlie Rose about Facebook's embattled privacy settings: "Google, Yahoo, Microsoft—they are all collecting information about you behind your back. We do it very openly, very transparently. They have way more info about you than Facebook has. On Facebook, at least you have control."[20] Google, for its part, accuses major competitors like Facebook of building closed systems that no one can penetrate. To some extent, these ideological battles are fought out in the open. But most of the normative stakes are hidden: buried in the defaults and algorithms of each platform's interface design; in the filtering of users and content; in ownership strategies and governance policies; and last but not least, in business models. Although each platform is different, all platforms operate from ideological tenets that appear remarkably compatible and complementary and yet difficult to recognize as a cogent system of principles: the principles of popularity and neutrality, connectedness and connectivity, quick turnovers and constant data flows, winner-takes-all and interoperability, a user-ranking ecosystem and a star-ranking Hollywood. The ecosystem of connective media does not *reflect* social norms; interconnected platforms *engineer* sociality, using real-life processes of normative behavior (peer pressure) as a model for and an object of manipulation (popularity ranking).

"Opting out" requires awareness and vigilance on at least two levels. First, it requires permanent alertness toward platforms and companies and how they operate. How do platforms code certain forms of sociality, to what ends, and for whose benefit? There are several nonprofit organizations, aside from regulatory public agencies, whose aim is to guard the public and individual's interest vis-à-vis corporate stakes, such as Bits of Freedom (Amsterdam), European Digital Rights (Brussels), and the Electronic Frontier Foundation (San Francisco). Several consumer protection organizations, such as the American Center for Digital Democracy, defend consumers and promote media education to empower consumers. Most advocacy groups and regulatory bodies that have been around for a decade or more have stepped up their vigilance in recent years as the landscape of platform providers has gotten increasingly crowded and more complicated. As we have seen in the previous chapters, questions of privacy and information control are premised on historically changing and ideologically informed definitions of the public, the private, and the corporate. Regulatory control and watchdogs are of vital importance when it comes to guarding the legal infringements of private space or the commercial invasions of public space.

The second level of awareness and vigilance pertains to social and cultural norms. From my reconstruction of the histories of individual microsystems, I have tried to distill a process of *normalization*—of how certain meanings of "sharing," "friending," "liking," "trending," and "following" managed to gain a dominant meaning. The culture of connectivity has manifested itself in the intense negotiations among platform operators and users over the meaning of online sociality and creativity. Disassembling five big platforms, taking apart their techno-cultural and socioeconomic actors, I have tried to reveal how code, interfaces, users, content, governance, and business models formed the tools to shape the new ecosystem of connective media. Reassembling sociality takes more than putting together a sum of its parts: harder than recognizing power strategies and instruments is pinpointing the norms that undergird culture. Normalization commonly takes the shape of the obvious, of what is implicit in structures, defaults, or rhetoric. It takes an effort to disclose what is considered evident: of course you "like" Facebook, of course you participate in online sociality unless you are old, odd, or underage. Connective media have almost become synonymous with sociality: you can check out any time you "like," but you can never leave.

Particularly now that a generation is coming of age for whom social media simply seem to be a given—an infrastructure they do not question—it is important to make explicit the ideological structures that undergird microsystems and their ecology. Many of the mechanisms and economics explained in the previous chapters are as of yet underexamined and call for more and more thorough critical inspection. There is an urgent need for sustained media education, not just in terms of teaching youngsters how to code, but also how to think critically. A critical history of the first decade of connective media is just a primer. While the ecosystem is evolving with few global players as its prime movers and shakers, we will soon be facing the emergence of more advanced intelligent systems in which networks define the production and distribution of (social and scientific) knowledge. In order to ensure future generations have a core of critical and knowledge-able citizens in their midst, we need to teach information literacy enriched with analytical skills and critical judgment.

Having said that, it is crucial to emphasize the rich cultural diversity of platforms that still populates the Web, as well as to point to the enormous reservoir of mostly young enthusiastic users who work on a balanced eco-system and a diversified online sociality. Besides a few big players that dominate the ecosystem—and which have formed the focus of this book—there are many smaller, specialized, both profit- and nonprofit-based plat-forms that seem to be pushed away from public view. These platforms are very important, as they cultivate specific niches; in fact, they warrant another book. A new generation of activists, entrepreneurs, and "creatives" is taking the social Web to the next level: some of them regard the layer of connective platforms simply as an infrastructure to build on; some are quite critical of how Facebook, Google, and Twitter steer their online rela-tionships, and they take on the challenge of working with or around them. In both ideological views, cultural diversity is vital to a thriving ecosystem.

Meanwhile, in the Alvin home, Pete's and Sandra's distinctive view-points have led to fierce discussions—debates about the impact of social media on society and on their everyday lives. Their deliberations have led to a compromise about how to feed their teenagers a healthy diet of engaged enjoyment and pragmatic criticism in their daily use of connective media. Pete teaches them about walled gardens and cultivating private space, while Sandra is more inclined to show her enthusiasm for growing net-works and harvesting connections. It is a workable compromise, prompt-ing Pete to choose a simple, age-old motto to counterbalance the corporate credos of doing no evil and making the world transparent: *Il faut cultiver notre jardin*. The ecosystem of connective media needs watchful caretakers and diverse gardeners in order for it to be sustained. A critical history is just a first step toward such sustainable future.

NOTES

CHAPTER 1

1. It is very difficult to find unambiguous facts about overall social media use. The numbers mentioned are cited from the CommScore report 2011. Available at http://www.comscore.com/Press_Events/Presentations_Whitepapers/2011/it_is_a_social_world_top_10_need-to-knows_about_social_networking. Last checked May 24, 2012. These numbers serve as a general trend indicator.

2. The verb "twittering" is used in a number of European languages, such as Dutch and German, whereas the verb "tweeting" is preferred in English.

3. Google Search and the company's specialized services (Maps, Scholar, Earth, Streetview, etc.) have conquered by far the largest share of the search engine market (82 percent); Yahoo (6 percent), the Chinese engine Baidu (5 percent), and Microsoft's Bing (4 percent) are Google's main competitors. Source: Wikipedia overview of search engine markets. Available at http://en.wikipedia.org/wiki/Search_engines#Market_share. Last checked May 27, 2012. The market for web browsers, intended to access the WWW, is divided much more equally: in June 2012, Internet Explorer (MS) has 26 percent of the market, Google Chrome 25 percent, Firefox 22 percent, and Safari 14 percent. Web directories specialize in linking to websites and categorizing those links; two examples are Yahoo! Directory and the Open Directory Project, in partnership with AOL search. Available at http://www.dmoz.org/. Last checked May 31, 2012.

4. Search engines and web browsers have arguably become an invisible layer of applied services, as they are often overlooked in terms of their technological and ideological steering of users. For instance, Eric Schmidt, one of Google's cofounders, in a lecture delivered to a symposium at the Royal Dam Palace in Amsterdam on May 24, 2012, talked about all Google platforms as "utilities," a term he used interchangeably with the Web itself. As I will argue later on (chapters 6 and 7), search engines and web browsers are central applications on which many social media platforms depend for their distribution.

5. The term "Web 2.0" was coined in 1999 and made popular by Tim O'Reilly in 2004. The term suggests a technical overhaul or changed specification of the WWW, but according to Tim Berners-Lee, there was no such reorientation, as its founder always intended the Web to become a two-way medium ("the Read/Write Web"); what gradually changed after 2003 is the way software engineers and users developed applications for the Web.

6. See *Time* magazine, December 16, 2006. Available at http://www.time.com/time/covers/0,16641,20061225,00.html. Last checked May 27, 2012.

7. See *Time* magazine, December 27, 2010. Available at http://www.time.com/time/covers/0,16641,20101227,00.html. Last checked May 27, 2012.

8. Mark Zuckerberg has stated Facebook's mission in numerous interviews, both in newspapers and on television. See for instance an interview with Zuckerberg and Sheryl Sandberg (Facebook's COO) with Charlie Rose on KQED, broadcast November 11, 2011. Zuckerberg explained the company as "completely open, transparent; everyone is connected to each other. You grow more when you're connected."

9. Please note the distinction between "engineering sociality" and "social engineering." The latter term is rooted in political science, where it refers to efforts of governments or private groups to massively influence social behaviors and popular attitudes. The engineering of sociality (my term) refers to social media platforms trying to exert influence on or directing user behavior.

10. The popularity principle was first established with regard to search engines: queries tend to reward sources already cited over sources that are less well connected; this "rich get richer" or "winner takes all" effect—much-cited sources gain prominence at the expense of less connected sources—is a well-researched yet disputed phenomenon in search engine research. See also van Dijck (2010).

11. I find the term "connective media" more suitable than the generic label "social media." In the remainder of the book, I will still deploy the term "social media" to alternate with "connective media." The term "social media" has become so ingrained in everyday language that it is hard to avoid.

12. Marc Zuckerberg, in David Kirkpatrick's book *The Facebook Effect* (2010: 199), is quoted as saying: "You have one identity. The days of you having a different image for your work friends or co-workers and for the other people you know are probably coming to an end pretty quickly. . . . Having two identities for yourself is an example of a lack of integrity."

13. For a detailed analysis of Web 2.0 business manifestos transferring the meaning of nonmarket peer production into for-profit enterprises, see van Dijck and Nieborg (2009).

14. The top 100 Web 2.0 platforms, ranked on the basis of number of average page views over the past three months and the number of average visitors, shows only two sites that are nonprofit: Wikipedia (no. 6) and Pirate Bay (no. 75). Source: Alexa Rankings. Available at http://www.alexa.com/topsites/global;0. Last checked May 27, 2012. For an analysis of profit versus nonprofit web 2.0 platforms, see Fuchs (2009b).

15. Evgeny Morozov sharply attacked Jeff Jarvis's assumptions on social media platforms as the saviors of humankind in a review in the *New Republic*. See E. Morozov, "The Internet Intellectual," *New Republic*, October 12, 2011. Available at http://www.tnr.com. Last checked May 27, 2012.

16. Information experts such as Poritz (2007) are rightly concerned about the accumulation not only of personal data but also of aggregated information—all valuable intelligence prone to being manipulated and sold. Jakobsson and Stiernstedt (2010), more profoundly, are concerned about sociability as such.

17. Hetcher (2004) provides a very thorough and early theoretical work on the importance of norms in the world of Internet and online sociality. Drawing on social science as well as moral and political philosophy, Hetcher explores how norms, understood as patterns of rationally governed behavior maintained in groups by acts of conformity, fill the gap between the law on the one hand and

informal social practices on the other. He applies these insights to tort law and Internet privacy laws.

18. See, for instance, Levy (2011), Auletta (2009), and Jarvis (2009) on Google; Comm and Burge (2009) on Twitter; and Jarvis (2011) and Kirkpatrick (2010) on Facebook.

19. YouTube was the subject of several multidisciplinary efforts (Burgess and Green 2009; Lovink and Niederer 2008), and so was Wikipedia (Lovink and Tkacz 2011). American media theorist Siva Vaidhyanathan (2011) published an incisive analysis of how Google, by operating a multitude of platforms, has become a dominant player in the connective media ecosystem.

20. These particular five platforms where selected for various reasons besides the fact that all are dominant platforms ranked (or previously ranked) in the top ten. First, two platforms are predominantly SNS (Facebook and Twitter), while the other three are in essence UGC sites. Second, they do not all represent successful, triumphant enterprises: Flickr is an example of a struggling, failing platform (I could have chosen Myspace instead). Third, I wanted to include at least one platform with a nonprofit ownership structure (Wikipedia) to highlight its difference from for-profit sites.

21. Futurists and information specialists consider Web 3.0 to be the Semantic Web, which will involve, among other developments, the rise of statistical, machine-constructed semantic tags and complex algorithms to enhance the personaliza-tion of information, driven by conversational interfaces. Some also imagine the simultaneous integrated development of TV-quality open video, 3D simulations, and augmented reality, in addition to pervasive broadband, wireless, and sensor-directed online activity. See, for instance, Hendler and Berners-Lee (2010) and Siegel (2009) for Web 3.0 explanations and prophecies.

CHAPTER 2

1. The story of the iPod, iTunes, and the integrated development of software, hard-ware, content, and the music industry is insightfully described in Walter Isaacson's biography of Steve Jobs (2011), more specifically in chapters 30, 31, and 32.

2. Actor-network theory has drawn criticism particularly in terms of its usefulness for analyzing *digital* networks. For one thing, ANT is said to overemphasize the relation between human and nonhuman forms of agency, while the complexity of Web 2.0 platforms forces its analysts to move beyond this binary configura-tion (Rossiter and Lovink 2010). Although I agree that there might be too much weight put on the human versus nonhuman actor in ANT, this criticism ignores the fact that ANT is explicitly leveled at the fluid relationships between humans, technologies, and ideas. About the fluidity of the (human/nonhuman) actor, Latour (1998, n.p.) explains: "There is no model of (human) actor in ANT nor any basic list of competences that have to be set at the beginning because the human, the self and the social actor of traditional social theory is not on its agenda. So what is on its agenda? The attribution of human, unhuman, non-human, inhuman, characteristics; the distribution of properties among these entities; the connections established between them; the circulation entailed by these attributions, distributions and connections; the transformation of those attributions, distributions and connections, of the many elements that circulates [*sic*] and of the few ways through which they are sent." It is exactly this notion of fluidity between various actors that I am looking for when trying to define connectivity.

3. For a more detailed critique of Castells's *Communication Power*, and in particular his theoretical framework, see, for instance, Fuchs (2009b) and Preston (2010).

4. According to Tarlton Gillespie (2010) the term "platform" has a semantic richness that helps position it as a computational and architectural concept, while its meaning can also be understood figuratively, in a sociocultural and a political sense. Social media sites are platforms "not necessarily because they allow code to be written or run, but because they afford an opportunity to communicate, interact, or sell" (Gillespie 2010: 351). Platforms aren't things; they *allow things to happen*. In contrast to terms like conduit, network, carrier, or distributor, the word platform avoids the suggestion of neutrality, Gillespie contends.

5. Hardware is beyond the scope of this book, mostly because of space constraints. It's not that hardware is not important for a thorough analysis of platforms—indeed, if Apple's iTunes had been one of the major case studies, hardware would have been an indispensable element of analysis—but including hardware would further expand the already broad focus of this book. I agree that, as more social media companies begin to buy up hardware firms and vice versa, and traditional hardware producers initiate partnerships with social media companies, hardware will be an equally important element of analysis. One might object that, besides hardware, the elements of design and marketing are relevant, too. And while these elements are not altogether absent—design is included in its specific meaning of software design; marketing has been included when specifically pertaining to business models—they are not identified as separate factors in the process for the same reasons as hardware.

6. Besides Berry and Fuller, software studies specialists Wendy Chun (2011) and Adrian Mackenzie (2006) have theorized software as a historically media-specific distribution of agency. Both highlight the historical, material specificity of code and point to the intricate relations among people, machines, and symbolic environments carried as code.

7. Literally, the word "code" refers to a platform's computational architecture; more figuratively, coding also relates to the inscription of social and cultural acts into machine language. As Galloway (2004) has eloquently described it, code "draws a line between what is material and what is active, in essence saying that writing (hardware) cannot do anything, but must be transformed into code (software) to be effective. . . . Code is the only language that is executable" (165). Like natural language, computer language codes meaning into action, but unlike natural language, computer code actually *executes* its commands.

8. In the vocabulary of actor-network theory, intermediaries transport forces without transforming them, whereas mediators translate meaning and transform the elements they are supposed to carry (Latour 2005: 108). Platforms are transformers of everyday life, even if they appear to be merely transporting user-generated content or communicative messages. A platform can be seen as a content-hosting, user-driven mediator, while it is also a regulative, political-economic mediator.

9. Metadata are often called "data about data" or "information about information." There are a number of different types of metadata, such as descriptive (data about the content of data), structural (information about the containers of data), and administrative (referring to technical information such as file type).

10. For instance, Google is known to pay $100 million per year for having its search engine the default on the Firefox browser—the third most popular browser in

the world, owned by Mozilla Corporation. Google argues that defaults do not deter competitors, but as I will argue in chapter 8, research shows that users are unlikely to manually change defaults.

11. A term often deployed for technological affordance or implicit use is *usage* (Hutchby 2001; Wellman 2003).

12. These comments can mostly be found in blogs—personal or group blogs—as bloggers tend to be vocal participants in social media platforms; but they can also be found on special user pages provided by a platform (e.g., Flickr's Discuss Page). YouTube's collection harbors a number of creative videos made by critical users responding to changes. Furthermore, user responses can be traced though journalistic sources.

13. As stated in the previous chapter, only two platforms can be considered nonprofit, nonmarket enterprises: Wikipedia and Pirate Bay. Craigslist.org is often mentioned as an example of a nonprofit, nonmarket platform, although its status is disputable; since Craigslist is not a UGC or SNS site, but a marketing and trade site, I do not take it into account. Needless to say, there are numerous smaller sites to which the status of nonprofit or nonmarket can be attributed.

14. The purchase of YouTube by Google for a reported $1.6 billion in 2006 (YouTube at that time was not even two years old and generated no income) raised many eyebrows; Facebook's takeover of Instagram (one year old, no profits, 13 employees) in 2012 for a reported $1 billion was considered a bargain.

15. Facebook's net worth, at the time of its IPO, was calculated at $4.69 per member. During the first quarter of 2012, Facebook's earnings were set at $1.21 per member.

16. In March 2012 Google introduced Google Play, a multimedia-content service for distributing music, movies, books, (Android) apps, and games. The service also offers a media player that operates from cloud distribution. Google Play is accessible from the Play Store and from all Android mobile apps as well as Google TV. See Google Play site. Available at https://play.google.com/store. Last checked June 6, 2012.

17. For instance, Facebook imposes a "real name policy" on its users through its EULA; in order to join, you must be 13 years of age or older, and proper identification is required. You must provide your real first name and last name; it is a violation of Facebook policy to maintain more than one account on the site. As a matter of fact, though, a substantial percentage of all Facebook users undermine this requirement. Nancy K. Baym (2010: 110), quoting Gross and Acquisti (2005) observes that 89 percent of all Facebook users appeared to be real; other sources put subversion of Facebook's real-name policy at 20 percent. The documentary *Catfish*, released at the Sundance Festival in 2010, painfully dismantles the fallacy of Facebook's real-name policy: the documentary fascinatingly exposes how the simple ingenuity of an ordinary Facebook user can undermine the site's regulatory policy. See also van Dijck (2012a).

18. Exploiting social capital in commercial environments is obviously a totally different game than managing social capital in nonprofit environments, such as Wikipedia. The term "business model," commonly applied to commercial organizations, will also be applied to nonprofit organizations, as its meaning is also appropriate for nonmarket forms of organization: who is in control of fund-raising vis-à-vis who operates and "owns" the platform?

19. Vincent Mosco (2009) defines commodification as "the process of transforming use values into exchange values, of transforming products whose value is

determined by their ability to meet individual and social needs into products whose value is set by what they can bring in the marketplace" (143–44).

20. More principally, researchers are part of the same culture of connectivity that involves software developers, platform owners, users, and regulators. Research results are never neutral but derive from a specific approach; for instance, researchers may a priori assume social networking sites to be "a new type of online public sphere" or a "context that encourages civic discourse and debate" (Robertson, Vatapru, and Medina 2009: 6). When information scientists develop algorithms for linking patterns to "help make the world a more connected place" or to "advance communities," an explicit belief in social media's efficacy belies their scholarly aims. In other words, academics, like other mediators, help shape the object they research. Where relevant, I will highlight how research is grounded in a particular (ideological) view on the subject matter.

CHAPTER 3

1. Dan Fletcher, "How Facebook Is Redefining Privacy," *Time*, May 20, 2010. Available at http://www.time.com/time/magazine/article/0,9171,1990798,00. html. Last checked June 7, 2012.

2. Marshall Kirkpatrick, "Why Facebook Changed Its Privacy Strategy," *ReadWriteWeb*, December 10, 2009. Available at http://www.readwriteweb.com/archives/ why_facebook_changed_privacy_policies.php. Last checked June 7, 2012.

3. Chris Tryhorn, "Evangelical Networker Who Wants Facebook to Open Up the World," *Guardian*, August 20, 2009. Available at http://www.guardian.co.uk/ business/2009/aug/20/facebook-ceo-sheryl-sandberg-interview Last checked June 7, 2012.

4. See Facebook's pre-IPO roadshow video. Available at http://www.youtube.com/ watch?v=wA81tRwvoPs. Last checked June 7, 2012.

5. These figures are provided by Facebook Internet Stats. Available at http://www. internetworldstats.com/facebook.htm. Facebook occupies second position in the Alexa rankings, behind Google Search. See http://www.alexa.com/siteinfo/ facebook.com. Last checked June 7, 2012.

6. Caroline McCarthy, "Facebook F8: One Graph to Rule Them all." *CNET*, April 21, 2010. Available at http://news.cnet.com/8301-13577_3-20003053-36.html. Last checked June 7, 2012.

7. When Facebook announced having surpassed the landmark of 800 million users worldwide in September 2011, it also emphasized that, in the United States alone, the site attracts over 140 million unique monthly users. See announcement on home page, available at http://www.facebook.com/notes/ statspotting/facebook-now-has-more-than-800-million-active-users/ 204500822949549. Last ckecked June 12, 2012.The announcement was picked up by many news outlets across the world. For statistics on monthly visitors, see Quantcast, at http://www.quantcast.com/facebook.com/traffic. Facebook regularly publishes users' facts and figures, so we can get an idea of who Facebook users are and in what quantities they flock to the site. For instance, over 60 percent of all global users are younger than 35, and 75 percent are below the age of 45. Americans comprise 66 percent of Facebook's global audience, and of all American users, 45 percent are male (see http:// www.checkfacebook.com/). Penetration of Facebook in Europe is less than in the United States: of all Internet users, almost 50 percent use Facebook in the United States, as compared to 25 percent in Europe. For a comparison between

European and American statistics, see http://www.internetworldstats.com/facebook.htm. Last checked June 7, 2012.

8. Mass self-communication platforms, such as Facebook, operate in the same economical, political, and legal space as personal media and mass media—a space dominated by powerful telecom and media industries. As Castells (2009) explains in *Communication Power*: "It is mass communication because it can potentially reach a global audience, as in the posting of a video on YouTube, a blog with RSS links to a number of web sources, or a message to a massive e-mail list. At the same time, it is self-communication because the production of the message is self-generated, the definition of the receiver(s) is self-directed, and the retrieval of specific messages or content from the WWW and electronic networks is self-selected" (55).

9. A USA Today–Gallup poll held in the fall of 2011 indicated that nearly 70 percent of all Facebook members surveyed—and 52 percent of Google users—say they are either "somewhat" or "very concerned" about their privacy while using the world's most popular social network and dominant search engine. Users who frequent the site more often cared less about privacy than those respondents who used the site less frequently. See http://www.usatoday.com/tech/news/2011-02-09-privacypoll09_ST_N.htm. Last checked June 7, 2012.

10. See, for instance, a news article "Facebook Users Protest over News Feed," *Guardian*, October 27, 2009. Available at http://www.guardian.co.uk/media/pda/2009/oct/27/new-facebook-newsfeed-protest. Last checked June 7, 2012.

11. For more information on the hackers' activities, see "Facebook Tracks Your Cookies Even after Logout," *HackerNews*, September 25, 2009. Available at http://thehackernews.com/2011/09/facebook-track-your-cookies-even-after.html. Last checked June 8, 2012. When confronted with the hackers' revelation, Facebook defended these practices, saying that the cookies are needed to protect their users' privacy and safety.

12. See home page of Userscripts.org, available at http://userscripts.org/scripts/show/76037. Last checked June 12, 2012.

13. UnFuck Facebook is run on Userscripts.org, available at http://userscripts.org/scripts/show/11992. Last checked October 2011; the text has since been changed.

14. Most users never change default settings, which is why they are so important. Moreover, most users know so little about defaults that they are unaware of the alternatives for privacy settings. A Columbia University study found that 94 percent of all college students were sharing personal information on Facebook that they never intended to make public. See http://academiccommons.columbia.edu/catalog/ac:135406. Last checked June 8, 2012.

15. See S. Kessler, "Facebook Reveals Its User-Tracking Secrets," *Mashable*, November 17, 2011. Available at http://mashable.com/2011/11/17/facebook-reveals-its-user-tracking-secrets/. Last checked June 12, 2012.

16. Net activist site Gizmodo published "Top Ten Reasons You Should Quit Facebook" on May 3, 2010. Available at http://gizmodo.com/5530178/top-ten-reasons-you-should-quit-facebook. Last checked June 8, 2012.

17. See the Quit Facebook Day initiative's website at http://www.quitfacebookday.com/. Last checked June 8, 2012.

18. Jodie O'Dell, "Once Facebook Launches Timeline, You'll Never Want to Leave," *VB Social*, October 6, 2011. Available at http://venturebeat.com/2011/10/06/facebook-timeline-lessin/. Last checked June 8, 2012.

19. As we can read on the Facebook Timeline site: "When you upgrade to timeline, you'll have seven days to review everything that appears on your timeline before anyone else can see it. If you decide to wait, your timeline will go live automatically after seven days. Your new timeline will replace your profile, but all your stories and photos will still be there." Available at http://www.facebook.com/blog/blog.php?post=10150408488962131. Last checked May 2, 2012.

20. See the blog NakedSecurity, which also released a survey among 4,000 Facebook users showing that 51 percent were worried by the Timeline feature, while 32 percent wondered why they were still on Facebook. Available at http://nakedsecurity.sophos.com/2012/01/27/poll-reveals-widespread-concern-over-facebook-timeline/. Last checked May 4, 2012.

21. On March 30, 2012, John Brownlee posted an interesting story on the daily news site Cult of Mac about the app Girls Around Me, which simply connects Facebook profiles to Google Maps and can be used in very simple ways to deceive naive girls into releasing an astonishing amount of information. See http://www.cultofmac.com/157641/this-creepy-app-isnt-just-stalking-women-without-their-knowledge-its-a-wake-up-call-about-facebook-privacy/. Last checked June 8, 2012.

22. A number of national SNSs have dwindled in the wake of Facebook's exponential growth. The Dutch network Hyves, for instance, was the largest SNS in the Netherlands until mid-2011, when Facebook took over its lead position. After this, Hyves lost substantial numbers of users each year, with a 38 percent loss in 2012 down to 3 million users, while Facebook's Dutch membership surged 45 percent to 7 million. See "Gebruik Hyves met 38 procent gedaald; Facebook met 45 procent gestegen," *De Volkskrant*, May 3, 2012. Available at http://www.volkskrant.nl/vk/nl/2694/Internet-Media/article/detail/3250173/2012/05/03/Gebruik-Hyves-met-38-procent-gedaald-Facebook-met-45-procent-gestegen.dhtml. Last checked May 6, 2012.

23. See Google+, available at https://www.google.com/intl/en-US/+/learnmore/index.html#circles. Last checked May 31, 2012. Six months after its introduction, Google+ had attracted some 40 million subscribers, while Facebook had just tipped 800 million registered users.

24. See M. Ramos, "Facebook Responds to Google Plus," *ByteLaunch*, June 7, 2011. Available at http://www.bytelaunch.com/bytelaunch-blog/social-media/facebook-responds-to-google-3/. Last checked June 8, 2012.

25. Several weeks before the IPO, it became known that Facebook secured a substantial reduction in the number of its shares that would be sold to retail investors because it sees itself as a service for, and driven by, users. According to IPO insiders, Facebook views itself as "the people's company." See http://dealbook.nytimes.com/2012/05/03/small-investors-may-get-to-own-a-bit-of-facebook/ Last checked June 6, 2012.

26. See Mark Zuckerberg's reaction in the *Huffington Post*, July 7, 2011. Available at http://www.huffingtonpost.com/2011/07/07/facebook-ceo-mark-zuckerb_n_892202.html. Last checked June 8, 2012.

27. For Facebook Principles, see http://www.facebook.com/principles.php. For Statement of Rights and Responsibilities, see http://www.facebook.com/note.php?note_id=183538190300; for Privacy Policy, see http://www.facebook.com/note.php?note_id=10150740019045301; for data use policy, see http://www.facebook.com/about/privacy/. For Platform Policies, see http://developers.facebook.com/policy/. All parts of Facebook's terms of use cited in this chapter were checked on October 26, 2011.

28. As legal expert Grimmelmann (2009) concludes, the bottom line of Facebook's terms of service is that "consumers don't, can't, and shouldn't rely on Facebook's privacy policy to protect their information as they use the site" (1184).

29. For information on the Los Angeles lawsuit, see "Lawsuit Says Teens Too Young to 'Like' Facebook Ads," Agence Presse France, August 27, 2010, available at http://www.france24.com/en/20100827-lawsuit-says-teens-young-like-facebook-ads. For more information on the Canadian lawsuit, see http://www.cbc.ca/news/technology/story/2010/09/23/facebook-like-invitations. For more on the German allegation, see Cloe Albanesius, "German Agencies Banned from Using Facebook, Like Button," in *PCMag.com*, August 27, 2011, available at http://www.pcmag.com/article2/0,2817,2391440,00.asp#fbid=iWNc6eckuX3. All sites last checked June 4, 2012.

30. As the Europe vs Facebook group contends on its website: "It is almost impossible for the user to really know what happens to his or her personal data when using Facebook. For example 'removed' content is not really deleted by Facebook and it is often unclear what Facebook exactly does with our data. Users have to deal with vague and contradictory privacy policies and cannot fully estimate the consequences of using Facebook." Available at http://europe-v-facebook.org/EN/Objectives/objectives.html. Last checked June 8, 2012.

31. The establishment of such a Privacy Foundation, however, merely fulfilled a requirement already mandated by the FTC as a measure to promote online privacy and secure users' data. See Sarah Perez, "Facebook Settlement Gets Judges OK," *ReadWrite Web*, October 26, 2009, available at http://www.readwriteweb.com/archives/facebook_settlement_gets_judges_ok.php. Last checked June 8, 2012.

32. Facebook's press release is available at http://www.facebook.com/press/releases.php?p=85587. Last checked June 8, 2012.

33. Facebook plans to launch SocialAds, its own online advertising tool that is supposed to compete with Google's AdSense.

34. This statistic was provided in May 2011 by the company's own Inside Facebook page, available at http://www.insidefacebook.com/2011/05/03/sponsored-stories-ctr-cost-per-fa/. Last checked June 7, 2012.

35. A branch of economics called "social economics" emphasizes the importance of social action and interaction as the microfunctions of business model performance, and considers their impact to be part of their monetizing capacity (Bates 2008; Zott and Amit 2009).

36. Facebook's ideology of sharing has also been strongly criticized from a political economy perspective by media scholar Fuchs, who observes: "Sharing on Facebook in economic terms means primarily that Facebook 'shares' information with advertising clients. And 'sharing' is only the euphemism for selling and commoditizing data" (2011a, 160).

37. See, for instance, Facebook's official (public) IPO registration statement offered by Morgan Stanley, J.P. Morgan, and Goldman & Sachs. Available at http://sec.gov/Archives/edgar/data/1326801/000119312512034517/d287954ds1.htm. Last checked June 7, 2012.

38. This statement by Sheryl Sandberg, Facebook's COO, is made in the pre-IPO video, available at http://www.youtube.com/watch?v=wA81tRwvoPs. Last checked June 7, 2012.

39. In 2005, the word "Facebooking" shortly came into vogue to describe the activity of browsing others' profiles or updating one's own. Unlike Google, Facebook

does not promote the use of its name as a verb; its Advertisement Policy includes the rule: "Do not use Facebook, or any other of our trademarks, as a verb. And don't pluralize them either. Trademarks may not be modified in that manner." See Facebook Ad Policies, available at http://www.facebook.com/brandpermissions/. Last checked May 3, 2012.

40. See The Privacy and Security Information Law Blog, December 15, 2011. Available at http://www.huntonprivacyblog.com/tag/video-privacy-protection-act/. Last checked January 3, 2012.

41. A Reppler survey among 300 hiring professionals in 2011 showed that 91 percent of employers actually screened prospective employees on social networks sites—76 percent by looking at Facebook and 48 percent by looking at LinkedIn profiles. For more details, see http://mashable.com/2011/10/23/how-recruiters-use-social-networks-to-screen-candidates-infographic/. Last checked June 7, 2012. Journalists interviewed prospective employees who were asked to release their Facebook password during a job interview. See "It's Akin to Requiring Someone's House Keys: Employers Ask Job Seekers for Facebook Passwords," *Sydney Morning Herald*, March 21, 2012. Available at http://www.smh.com.au/technology/technology-news/its-akin-to-requiring-someones-house-keys-employers-ask-job-seekers-for-facebook-passwords-20120321-1vioi.html. Last checked May 5, 2012.

42. According to Jenna Wortham in her article "The Facebook Resisters" the rebels say that "their no-Facebook status tends to be a hot topic of conversation—much as a decision not to own a television might have been in an earlier media era." *New York Times*, December 13, 2011, Technology section. Available at http://www.nytimes.com/2011/12/14/technology/shunning-facebook-and-living-to-tell-about-it.html. Last checked December 21, 2011.

43. A Pew study released in February 2012 showed that a rising number of users, especially women and younger users, are becoming more selective in listing friends and are pruning their friend lists; unfriending and untagging people has become more popular. See "Facebook Defriending Is on the Rise," in *ReadWriteWeb*, Feburary 24, 2012. Available at http://www.readwriteweb.com/archives/study_facebook_unfriending_is_on_the_rise.php. Last checked June 8, 2012.

44. A 2012 study on the value of personal information and people's willingness to pay for privacy, conducted by the European Network and Information Security Agency, shows that less than 30 percent of users are willing to pay extra for keeping information out of the hands of data collectors. See the report at http://www.enisa.europa.eu/activities/identity-and-trust/library/deliverables/monetising-privacy. Last checked June 8, 2012.

CHAPTER 4

1. See C. McCarthy, "Twitter Co-founder: We'll Have Made It When You Shut Up about Us," *CNet*, June 3, 2009. Available at http://news.cnet.com/8301-13577_3-10256113-36.html. Last checked May 16, 2012.

2. For the announcement of Twitter's member milestone, see Mashable: http://mashable.com/2012/02/22/twitters-500-million-user/. An update on the latest Twitter figures, both in the United States and worldwide, see http://www.quantcast.com/twitter.com#summary. Twitter is ranked number 8 in the global Alexa rankings. See http://www.alexa.com/siteinfo/twitter.com. Last checked May 8, 2012.

3. In an impressive piece of ethnographic journalism, Joe Hagan interviews Twitter's CEO and observes the "management control room." Managers explain the platform's transforming ambition, from a social network into an information network. See J. Hagan, "Tweet Science," *New York Magazine*, October 2, 2011. Available at http://nymag.com/news/media/twitter-2011-10/. Last checked May 16, 2012.

4. Twitter's capacity to deliver messages to various different hardware platforms has been essential to its success. In a Pew Internet study, Lenhart and Fox (2009) reported that Twitter users are most likely to access the service through wireless Internet on mobile devices.

5. Early research examines Twitter's usage as a tool for daily conversation between friends and for sharing information and news alerts at a community level (Java et al. 2007; Mischaud 2007).

6. Behavioral scientists Zhao and Rosson (2009: 243) concentrate on Twitter's role as an informal communication medium in the workplace; they find that the web service can be used to enhance a feeling of connectedness and to build common ground for collaboration. Information scientists Honeycutt and Herring (2009: 9), while acknowledging that Twitter may not have been especially designed for informal collaborative purposes, suggest that "design modifications could make microblogging platforms such as Twitter more suitable for collaboration."

7. Over the past decade, there have been over 100 microblogging sites active worldwide. Besides Twitter, sites such as whatyadoin.com, Tumblr, Beeing, PingGadget, Jaiku, and Plurk emerged and disappeared over the years. Competing services usually occupy specific niches of microblogging, incorporating various SNS elements; Plurk, for instance, combines microblogging with video and picture sharing. Pownce integrates microblogging and file sharing.

8. For an introduction to the new Twitter interface, see, for instance, J. O'Dell, "Here's a first Look at the New-New Twitter," *VB News*. Available at http://venturebeat.com/2011/12/08/new-new-twitter/. Last checked May 16, 2012. As Twitter's CEO, Jack Dorsey, commented in *VB News*: "A lot of this is around education. . . . We saw the same thing ten years ago when people first encountered URLs. [People needed] an interface that made entry into some of these new things easier, less scary. . . . Our users invented this syntax, and we're honoring that."

9. For the list of most notable Twitter uses, see Wikipedia. http://en.wikipedia.org/wiki/Twitter#cite_note-72. Last checked August 14, 2010. This link is no longer available.

10. Evan Williams, one of Twitter's cofounders and chief executives, said in an interview with the *New York Times:* "Many people use it for professional purposes—keeping connected with industry contacts and following news. . . . Because it's a one-to-many network and most of the content is public, it works for this better than a social network that's optimized for friend communication." See C. Miller, "Who Is Driving Twitter's Popularity? Not Teens," *New York Times*, August 25, 2009, technology section. Available at http://www.nytimes.com/2009/08/26/technology/internet/26twitter.html. Last checked May 16, 2012.

11. See A. Lipsman, "What Ashton vs CNN Foretold about the Changing Demographics of Twitter," *ComScore*, September 2, 2009. Available at htt://blog.comscore.com/2009/09/changing_demographics_of_twitter.html. Last checked May 16, 2012.

12. According to a statistical analysis of some 300,000 Twitter users in 2009, Harvard researchers Heil and Piskorski found that men comprise a minority of

users (45 percent), while they have 15 percent more "followers" than women and also have more reciprocated relationships. Both men and women are more likely to follow men than women; in fact, an average man is 40 percent more likely to be followed by a man than by a woman, while both tweet at the same rate. This gender division is unlike other social network sites, where most of the activity is "focused around women and where men follow content produced by women they do and do not know, and women follow content produced by women they know" (Heil and Piskorski 2009, n.p.).

13. According to Joe Hagan, in his article "Tweet Science" (see note 3), a recent Yahoo study found that in a random Twitter user's feed, roughly 50 percent of the tweets came from one of just 20,000 users. Twitter's management duly recognizes the impact of a small number of so-called "hyperconnected" twitter-ers (also known as "power users" or "influencers") as one of its greatest assets.

14. Information scientist Christian Christensen (2011) sharply interrogates Western governments' enthusiastic promotion of American social media brands as a technological boost to democratic struggle, raising fundamental questions regarding the "increasingly blurred lines among policy, development aid, technological determinism, and commodification" (250).

15. The considerable drift toward popular Twitter lists and their following is underscored by public rankings of "The Top 100 Twitterholics Based on Followers." Available at http://twitterholic.com/. Last checked May 16, 2012.

16. See J. Hagan, "Tweet Science," *New York Magazine*, October 2, 2011 (see note 3).

17. The start-up Klout, which started in 2011, offers a service for measuring individual's influence across all social networks (Facebook, Twitter, Google+, LinkedIn); a Klout score is a number between 1 and 100, with scores over 50 beginning to indicate a high degree of influence. For more information on Klout's measuring philosophy, see http://klout.com/corp/kscore. Last checked May 16, 2012.

18. A study performed by Pear Analytics in August 2009 (Kelly 2009) analyzing 2,000 tweets over a two-week period found that approximately 83 percent of all tweets involved short conversational, expressive, and promotional statements that form the heart of "pointless babble." This outcome was disputed by social networking researcher danah boyd, who responded to the survey in a blog post, stating that "pointless babble" is better characterized as "peripheral awareness" or "social grooming." See d. boyd, "Twitter: 'Pointless Babble' or Peripheral Awareness + Social Grooming?" *Apophenia*, 2009. Available at http://www.zephoria.org/thoughts/archives/2009/08/16/twitter_pointle.html. Last checked June 12, 2012. In earlier work, boyd and Ellison (2007) argued that the flow of tweets reflects a form of "networked sociability" aimed at maintaining intimate relationships with friends, following high-profile users, and connecting with other people—close and remote (cf. boyd and Ellison 2007).

19. While early observers emphasized the conversational nature of tweets, later researchers focused more on tweets' informational content, by looking at Twitter's function either as a headline-news distribution system (Kwak et al. 2010) or as a journalistic tool (Emmett 2008; Hermida 2010; Hirst 2011; Murthy 2011). A Pew State of the News Media report published in 2012 shows that only 9 percent of people get their news from social media. See http://pewresearch.org/pubs/2222/news-media-network-television-cable-audioo-radio-digital-platforms-local-mobile-devices-tablets-smartphones-native-american-community-newspapers. Last checked May 16, 2012.

20. As one study by information scientists phrased it: "Twitter has shown how a medium for social networking and microblogging can be used as both a tool for delivering essential information, i.e., news, as well as a medium for delivering non-essential information, i.e., personal messages" (Blake et al. 2010: 1260).

21. For stats and figures on Twitter use, see http://blog.twitter.com/2011/03/numbers.html. Last checked May 16, 2012.

22. Twitter's CEO Dick Costello quoted in J. Hagan, "Tweet Science," in *New York Magazine*, October 2, 2011 (see note 3).

23. Rumors of Twitter's impending takeover by Google or Facebook in early 2011 were quickly denied by the site's owners. See, for instance, Rupert Neate, "Twitter Denies $10bn Takeover Talks with Google and Facebook," *Telegraph*, February 14, 2011. Available at http://www.telegraph.co.uk/technology/twitter/8324438/Twitter-denies-10bn-takeover-talks-with-Google-and-Facebook.html# . Last checked February 22, 2011.

24. Alan Rusbridger, editor-in-chief of *The Guardian*, explains why Twitter has become an indispensable news source for journalists by listing 15 features. See A. Rusbridger, "Why Twitter Matters for News Organisations," *Guardian*, November 19, 2010, http://www.guardian.co.uk/media/2010/nov/19/alan-rusbridger-twitter. Last checked April 17, 2011.

25. In July 2012, Apple reportedly considered taking a stake in Twitter. Apple has tightly interwoven Twitter features into its software for phones, computers, and tablets. I will return to these partnerships between social media, software, and hardware firms in the last chapter

26. Since 2006, Twitter has relied primarily on investments from investors like Fred Wilson, a venture capitalist and principal of Union Square Ventures. In a 2010 round of funding, six investors, including T. Rowe Price (TROW), Insight Venture Partners in New York, and Spark Capital in Boston, reportedly pumped $100 million into the company.

27. Journalist Claire Miller (2009) reports about market analysts getting impatient with Twitter. See C. Miller, "The Obsession with Twitter's Business Model," *New York Times*, March 26, 2009, Business section. Available at http://bits.blogs.nytimes.com/2009/03/26/the-twitterverses-obsession-with-twitters-business-model/. Last checked May 16, 2012. See also D. L. Smith (2009), "Twitter's Business Model: Brilliant or Non-existent?" *Harvard Business Review*, October 26. Available at http://bx.businessweek.com/twitter-business-model/twitters-business-model-brilliant-or-non-existent/1376625150997754291-aecc46f-cc0cdeefdd60745fe01e68cb9/. Last checked May 16, 2012.

28. Besides Tweetdeck, a San Francisco-based start-up called CoTweet successfully developed services to manage large companies' Twitter accounts (e.g., Coca-Cola) by tracking interactions with customers and letting employees respond. See C. Miller, "Tensions Rise for Twitter and App Developers," *New York Times*, April 11, 2010, Technology section. Available at http://www.nytimes.com/2010/04/12/technology/12twitter.html. Last checked May 16, 2012.

29. Promoted Tweets and Promoted Trends work as follows: if you look at the right side of users' Twitter feeds, one "promoted trend" is added to the traditional top ten of most popular tweeted topics. By adding a paid-for eleventh trend to the list—for instance Disney-Pixar's most recent movie title—the sponsor hopes the item will rise up the list. In addition to Promoted Tweets and Trends, companies have already started to use Twitter to engage viewers in their broadcast ads; during the 2011 Superbowl, for instance, car maker Audi

promoted a Twitter hashtag in its commercial, inviting viewers to join a conversation about the meaning of the concept of "progress."

30. M. Evans, "Is Twitter's Business Model the 'Firehose'?" Blog post on Twitterati, April 26, 2011. Available at http://www.twitterrati.com/2011/04/26/is-twitters-business-model-the-firehose/. Last checked May 16, 2012.

31. Much to the company's credit, Twitter offers an archive of its terms of service on the bottom of its website, which makes it easy to track how their policies have changed over the years. See http://twitter.com/tos. Last checked November 3, 2011. All further references to Twitter's terms of service refer to this website.

32. In Western countries, legislators may demand that social network services hand over their data, in order to help central governments carry out their own "citizen intelligence" programs. In 2011, Twitter lost a case where it refused a subpoena to deliver the tweets of an Occupy protestor to the California courts. In an unexpected move, Twitter took on the court's decision by delivering an ingenious argument why it was not legally forced to deliver these data. Many users praised the company's defense strategy on behalf of its users. See, for instance, Zach Walton, "Twitter Defends User in Court over Occupy Tweets," *WebProNews* May 10, 2012. Available at http://www.webpronews.com/twitter-defends-user-in-court-over-occupy-tweets-2012-05. Last checked May 16, 2012.

33. See, for instance, C. Arthur, "Twitter Faces Censorship Backlash," *Guardian*, January 27, 2012. Available at http://www.guardian.co.uk/technology/2012/jan/27/twitter-faces-censorship-backlash. Last checked May 12, 2012.

34. Twitter director Ryan Sarver quoted by D. Taft, "Users lash out at new Twitter restrictions." *TechWeek Europe*, March 14, 2011. Available at http://www.techweekeurope.co.uk/news/developers-lash-out-against-new-twitter-restrictions-23678. Last checked May 15, 2012.

35. This comment comes from a Google groups user by the name of Klondike. Available at https://groups.google.com/forum/#!msg/twitter-development-talk/yCzVnHqHIWo/gYUpkfrGXvwJ. Last checked May 16, 2012.

36. In parliamentary elections in the Netherlands in September 2012, Twitter was claimed to be as accurate as most election polls because it "echoed" the real voice of the people. See "Politieke peiling kun je net zo goed via Twitter doen," *De Volkskrant*, September 9, 2012. Available at http://www.volkskrant.nl/vk/nl/10637/VK-Dossier-Verkiezingen-van-2012/article/detail/3314680/2012/09/11/Politieke-peiling-kun-je-net-zo-goed-via-Twitter-doen.dhtml Last checked September 12, 2012.

37. Charles Duhigg in his book *The Power of Habit* (2012) insightfully maps the market of predictive analytics. One of his persuasive examples is a mathematician employed by Target who designed an algorithm that predicts on the basis of 20-some variables whether a female customer is pregnant, and lets interviewers avoid asking this impertinent question. When the father of a 17-year-old girl complained about Target's uncalled-for ads for diapers and baby stuff targeted at his daughter, he apologized three weeks later, after he found out about his daughter's pregnancy—a state that she had carefully hidden from her parents.

38. See D. Carr, "Hashtag Activism and Its Limits," *New York Times*, March 25, 2012. Available at http://www.nytimes.com/2012/03/26/business/media/hashtag-activism-and-its-limits.html?pagewanted=all. Last checked May 16, 2012.

39. Such was the case in the Kony 2012 affair, when an activist's video produced by Invisible Children urging the indictment and incarceration of Ugandan war criminal Joseph Kony went viral through Twitter, YouTube, Facebook, Flickr,

and Vimeo and was picked up by virtually every offline news organization in the world.

40. Part of a growing market for Twitter-based predictive analytics, companies like Topsy Labs use the tweet streams of millions of people to help predict the future—from the spread of disease and financial fluctuations to elections and revolutions. Using the incessant flow of tweets, marketers get a real shot at engineering trends, popular topics, and the popularity of people. See M. Ingram, "Can Watching Twitter Trends Help Predict the Future?" Available at http://gigaom.com/2011/10/19/can-watching-twitter-trends-help-predict-the-future/. Last checked May 16, 2012

CHAPTER 5

1. See blogger Lucian Marin's post January 7, 2012. Available at http://lucianma-rin.com/archive/a-dash-in-space-time-continuum. Last checked May 15, 2012.

2. In May 2012, Flickr ranked 48th on the global Alexa list. Available at http://www.alexa.com/siteinfo/flickr.com. The site started to decline in terms of monthly users after 2009, and in 2011, it had declined by a reported 18 percent. For these stats and figures, see http://siteanalytics.compete.com/flickr.com/. Last checked May 15, 2012.

3. The Yahoo ID was already optional in 2005 and became mandatory in 2007, much to the chagrin of its "old school" users. See J. Twist, "Flickr Fans Have Yahoo Fear Eased," *BBC News*, September 2, 2005. Available at http://news.bbc.co.uk/2/hi/technology/4201438.stm. See also "Flickr to Require Yahoo! User Names," *BBCNews*, February 1, 2007. Available at http://news.bbc.co.uk/2/hi/technology/6316761.stm. Last checked May 18, 2012.

4. In 2009, Flickr added the ability to upload and view high-definition videos.

5. See Flickr home page, available at http://www.flickr.com/about/. Last checked May 17, 2012.

6. See V. G. Kopytoff, "Flickr Builds an Online Photo Album for Sharing," *New York Times*, September 28, 2011, Technology section. Available at http://bits.blogs.nytimes.com/2011/09/28/flickr-builds-an-online-photo-album-for-sharing/. Last checked May 15, 2012.

7. See Flick Galleries home page. Available at http://www.flickr.com/help/galleries/. Last checked May 17, 2012.

8. Flickr groups can either be public (open to all), semipublic (invite only), or completely private, and every group is a discussion board for talking with members (for introduction, see Flickr home page. Available at http://www.flickr.com/groups/. Last checked May 15, 2012). A group's initiator automatically becomes the host of a pool of photos posted by users who have joined the group, as well as the administrator of the accompanying discussion forum. Users can shift photos from a user's photostream to a "group pool." Flickr has a bias toward high-degree users who constantly link to other users and who respond to incoming links (Mislove et al. 2008). As Negoescu and Gatica-Perez (2008) found in their statistical group analysis, almost 60 percent of Flickr users share at least one photo in one group, but it is unclear how groups function as an organizing feature for the website. At least half of all Flickr-Pro users participate in at least one group.

9. In the late twentieth and early twenty-first century, digital cameras began to be used increasingly as communication devices—instruments for peer bonding and social interaction—and personal pictures were now distributed more outside private circles (van Dijck 2007a; Pauwels 2008).

10. Flickr always had a rather old demographic, with most of its users aged between 35 and 44, with fairly high educational levels and belonging to above-average income levels. For statistics on Flickr's demographics 2008–11, see the Ignite Social Media report. Available at http://www.ignitesocialmedia.com/social-media-stats/2011-social-network-analysis-report/. Last checked May 18, 2012.

11. Huang and Hsu (2006) reconstructed personal social networks by connecting people pictured in the photos, events tagged, time stamp, location, and owner-ship of the upload. A personal network indicates a social structure between actors through various social bonds, which can be any kind of relationship (kinship, social, professional, affective), a material exchange, a common behavior, etc. For instance, a person showing up in *x* number of pictures at close distance to two other persons, showing up in the same location, or sharing a pattern of browsing behavior with a number of other users, betrays much about his or her social kinships.

12. Since the emergence of photo-sharing sites like Flickr, electronic platforms by default encourage the exchange of personal pictures with total strangers. Prieur et al. (2008) tout this transformation as a change from a "Kodak culture"—referring to a small group of friends and family sharing oral stories *around* or *about* images—to a "Snaprs culture"—referring to photographs being used to tell stories *with* images to anonymous audiences.

13. As Mortensen (2011) explains, it was in fact mainstream media, not social media, that turned the young woman into a symbolic icon—an attempt to illustrate a complex political situation in the Middle East to Western viewers.

14. Flickr Central is a forum for the exchange of user responses. See http://www.flickr.com/search/groups/?w=34427469792%40N01&q. Last checked May 17, 2012.

15. For instance, as Australian-British blogger James Offer comments: "And I think that's really where the crux of Flickr's problems lie: the site is now so massive that no real thought has gone into how to inspire and showcase the best the site has to offer. Groups are so flooded with photos that keeping track of them is almost impossible. And unfortunately, if a stranger does comment on your photo, the chances of ending up with a page full of badly animated GIFs is quite good." Available at http://www.codehesive.com/index.php/archive/the-slow-decline-of-flickr/. Last checked May 31, 2012.

16. Blogger Thomas Hawk is one of Flickr's most fervent and critical users. This blog was posted on his site *Thomas Hawk's Digital Connection*, February 8, 2008. Available at http://thomashawk.com/2008/02/why-microsoft-owning-flickr-is-no-worse.html. Last checked May 17, 2012.

17. In a carefully researched journalistic report, Mat Honan cites an anonymous former member of the Flickr development team. See M. Honan, "How Yahoo! Killed Flickr and Lost the Internet," *Gizmodo*, May 15, 2012. Available at http://gizmodo.com/5910223/how-yahoo-killed-flickr-and-lost-the-internet. Last checked May 18, 2012.

18. People who spend energy on managing and cultivating their Flickr groups unconsciously release profiling information on what they like, whom they relate to, and for what purposes. Even if a Flickr user's profile remains private, links to groups and group affiliation are visible to the public because Flickr does not allow users to hide their group memberships (Zheleva and Getoor 2009).

19. Information derived from these data analyses may in turn be used to develop automated personal recommendation systems featured by the button "Explore" (Jin et al. 2010).

20. For instance, researchers Kennedy et al. (2007: 631) claim that their main goal is to analyze, extract, and interpret patterns from random, user-generated data in order to "enhance . . . our understanding of the world." Along similar lines, information scientists argue that new knowledge about geographical sites or cultural heritage is created out of thousands of pictures taken by Flickr users and repurposed to form our "common knowledge" of the world's popular places and cultural treasures (Snavely, Seitz, and Szeliski 2008).

21. In a popular webcast TED-talk, Microsoft engineer Blaise Aguera y Arcas commends Photosynth's potential to take data "from our social environment" and make something emergent that is "greater than the sum of its parts" Aguera y Arcas's demonstration of the Photosynth software for TED can be viewed on TED's website, available at www.ted.com/talks/blaise_aguera_y_arcas_demos_photosynth.html. Last checked May 19, 2012. The software package draws on visual data enriched by a variety of metadata (e.g., added tags and comments vis-à-vis automatic time stamps and geotags, source information) from large databases such as Flickr.

22. The conjecture of individual pictures resulting in collective experiences or common viewpoints raises several concerns. To be sure, Photosynth is not the outcome of a process of negotiating various views but is the result of a process of *manipulating* individual takes into an artificially unified perspective. Photosynth, just like Photoshop, may be used to *doctor* photographic representations of public events, which may in turn affect the way we experience or watch the world (Sacchi, Agnoli, and Loftus 2007). Moreover, the convergence of imagery from different individual sources is always mediated by an interface that strategically selects and combines images, linking them according to semantic, geometric, or perspectivist principles translated into algorithms. William Uricchio (2011) has explained how applications like Photosynth rely on algorithmically defined relations between the viewing subject and the world viewed, a visual regime he calls the "algorithmic turn."

23. Photobucket, a photo-sharing service, was started in 2003 and acquired by Fox in 2007. Snapfish, owned by Hewlett-Packard, was launched in 2000. Picasa, a tool for organizing, editing, and sharing photos, was started in 2002 and taken over by Google in 2004.

24. For instance, a comment by Sherry Turkle in *Wired* on the news of the Yahoo takeover: "So many of us don't have a gathering place that feels comfortable and communal," she said. "For those who found that on Flickr.com, its transformation into a 'service' on Yahoo is a loss; they are losing something important to them." See "Flickr Fans to Yahoo: Flick Off!" *Wired*, August 29, 2005. Available at http://www.wired.com/techbiz/media/news/2005/08/68654. Last checked May 16, 2012.

25. A blog post from longtime Flickr member Thomas Hawk is illustrative in this respect: "Now for those of you who say, ewwwww, who wants all this extra exposure and money from stock photography, I want my little community watering hole that Flickr used to be. I don't want Flickr to go mainstream. To you I say this is too late. Flickr lost the small community of photographers a long time ago. When Flickr merged Yahoo photos into Flickr they pushed the mainstream smack dab in the middle of it all. Your experience on Flickr today would be no different than it would be with Microsoft owning it." Available at http://thomashawk.com/2008/02/why-microsoft-owning-flickr-is-no-worse.html. Last checked May 17, 2012.

26. See D. F. Gallagher, "Flickr Users Consider Their Potential Microsoft Overlords," *New York Times*, February 1, 2008, Bits section. Available at http://bits.blogs. nytimes.com/2008/02/01/flickr-users-consider-their-potential-microsoft-over-lords/. Last checked May 16, 2012.

27. According to ComScore, in December 2010 the number of unique visitors to Flickr in the United States fell to 21.3 million, 16 percent lower than a year earlier. Meanwhile, for that same time frame, use of Facebook's photo features grew 92 percent, to 123.9 million users. See V. G. Kopotoff, "At Flickr, Fending Off Rumors and Facebook," *New York Times*, January 30, 2011. Available at http://www.nytimes.com/2011/01/31/technology/31flickr.html. Last checked September 1, 2012.

28. See N. Carlson, "Yahoo, Not Facebook, Is Bleeding Flickr to Death," *Business Insider*, January 31, 2011. Available at http://www.businessinsider.com/ yahoo-not-facebook-is-bleeding-flickr-to-death-2011-1. Last checked May 12, 2012.

29. See, for instance, D. Rushe, "Is Instagram the Next YouTube or the Next Flickr?" *Guardian*, April 10, 2012. Available at http://www.guardian.co.uk/tech-nology/2012/apr/10/instagram-next-youtube-flickr. Last checked May 18, 2012.

30. For the Commons project on Flickr see http://www.flickr.com/commons?GXHC_ gx_session_id_=6afecb2055a3c52c. Last checked May 12, 2012. Participants include George Eastman House, Library of Congress, Brooklyn Museum, Nationaal Archief, National Archives and Records Administration, State Library of New South Wales, and Smithsonian Institution. "Heritage institutions" such as archives, libraries, and museums increasingly invite individual photographic collections as building blocks for recreating communal historical experiences.

31. During the first two years, over 67,000 tags were added by 2,500 unique Flickr users, and information on 500 photos was verified by the Library of Congress and moved into its permanent records. Two collections of historical photographs were made public on Flickr Commons to increase "common knowledge of the past" by adding tags or comments to items from the Library's visual collections (Springer et al. 2008).

32. Both European and American supporters euphorically claimed that the project allowed a cultural heritage to emerge "at the click of a mouse," suggesting that information is "out there" waiting to be collected, and that sites like Flickr Commons magically turn all uploaded data into knowledge about the past. See, for instance, "European Commission Steps Up Efforts to Put Europe's Memory on the Web via a European Digital Library," available at http://europa.eu/rapid/ pressReleasesAction.do?reference=IP/06/253 and "Europe's Cultural Heritage at the Click of a Mouse," available at http://ec.europa.eu/information_society/ activities/digital_libraries/index_en.htm. Last checked May 19, 2012. Obviously, such claims ignore the fact that individual uploads only acquire meaning and impact through the connective work of human contributors, and through nonhuman actors, such as networked technologies and protocols (e.g., selection mechanisms)—which are in turn already prefigured in the institutional modus operandi for defining what cultural heritage actually is (Manzuch 2009).

33. Professional photographer Jim Goldstein, for instance, argued on his blog that the photographers had little to win from this deal if they were already represented by an agent. See Jim Goldstein's blog. Available at http://www.jmg-galleries.com/ blog/2009/01/22/flickr-collection-on-getty-why-im-not-taking-part/. Last checked May 18, 2012.

34. See Yahoo terms of service at http://info.yahoo.com/legal/ie/yahoo/utos.html. Last checked May 19, 2012.

35. For Flickr API terms of service, see http://www.flickr.com/services/api/tos/. Last checked May 18, 2012.

36. See Flickr's terms of service, available at http://info.yahoo.com/legal/us/yahoo/utos/utos-173.html.

37. In 2009, the blog Social Photo Talk, a platform for photographers and social media marketing, featured a discussion about Flickr's confusing policies. See http://www.socialphototalk.com/flickr-permanently-deletes-yet-another-user-without-warning/. Last checked May 18, 2012.

38. See, for instance, an article by C. Cheesman, "Getty Hits Back at Flickr-Deal Critics," *Amateur Photographer*, June 21, 2012. Available at http://www.amateurphotographer.co.uk/photo-news/535644/getty-hits-back-at-flickr-deal-critics. Last checked May 19, 2012.

39. See Yahoo terms of service. Available at http://info.yahoo.com/legal/us/yahoo/utos/utos-173.html. Last checked May 19, 2012.

40. See "Flickr Terms of Service, Unwritten Guidelines and Safety Levels." Anonymous blog post, Spellbound Blog. Available at http://www.spellboundblog.com/2008/07/06/flickr-terms-of-service-unwritten-guidelines-safety-levels/. Last checked May 18, 2012.

41. See an interview with Stewart Butterfield, one of Flickr's cofounders, with CNN on January 20, 2007. Available at http://edition.cnn.com/2007/TECH/01/17/global.office.flickr/index.html. Last checked May 18, 2012.

42. See Thomas Hawk's blog post dated March 30, 2009. Available at http://thomashawk.com/2009/03/should-yahooflickr-be-advertising-paid-pro-memberships-as-ad-free-browsing-and-sharing-when-they-in-fact-plan-on-advertsing-at-them.html. Last checked May 18, 2012.

43. Having said that, Flickr users are also interested in the site's profitability: users regularly discuss the topic on the Flickr Help Forum and Flickr Central Discuss forum. Available at http://www.flickr.com/groups/central/discuss/72157608259101283/. Last checked May 18, 2012.

44. Along these lines, photo-sharing sites are hybrid instruments that fall between "an information system that might be understood within the paradigms of information studies and a mass medium that can be approached by methods prevalent within media or cultural studies" (Cox, Clough, and Marlowe 2008, n.p.).

45. WikiCommons differs from commercial platforms not only because it is nonprofit, but because photos uploaded must be potentially useful on any of the Wikimedia projects, thus excluding personal pictures and artwork.

46. See A. Eiler, "How Photographs on Instagram Differ from Flickr," *ReadWriteWeb*, April 27, 2012. Available at http://www.readwriteweb.com/archives/how_photographs_on_instagram_differ_from_flickr.php. Last checked May 19, 2012.

47. See Thomas Hawk's blog post on May 15, 2012, where he states: "I'm more hopeful on Flickr than I've been in a long, long time. They still have the best image search in the business. They still have the best photo organizational tools in the business. They seem to have positive leadership." Available at http://thomashawk.com/2012/05/my-thoughts-on-mat-honans-gizmodo-article-on-how-yahoo-killed-flickr-and-lost-the-internet.html. Last checked May 19, 2012.

CHAPTER 6

1. YouTube's Alexa ranking (no. 3 worldwide, after Google and Facebook) concerns its measurement in May 2012. For more facts and figures, see YouTube's own stats page, available at http://www.youtube.com/t/press_statistics. Last checked May 20, 2012.

2. Even a decade before the emergence of YouTube, the Internet's emphasis on interactivity was promoted to depreciate the amenities of a one-way transmission system. Building on a simple replacement theory of consecutive media constellation, early technology gurus had long prophesied the "postbroadcasting age"—the decline and eventual demise of broadcasting as a result of the Internet's popularity (Gilder 1994; Miller and Allen 1995). Yet despite ominous predictions, TV never faced the serious threat of disappearance. Instead, YouTube ushered television into yet another stage of evolutionary contestation, which is nothing new for a medium that has been going through "a series of definitional crises over its long history" (Uricchio 2009: 31).

3. Lisa Parks (2004: 135) introduced the term "flexible microcasting" to refer to a "set of industrial and technological practices that work to isolate the individual cultural tastes of viewers/consumers in order to refine direct marketing in television—that is, the process of delivering specific audiences to advertisers." Narrowcasting and microcasting are described in terms of reaching specific targeted audiences for specific audiovisual contents, a feature they have in common with homecasting.

4. Like "webcasting," the term "homecasting" indicates the technological convergence of TV and PC in the homes of individual users (Ledoux Book and Barnett 2006; Ha, Dick, and Ryu 2003), yet the word "home" has more intimate, social connotations than the word "web."

5. For three years, Google also deployed its own platform GoogleVideo, which was significantly less popular; during the first couple of years, features of Google-Video were implemented in YouTube, and in 2009 Google's video service was discontinued.

6. YouTube's coding architecture promotes the formation of groups, for instance by author-applied tags and comments (Paolillo 2008). In addition, profiling metadata connect video content to users and users to each other, thus automating sociality (Jakobsson 2010). Since YouTube never became a real competitor in the SNS market, Google finally launched its own social networking site, in direct competition to Facebook. GooglePlus (Google+) was launched in June 2011, and was heavily promoted through YouTube; see http://www.youtube.com/watch?v=xwnJ5Bl4kLI. Last checked June 8, 2012.

7. See, for instance, Cheng, Dale, and Liu (2008), who present a systematic and in-depth measurement on the statistics of one million YouTube users. They find that 58 percent of users have "no friends," but there is a stronger correlation between videos than there is between users. A later study by Siersdorfer et al. (2010) shows how the metadata of user behavior (ratings, comments) in relation to video contents can be used to predict user behavior and enhance ratings performance.

8. The term "produsage" was introduced by Axel Bruns (2008) to indicate a new group of users who also produced (created and uploaded) videos.

9. For statistics, see YouTube's home page. Available at http://www.youtube.com/t/press_statistics. Last checked May 21, 2012.

10. As Ding et al. (2011: 363) conclude: "We find that there are more than three times the number of male uploaders than female uploaders. Consistent with the

number of uploaders, male uploaders contribute more than three times the number of videos and attract more than three times the number of views than female uploaders. We also observe that the uploaders with ages from 20 to 30 are the most active uploaders, contributing approximately 40.0 percent of YouTube videos."

11. As we can read on the YouTube Partnership home page: "The YouTube Partner Program provides creators with resources and opportunities to improve their skills, build larger audiences, and earn more money." Available at http://www.youtube.com/yt/creators/partner.html. Last checked May 22, 2012.

12. John Seabrook in his article on YouTube's changing strategies, "Streaming Dreams: YouTube Turns Pro," *New Yorker*, January 19, 2012, quotes Ben Relles, employee of YouTube NextLab, saying that most YouTube viral videos do not go viral by accident: "Although people tend to think that viral videos are serendipitous, in fact, Relles said, six of the top ten most-viewed YouTube videos in 2010 were scripted and produced just like TV shows. The difference is that the poetics of YouTube favors authenticity over production values. But what looks good enough on your desktop may look cheap in your living room." Available at http://www.newyorker.com/reporting/2012/01/16/120116fa_fact_seabrook. Last checked June 10, 2012.

13. An extensive report in the *New York Times* on June 28, 2012, describes how aspiring YouTube performers turn their hobby into a livelihood by entering competitions such as Next Up. See R. Walker, "On YouTube, Amateur Is the New Pro," *New York Times*, June 28, 2012.

14. This double bind of mediated dependency is part of a more general trend toward the public mediation of private life—a trend to which John Thompson (1995: 215) alerted us ten years before YouTube started. Social media further enhanced the trend toward mixing private worlds with mass media, turning audiovisual exposure into an integral part of everyday life. To bend a familiar cliché: if broadcast television opens up a window to the world, homecast video sharing provides the looking glass to have the world stare right back into the living room.

15. See protest video on YouTube: http://www.youtube.com/watch?v=sptj09iyuAM&feature=related. Last checked June 7, 2012. A number of remixes and variations of this video appeared on the site, as well as protest songs and personal video statements.

16. See for instance, "How to Change Back the Old YouTube Layout." Available at http://www.youtube.com/watch?v=LJ1ThFddbJU&feature=related. See also "I Want My Old Channel Back!" http://www.youtube.com/watch?v=KbvWlsa_ui8&feature=related and "Get Your Old Channel's Design Back!" at http://www.youtube.com/watch?v=tr6btWZh80U&feature=related. All checked January 7, 2012.

17. Formats—copyrighted descriptions of formatted television productions such as game shows—arrived on the television market in the late 1980s (Keane and Moran 2008).

18. According to Cheng, Dale, and Liu (2008), who conducted a systematic and in-depth measurement study on the statistics of 77 million uploaded videos on YouTube, almost 98 percent of all videos are less than ten minutes in length, and the average length is between three and four minutes.

19. As researchers Ding et al. conclude: "Perhaps the most surprising result in the paper is the discovery that much of the content in YouTube is not user

generated. We found that 63 percent of the most popular uploaders are primarily uploading UCC content, and that UCC uploaders on average upload many more videos than UGC uploaders" (Ding et al. 2011: 366).

20. The question whether Google (YouTube) was a rival or potential ally of the media entertainment industry was asked many times between 2005 and 2008. See, for instance, Laura M. Holson, "Hollywood Asks: Is Google a Friend or Foe?" *New York Times*, Technology section, January 14, 2007. Available at http://www.nytimes.com/2007/01/15/technology/15youtube.html. Last checked June 10, 2012.

21. McDonald (2009: 395) lists at least 12 content deals between YouTube and major copyright owners between 2006 and 2009, including ABC, NBC, Disney, and MGM, leaving only a few unsettled lawsuits. The Viacom versus YouTube case is still pending. Viacom sued YouTube for $1 billion in damages, claiming 160,000 copyrighted videos were illegally posted on the site. However, there are documented cases of Viacom itself uploading its copyrighted clips on YouTube in an attempt to promote their TV shows while at the same time incriminating the Google subsidiary. Moreover, Viacom-owned site Spike.com routinely monetizes videos from independent content producers by placing commercials without permission.

22. Compared to the five hours a day Americans spend watching television, people spend fifteen minutes watching videos online. Short videos average between three to six minutes in length, and a typical user watches six videos a day. Such a sequence is unlikely to hold the attention span of viewers because the short length of videos presents too many opportunities to leave the flow. See Randall Stross, "YouTube Wants You to Sit and Stay Awhile," *New York Times*, May 28, 2010, Business section. Available at http://www.nytimes.com/2010/05/30/business/30digi.html?partner=rss&emc=rss. Last checked June 12, 2012.

23. Next New Networks promotes itself as a leading provider of original entertainment programming for the Internet, "redefining entertainment by championing the next generation of show creators, helping build their audiences, capabilities, and paths to revenue." See http://www.nextnewnetworks.com/. Last checked May 31, 2012. NowMov, a San Francisco start-up, introduced a service combining Twitter and YouTube in order to elongate viewers' attention span. The site uses Twitter feeds to determine which YouTube videos are appearing with the greatest frequency in Tweets, and NowMov starts playing these most-played videos as soon as a visitor arrives at its site.

24. Netflix launched an online version of the traditional pay-per-rental system in 1998, which it changed in 2000 into a flat-fee rental service. Netflix first focused on movie rentals, but started to include TV content after 2008. Hulu started as a subscription service offering ad-supported streaming video of TV shows, movies, webisodes, and other new media, trailers, clips, and behind-the-scenes footage in March 2008. Hulu is a joint venture initiative empowered by AOL, MSN, Facebook, and Yahoo; Disney later bought a 27 percent stake in the joint venture.

25. In March 2011, Netflix announced plans to begin acquiring first-run original content for its popular Watch Instantly subscription service. This business model has yet to be implemented.

26. For YouTube's terms of service, see http://www.youtube.com/static?gl=US&template=terms. Last checked June 10, 2012. Under clause 6C, the terms of service state: "For clarity, you retain all of your ownership rights in your Content. However, by submitting Content to YouTube, you hereby grant YouTube a worldwide, non-exclusive, royalty-free, sublicenseable and

transferable license to use, reproduce, distribute, prepare derivative works of, display, and perform the Content in connection with the Service and YouTube's (and its successors' and affiliates') business, including without limitation for promoting and redistributing part or all of the Service (and derivative works thereof) in any media formats and through any media channels."

27. Users can still post videos to YouTube under a Creative Commons license; however, users who do so can use exclusively material they themselves created or recycle material from other videos issued under a CC license. For a precise description of these conditions, see the YouTube Creative Commons website. Available at http://www.youtube.com/t/creative_commons?hl=en. Last checked June 12, 2012.

28. See, for instance, the Google Privacy Policy Update on YouTube. Available at http://www.youtube.com/watch?v=KGghlPmebCY&feature=related. Last checked May 22, 2012.

29. See, for instance the video "Google Has an Evil Plan," posted on January 28, 2012. Available at http://www.youtube.com/watch?v=aq219NGjjWM&feature= related. Last checked May 22, 2012. See also the funny video clip "Google's Privacy Policy Change Is Freaking Me Out," posted on January 31, 2012. Available at http://www.youtube.com/watch?v=7jHxfJW7Zww&feature=related. Last checked May 22, 2012.

30. See, for instance, an article by N. Cohen, "Professor Makes the Case That Google Is a Publisher," *New York Times*, May 20, 2012, where the journalist asks: "Is Google search an intermediary like the phone company—simply connecting people with the information they seek? Or is Google search a publisher, like a newspaper, which provides only the information that it sees fit and is protected by the First Amendment?" Available at http://www.nytimes.com/2012/05/21/ business/media/eugene-volokh-ucla-professor-makes-a-case-for-google-as-publisher.html?pagewanted=all. Last checked May 23, 2012.

31. The ads in this campaign all center around people creating and connecting their own communicative environments, such as an ad showing a young father patching and pasting photos of his daughter ("Dear Sophie") from Picasa to home videos on YouTube and text messages on Gmail as a means of document-ing his daughter's early life. For more details, see Claire Miller, "Google Takes to TV to Promote Browser," *New York Times*, May 3, 2011, Technology section. Available at http://www.nytimes.com/2011/05/04/technology/04chrome.html. Last checked May 4, 2011.

32. As researchers Ding et al. conclude: "YouTube incentivizes the very popular uploaders by sharing its ad revenue with them. To some extent, the number of views of an uploader influences its motivation to upload" (Ding et al. 2011: 363).

33. Read, for instance, the remarkable story by L. Ulanov, "You Tube Partnership Program: Opportunity or Witch-Hunt?" in *PC Magazine.com*, October 7, 2009. Available at http://www.pcmag.com/article2/0,2817,2353844,00.asp. Last checked May 21, 2012. Ulanov, the producer of the "carved pumpkin" videos wildly popular in 2009, describes in great detail how YouTube's Partnership program forced him to modify his goofy YouTube clips to meet Google's AdSense requirements at the risk of his videos being deleted altogether.

34. See videoclip by YouTuber Derek, posted May 8, 2007. Available at http://www. youtube.com/watch?v=NA6SMPXdAYU. Last checked May 21, 2012.

35. For the official Google blog, see http://googleblog.blogspot.com/2011/12/ get-more-into-what-you-love-on-youtube.html. Last checked December 8, 2011.

36. A notable exception is, for instance, Gooyong (2009), who argues that the future of YouTube is in the hands of users; they allegedly have the power to barter over the Internet's democratic potential and commercial control of the Net. New critical media pedagogies should enable students to become critical and active platform users.

CHAPTER 7

1. For Wikipedia's five core principles, see the home wiki page. Available at http://en.wikipedia.org/wiki/Wikipedia:Five_pillars.

2. In May 2012, Wikipedia was ranked number 6 on the Alexia rankings. Available at http://www.alexa.com/topsites. The latest updates on Wikipedia's facts and figures can be checked at the About Wikipedia page. Available at http://en.wikipedia.org/wiki/Wikipedia:About. Last checked May 27, 2012.

3. Germany's Wikipedia overseer, a member of the Wikimedia Foundation, came up with the idea of nominating the online encyclopedia for the World Heritage or Intangible Cultural Heritage List. Both nominations are ill fits not only because the project lacks the necessary maturity for listing, but also because the World Heritage List so far only includes historical monuments and natural sites (like the Amsterdam Canal district or the Great Barrier Reef), and the Intangible Cultural Heritage List only includes *endangered* traditions and practices (like flamenco). See K. O'Brien, "Worthy Online Resource, but Global Cultural Treasure?" *New York Times*, May 22, 2011. http://www.nytimes.com/2011/05/23/technology/23wikipedia.html?pagewanted=2. Last checked May 28, 2012.

4. The word "crowdsourcing" was launched by journalist Jeff Howe in 2006 in his article "The Rise of Crowdsourcing" in *Wired*. Available at http://www.wired.com/wired/archive/14.06/crowds.html. The term "collaborative knowledge" was first used by Marshall Poe in his September 2006 article "The Hive" in *The Atlantic*. Available at http://www.theatlantic.com/magazine/archive/2006/09/the-hive/5118/. Last checked May 28, 2012.

5. Journalist Nicolas Baker summed up the charms of Wikipedia in a style typical of such praise: "Wikipedia flourished partly because it was a shrine to altruism—a place for shy, learned people to deposit their trawls." See N. Baker, "The Charms of Wikipedia," *New York Review of Books*, March 20, 2008. Available at http://www.nybooks.com/articles/archives/2008/mar/20/the-charms-of-wikipedia/?pagination=false. Last checked May 28, 2012.

6. Jimmy Wales was cited in 2006 by blogger Aaron Swartz as downplaying the myth that Wikipedia was written by the masses, by doing the math: "I expected to find something like an 80-20 rule: 80 percent of the work being done by 20 percent of the users, just because that seems to come up a lot. But it's actually much, much tighter than that: it turns out over 50 percent of all the edits are done by just.7 percent of the users . . . 524 people. . . . And in fact the most active 2 percent, which is 1400 people, have done 73.4 percent of all the edits." The remaining 25 percent of edits, he said, were from "people who [are] contributing . . . a minor change of a fact or a minor spelling fix . . . or something like that." See A. Swarz (2006), "Who writes Wikipedia?" Raw Thought Blog. Available at http://www.aaronsw.com/weblog/whowriteswikipedia. Last checked May 28, 2012.

7. Researchers Ghosh and Prakash (2000) were among the first to disaggregate the "many minds" myth in the open software movement; their conclusion was that "free software development is less a bazaar of several developers involved in

several projects and more a collation of projects developed single-mindedly by a large number of authors" (1).

8. Internet critic Andrew Keen (2008) is one of these theorists in favor of the expert approach; he applauded Sanger for leaving the wiki model and for coming to his senses about the "debased value of amateur contributions" in favor of expert-professionals (186).

9. Journalist Marshall Poe, in his article "The Hive" in *The Atlantic* (September 2006), painstakingly described the evolution of Wikipedia's principles from the early Nupedia experiment to Wikipedia five years after its inception. Available at http://www.theatlantic.com/magazine/archive/2006/09/the-hive/5118/. Last checked May 28, 2012.

10. Sanger eventually, in March 2007, launched the Citizendium project, but it never really took off. According to the Wikipedia lemma on Citizendium: "As of July 2011, it had 15,920 articles, of which 155 had achieved editorial approval, and around 45 contributors making at least 20 edits a month, by October 27, 2011, the site had fewer than 100 active members." For more information on the Citizendium Beta project see http://en.citizendium.org/wiki/Welcome_to_ Citizendium. Last checked May 28, 2012.

11. Pulitzer Prize–winning journalist Stacy Schiff observed in her extensive Wikipedia profile that, curiously, mob rule did not lead to chaos: "Wikipedia, which began as an experiment in un fettered democracy, has sprouted policies and procedures." See S. Schiff, "Know It All: Can Wikipedia Conquer Expertise?" *New Yorker*, July 31, 2006. Available at http://www.newyorker.com/ archive/2006/07/31/060731fa_fact. Last checked May 28, 2012.

12. For a complete overview of user groups and their access and permission levels, see the Wikipedia page. Available at http://en.wikipedia.org/wiki/ Wikipedia:User_access_levels. Last checked May 27, 2012.

13. See Wikipedia System Administrators page. Available at http://meta.wikimedia. org/wiki/System_administrators.

14. See Wikipedia Bot Policy page. Available at http://en.wikipedia.org/wiki/ Wikipedia:Bot_policy. Last checked May 28, 2012.

15. See Wikipedia History of Bots page. Available at http://en.wikipedia.org/wiki/ Wikipedia:History_of_Wikipedia_bots. Last checked May 28, 2012.

16. See Wikipedia Editing Frequency of All Bots page. Available at http:// en.wikipedia.org/wiki/Wikipedia:Editing_frequency/All_bots

17. Some claim an even higher percentage of bots in Wikipedia: Geiger (2011), for instance, claims that "bots make about 50 percent of all edits, and users with semi-automated editing tools make another 30 percent" (79).

18. See Wikipedia Ram-Man User Page. Available at http://en.wikipedia.org/wiki/ User:Ram-Man. Last checked May 28, 2012.

19. See List of Wikipedians by Number of Edits. Available at http://en.wikipedia. org/wiki/Wikipedia:List_of_Wikipedians_by_number_of_edits

20. For the three Wikipedia's core principles, see the respective Wikipedia pages. Available at http://en.wikipedia.org/wiki/Wikipedia:Neutral_point_of_view. http://en.wikipedia.org/wiki/Wikipedia:No_original_research. http://en. wikipedia.org/wiki/Wikipedia:Verifiability All checked May 28, 2012.

21. Informatics researcher Alexander Halavais, for instance, intentionally contrib-uted incorrect information to Wikipedia entries; for his "Isuzu Experiment," he inserted 13 mistakes into 13 different entries, expecting that most of the errors would remain intact, but much to Halavais's surprise, his wrongful edits were all

corrected within a couple of hours. See A. Halavais, "The Isuzu Experiment," A Thaumaturgical Compendium, 2004. Available at http://alex.halavais.net/the-isuzu-experiment/. Last checked May 28, 2012. Halavais's approach was heavily criticized, mainly because he deliberately littered his object of study. One of the problems with these tests is that they treat isolated Wikipedia content as a static product, assessing its entries against other encyclopedic records. A technical problem was that Halavais made all changes from the same username and IP address, rendering it all too easy for bots and Wikipedians to undo his edits. Philosopher of science P. D. Magnus (2008) later provided a corrective to Halavais's research method by inserting inaccuracies distributed across IP addresses and fields of expertise. He found that one-third of the errors were corrected within 48 hours, and most others were "corrected by association," as was the case with Halavais's experiment. Halavais and Lackaff (2008) examine Wikipedia's reliability and completeness, assessing qualities of its users rather than those of its systems (see also Niederer and van Dijck 2010).

22. See "Wikipedia Survives Research Test," *BBC News*, December 15, 2005. Available at http://news.bbc.co.uk/2/hi/technology/4530930.stm. Last checked July 18, 2011.

23. In 2006 information systems researcher Thomas Chesney conducted empirical research into the accuracy of Wikipedia, asking a total of 258 experts (academics) and nonexperts to fill out a survey about a Wikipedia article from their area of expertise (or, for the laymen, in their realm of interest). The respondents found mistakes in 13 percent of the Wikipedia articles. But Chesney also found that the experts gave the Wikipedia articles a higher credibility rating than the nonexperts did. Contrary to the perceived inaccuracy of Wikipedia, the respondents found Wikipedia to be a reliable source of information on the Web. In 2011, a study from Brigham Young University proved the reliability of Wikipedia's sources in the field of political science. See http://www.sciencedaily.com/releases/2011/04/110414131855.htm. Last checked May 28, 2012.

24. The WikiScanner is a tool created by California Institute of Technology student Virgil Griffith in 2007, designed to reveal bias. Tools like the WikiScanner facilitate the tracking of anonymous users by revealing who and where they actually are; they also empower researchers and journalists trying to localize and expose biased content. Griffith collects the most spectacular results on his website, where he also states he created the WikiScanner (among other reasons) to "create a fireworks display of public relations disasters in which everyone brings their own fireworks, and enjoys." In the summer of 2008, Griffith launched the WikiWatcher suite, a set of tools designed for monitoring and maintaining Wikipedia. The suite includes a tool that makes it possible to de-anonymize users with a username whose IP addresses match that of other user(name)s or companies/institutions in a IP-to-Geo database. This stretches the notion of anonymity from the unregistered to the registered with a username. For more details, see Griffith's home page. Available at http://wiki-watcher.virgil.gr/ Last checked May 28, 2012.

25. See T. Messer-Kruse, "The 'Undue Weight' of Truth on Wikipedia," *Chronicle Review of Higher Education*, February 12, 2012. Available at http://chronicle.com/article/The-Undue-Weight-of-Truth-on/130704/. Last checked May 28, 2012.

26. See *The Colbert Report*, July 31, 2006. Available at http://www.colbertnation.com/the-colbert-report-videos/72347/july-31-2006/the-word—wikiality. Last checked May 28, 2012.

27. In an interview (Kamir and Niesyto 2011), Israeli Wikipedia developer Dor Kamir explains how the NPoV principle and the No Original Research (NOR) principle are sometimes at odds. For instance, in Hebrew there are several optional names for the territories known in English as the West Bank and the Gaza Strip, and yet choosing a "neutral" or new name is impossible because it would violate the NOR principle.

28. The Wikimedia Foundation is a nonprofit charitable organization "dedicated to encouraging the growth, development and distribution of free multilingual content, and to providing the full content of these wiki-based projects to the public free of charge." See http://wikimediafoundation.org/wiki/Home. Last checked May 28, 2012. The board of trustees has the power to direct the activities of the foundation and also has the authority to amend the corporate bylaws. At full membership, the board has eighteen trustees, including one seat designated for Jimmy Wales.

29. Wikipedia's Mediation Committee (MedCom) is "a panel of editors who resolve disputes about the content of Wikipedia articles by providing formal mediation." It was established in January 2004, with the Arbitration Committee, and it is the "the last stage of formal content-dispute resolution on the English Wikipedia." See http://en.wikipedia.org/wiki/Wikipedia:Mediation_Committee. Last checked May 28, 2012.

30. See Wikipedia Mediation Committee and Mediation Policy. Available at http://en.wikipedia.org/wiki/Wikipedia:Mediation_Committee/Policy. Last checked May 28, 2012.

31. For the Wikipedia Arbitration Committee/Policy. Available at http://en.wikipedia.org/wiki/Wikipedia:Arbitration_policy#Admissibility_of_evidence. Last checked May 28, 2012.

32. See Information about Facebook's Community Pages. Available at http://www.facebook.com/help/?page=168393039888715. Last checked May 28, 2012.

33. See Google Cache, 2007, a blog by Russ Jones, an Internet search-engine optimization specialist, presenting himself as a "Google watcher." Available at http://www.thegooglecache.com/white-hat-seo/966-of-wikipedia-pages-rank-in-googles-top-10/. See also "Wikipedia Traffic, Mostly from Google" article featured on the Softmedia Blog, May 15, 2008, http://news.softpedia.com/news/Wikipedia-Traffic-Mostly-from-Google-85703.shtml. Last checked December 14, 2011.

34. See "Wikipedia Wins the Google Lottery—but Why?" *Guardian*, Technology Blog, February 18, 2010. Available at http://www.guardian.co.uk/technology/blog/2010/feb/18/wikipedia-google. Last checked December 14, 2011.

CHAPTER 8

1. Yonoo, an app powered by Mozilla, was introduced in 2011; similar apps connecting social media platform input are surfacing every day.

2. Google's CEO Eric Schmidt used the concept of "augmented humanity" when delivering a talk about his vision for the next decade at the Digital Life Design conference in Munich in January 2011. He anticipates computers getting smart enough to help humans on everything from translating speech to driving cars. See the techno-blog Mediabeat, January 27, 2011. Available at http://venturebeat.com/2011/01/27/eric-schmidts-talk-on-age-of-augmented-humanity-at-dld-video/. Last checked June 12, 2012.

3. The term "switching costs" stems from microeconomics, where it refers to any impediments to a customer's changing of suppliers (Shapiro and Varian 1999).

With regard to social media, the costs of switching are not so much financial as psychological, social, and emotional: if you quit Facebook, for instance, you may lose a large network of contacts built up over many years. To many critical users, switching costs may be a major barrier as long as they cannot take their personal data and network to another supplier.

4. For Indymedia Independent news centers, see http://www.indymedia.org/nl/index.shtml. Global Voices is an international network of citizen journalists and bloggers that follow current affairs in the global blogosphere; see http://www.global-voices.info/. Diaspora is "an international community of people who are passionate about making the social web work for everyone" and which gives users control of their data. See http://diasporaproject.org/. Last checked June 12, 2012.

5. As Internet researcher Eli Pariser (2011) argues, the dynamics of personalization and customization cause so-called filter bubbles: algorithmic induction "can lead to a kind of information determinism in which our past clickstreams entirely define our future" (135). Because users are locked into a flow, they tend to click on content preselected by platforms and reaffirmed by their friends' clicking behavior. Filter bubbles give us an emotional world, because strong feelings and emotions are more easily shared than more important but complex or unpleasant pieces of content, which will subsequently be blocked out (Pariser 2011: 150–51).

6. See the takeover announcement "Microsoft buys Skype" on the tech-site Geek. com on May 10, 2011. Available at http://www.geek.com/articles/geek-pick/microsoft-buys-skype-20110510/. Last checked June 12, 2012.

7. These four platforms also go by the acronym of GAFA. As explained in the first chapter, I have limited my focus to SNS and UGC platforms, and therefore Apple and Amazon are beyond the scope of this book. As will become clear in this chapter, though, it is impossible to reflect on major chains in the ecosystem without including Apple—which is increasingly including software and apps in its hardware imperium and builds partnerships with social media sites. For instance, in June 2012, it was also rumored that Apple was interested in buying stakes in Twitter. Amazon, for its part, connects to a host of vertically integrated services, but its core business is to provide offline businesses, such as Toys "R" Us and Target, with online sales and marketing services.

8. As two *New York Times* reporters observed, the two competing moguls are changing the way people engage in online activities: "Facebook's moves sharpen the battle lines between the social networking giant and Google, the search giant, because Facebook is trying to change the way people find what they want online. Searching the Web is still the way most people discover content—whether it is news, information about wedding photographers or Swiss chard recipes. Facebook is trying to change that: in effect, friends will direct other friends to content. Google has its own social network product in Google+, but it is far behind Facebook." See S. Sengupta and B. Sisaro, "Facebook as Tastemaker," *New York Times*, September, 22, 2011, Technology section. Available at http://www.nytimes.com/2011/09/23/technology/facebook-makes-a-push-to-be-a-media-hub.html?pagewanted=all. Last checked June 12, 2012.

9. See S. Sengupta, "Facebook's Prospects May Rest on Trove of Data," *New York Times*, May 14, 2012, Technology section. Available at http://www.nytimes.com/2012/05/15/technology/facebook-needs-to-turn-data-trove-into-investor-gold.html?pagewanted=all. Last checked May 30, 2012.

10. Early June 2012, Apple's CEO Tim Cook announced that Apple had reached an agreement with Facebook to weave the social network deeper into Apple's mobile devices iPhone, iPod, and iPad, for instance by allowing people to share photos through Facebook without having to open a separate Facebook app.

11. The term "nirvana of interoperability" was used by Ted Cohen, a consultant and former digital executive, when commenting on the announcement that Facebook had made agreements with a number of media companies to develop a way for a user's profile page to display whatever entertainment he is consuming on those outside services. See B. Sisario, "Facebook to Offer Path to Media," *New York Times*, September 18, 2011, Business section. Available at http://www.nytimes.com/2011/09/19/business/media/facebook-is-expected-to-unveil-media-sharing-service.html. Last checked June 12, 2012.

12. Google's deal with browser Firefox to make Google Search its default browser led to an investigation by a U.S. Senate antitrust panel. In September 2011, Google's chairman, Eric Schmidt, testified before the panel that the Internet is the ultimate level playing field where users were "one click away" from competitors. The "one click away" adagio has been Google's consistent antitrust defense: the company that has 84 percent of the search market, cannot be a search monopoly as long as a user can click away to other search engines and browsers.

13. Law professor turned regulator Tim Wu (2010) warned that, in a relatively short period, a group of new monopolists has reined in big chunks of the Internet—Google controlling search, Facebook social networking, and Apple content delivery. According to Wu, media history shows regular patterns in which short periods of relative openness are followed by stagnant periods when one or two corporate winners employ the "master switch" to fence off their systems to competitors.

14. The United States lacks a comprehensive data privacy law. The European Union has a Data Protection Directive for its member states, regulating the processing of personal data and the free movement of such data to protect individuals. In 1995, the U.S. Federal Trade Commission (FTC) issued a set of nonbinding governing principles—the Fair Information Principles—for the commercial use of personal information. Although they provide guidance for drafting privacy policies, they do not mandate policy.

15. "Memology" refers to the study of how "memes," or new ideas and trends, spread on Facebook. See Facebook Memology Blog. Available at http://www.facebook.com/blog.php?post=215076352130. Last checked June 12, 2012.

16. For an introduction to the promises and benefits of the "free" model, see Anderson (2009). An interesting and critical review of Anderson's ideas is M. Gladwell, "Priced To Sell. Is Free the Future?" *New Yorker*, June 6, 2009. Available at http://www.newyorker.com/arts/critics/books/2009/07/06/090706crbo_books_gladwell. Last checked Jun12, 2012.

17. See European Network Information and Security Agency (ENISA), "Study on Monetizing Privacy. An Economic Model for Pricing Personal Information." Published February 27, 2012. Available at http://www.enisa.europa.eu/activities/identity-and-trust/library/deliverables/monetising-privacy. Last checked May 30, 2012.

18. Interestingly, Apple lashed out at Facebook's and Google's refusal to insert a "Do Not Track" option, and compared its own services favorably to its competitors. An article on the Apple Insider blog comments: "Because Apple earns its revenues almost entirely from hardware sales, it doesn't have the same

motivation to track users as other browser makers and Internet service providers do. Even Apple's own iAd network gains only limited benefits from reporting user behaviors, making it easy for Apple to offer legitimate opt out options. In contrast, Google, Facebook, Yahoo, Mozilla and Microsoft have made advertising and user tracking a key linchpin of the business model behind their browser software and online services." See D. E. Dilger, "Google, Facebook Working to Undermine Do Not Track Privacy Protections," *Apple Insider*, March 30, 2012. Available at http://www.appleinsider.com/articles/12/03/30/google_facebook_working_to_undermined_do_no_track_privacy_protections.html. Last checked May 30, 2012. Twitter announced on May 15, 2012 that it would offer a do not track option on its site, which means that Twitter will stop receiving page-visit information as users surf the Internet.

19. A group by the name of Consumers International calls for a different type of consumer rights activism by social media users. "Connected and part of the conversation, we're fast evolving from passive recipients, to active participants in the media of the masses." See Consumers International Blog, December 2011. Available at http://consumersinternational.blogspot.com/2011/12/three-social-media-challenges-for.html. Last checked June 12, 2012.

20. Interview with Facebook's Marc Zuckerberg and Sheryl Sandberg on *Charlie Rose*. Broadcast by KQED World, November 11, 2011.

BIBLIOGRAPHY

Adler, T., L. de Alfaro, I. Pye, and W. Raman. 2008. Measuring author contributions to Wikipedia. In *Proceedings of WikiSym 2008*, Porto, September 8–10. New York: ACM. Available at http://users.soe.ucsc.edu/~luca/papers/08/wikisym08-users. pdf. Last checked: April 16, 2012.

Anderson, C. 2009. *Free: The Future of a Radical Price*. New York: Hyperion.

Andrejevic, M. 2011. The work that affective economics does. *Cultural Studies* 25(4–5), 604–20.

Ang, I. 1991. *Desperately Seeking the Audience*. New York: Routledge.

Antin, J., and C. Cheshire. 2010. Readers are not free-riders: Reading as a form of participation in Wikipedia. *Proceedings of the 2010 ACM Conference on Computer Supported Cooperative Work*, February 6–10, 2010, Savannah, GA. Available at ACM, http://dl.acm.org/citation.cfm?id=1718942. Last checked June 12, 2012.

Arceneaux, N., and A. Schmitz Weiss. 2010. Seems stupid until you try it: Press coverage of Twitter, 2006–2009. *New Media & Society* 12(8), 1262–79.

Auletta, K. 2009. *Googled: The End of the World as We Know It*. New York: Penguin.

Bates, B. J. 2008. Framing media economic policy: A social economics approach. Paper presented at the Eighth World Media Economics Conference, Lisbon, Portugal, May 2008. Available at http://www.cci.utk.edu/~bates/papers/WME-2008-framingmediapol.pdf. Last checked September 7, 2012.

Baym, N. K. 2010. *Personal Connections in the Digital Age*. Cambridge: Polity Press.

Beer, D. 2008. Social network(ing) sites . . . revisiting the story so far: A response to danah boyd & Nicole Ellison. *Journal of Computer-Mediated Communication* 13, 516–29.

———. 2009. Power through the algorithm? Participatory web cultures and the technological unconsciousness. *New Media & Society* 11(6), 985–1002.

Benkler, Y. 2006. *The Wealth of Networks: How Social Production Transforms Markets and Freedom*. New Haven: Yale University Press.

Bermejo, F. 2009. Audience measurement in historical perspective: From broadcasting to Google. *New Media & Society* 11(1–2), 133–54.

Berry, D. M. 2011. *The Philosophy of Software: Code and Mediation in the Digital Age*. London: Palgrave.

Berry, D. M., and G. Moss. 2008. Libre Culture: Meditations on Free Culture. Pygmalion Internet Archive. Available at http://www.archive.org/search.php?query=publisher%3A%22Pygmalion+Books%22. Last checked June 13, 2012.

Berry, D. M., and J. Pawlik. 2008. What is code? A conversation with Deleuze, Guattari, and code. In *Libre Culture: Meditations on Free Culture*, ed. D. M. Berry and G. Moss. Pygmalion Internet Archive. Available at http://www.archive.org/search.php?query=publisher%3A%22Pygmalion+Books%22. Last checked September 1, 2012.

Bijker, W. E. 1995. *Of Bicycles, Bakelites, and Bulbs: Toward a Theory of Sociotechnical Change*. Cambridge: MIT Press.

Blake, B., N. Agarwal, R. Wigand, and J. Wood. 2010. Twitter quo vadis: Is Twitter bitter or are tweets sweet? Paper presented at the Seventh International Conference on Information Technology, Las Vegas, NV, April 12–14. 1257–60. Available at http://www.computer.org/portal/web/csdl/doi/10.1109/ITNG.2010.61, Last checked May 13, 2012.

Bollen, J., H. Mao, and A. Pepe. 2010. Determining the public mood state by analysis of microblogging posts. *Proceedings of the 12th International Conference on the Synthesis and Simulation of Living Systems*, Odense, Denmark, 2010. Available at http://pti.iu.edu/pubs/determining-public-mood-state-analysis-microblogging-posts. Last checked June 12, 2012.

boyd, d. 2007. None of this is real: Identity and participation in Friendster. Joe Karaganis, ed., *Structures of Participation in Digital Culture*. New York: Social Science Research Council. 132–57.

boyd, d., and N. Ellison. 2007. Social Network Sites: Definition, History, and Scholarship. *Journal of Computer-Mediated Communication* 13(1), 1–11.

Bruns, A. 2008. *Blogs, Wikipedia, Second Life and Beyond: From Production to Produsage*. New York: Peter Lang.

Bucher, T. 2012a. Want to be on the top? Algorithmic power and the threat of invisibility on Facebook. *New Media & Society*, Online First. Available at http://nms.sagepub.com/content/early/2012/04/04/1461444812440159.

———. 2012b. The friendship assemblage: Investigating programmed sociality on Facebook. *Television & New Media*. doi:10.1177/1527476412452800.

Burgess, J., and J. Green, eds. 2009. *YouTube: Online Video and Participatory Culture*. Cambridge: Polity Press.

Burke M., and R. Kraut. 2008. Taking up the mop: Identifying future Wikipedia administrators. *Proceedings of the 2008 CHI Conference, Florence*, April 5–10. New York: ACM. 3441–46. Available at http://portal.acm.org/citation.cfm?id=1358628.1358871. Last checked June 13, 2012.

Carr, N. 2011. Questioning Wikipedia. G. Lovink and N. Tkacz, eds., *Critical Point of View: A Wikipedia Reader*. Amsterdam: Institute for Network Cultures. 191–202.

Castells, M. 1996. *The Rise of the Network Society*. Vol. 1 of *The Information Age: Economy, Society and Culture*. Oxford: Blackwell.

———. 1997. *The Power of Identity*. Vol. 2 of *The Information Age: Economy, Society and Culture*. Oxford: Blackwell.

———. 1998. *End of Millennium*. Vol. 3 of *The Information Age: Economy, Society and Culture*. Oxford: Blackwell.

———. 2007. *Mobile Communication and Society*. Cambridge: MIT Press.

———. 2009. *Communication Power*. Oxford: Oxford University Press.

Certeau, M. de. 1984. *The Practice of Everyday Life*. Berkeley: University of California Press.

Cha, M., H. Haddadi, F. Benevenuto, and K. P. Gummadi. 2010. Measuring user influence in Twitter: The million dollar fallacy. *Proceedings of the Fourth International AAAI Conference on Weblogs and Social Media*. No page numbers Available at http://pdfcast.org/pdf/measuring-user-influence-in-twitter-the-million-follower-fallacy. Last checked June 12, 2012.

Cheng, X., C. Dale, and J. Liu. 2008. Statistics and Social Network of YouTube Videos. *Proceedings of the IEEE* 96(1), 229–38. Available at http://citeseerx.ist.psu.edu/viewdoc/summary?doi=10.1.1.150.7896. Last checked June 13, 2012.

Chesney, T. 2006. An empirical examination of Wikipedia's credibility. *First Monday* 11(11). No page numbers. Available at http://firstmonday.org/issues/issue11_11/chesney/. Last checked June 13, 2012.

Choi, B., K. Alexander, R. E. Kraut, and J. M. Levine. 2010. Socialization tactics in Wikipedia and their effects. *Proceedings of the 2010 ACM Conference on Computer Supported Cooperative Work*, February 6–10, Savannah, GA. Available at ACM Portal, http://dl.acm.org/citation.cfm?id=1718940. Last checked June 13, 2012.

Christakis, N. A., and J. H. Fowler. 2009. *Connected: How Your Friends' Friends' Friends Affect Everything You Feel, Think, and Do*. New York: Nack Bay Books.

Christensen, C. 2011. Discourses of technology and liberation: State aid to net activists in an era of "Twitter revolutions." *Communication Review* 14(3), 233–53.

Christofides, E., A. Muise, and S. Desmarais. 2009. Information disclosure and control on Facebook: Are they two sides of the same coin or two different processes? *CyberPsychology & Behavior* 12(3), 341–45.

Chun, W. 2011. *Programmed Visions: Software and Memory*. Cambridge: MIT Press.

Clemons, E. K. 2009. The complex problem of monetizing virtual electronic social networks. *Decision Support Systems* 48, 46–56.

Cohen, J. 2012. *Configuring the Networked Self: Law, Code and the Play of Everyday Practice*. New Haven: Yale University Press.

Cohen, N. S. 2008. The valorization of surveillance: Towards a political economy of Facebook. *Democratic Communiqué* 22(1), 5–22.

Comm, J., and K. Burge. 2009. *Twitter Power: How to Dominate Your Market One Tweet at a Time*. Hoboken, NJ: Wiley and Sons.

Cowhey, P. F., and J. D. Aronson. 2009. *Transforming Global Information and Communication Markets: The Political Economy of Innovation*. Cambridge: MIT Press.

Cox, A. M., P. D. Clough, and J. Marlow. 2008. Flickr: A first look at user behavior in the context of photography as serious leisure. *Information Research* 13(1). No page numbers. Available online at http://informationr.net/ir/13-1/paper336.html. Last checked June 13, 2012.

Deleuze, G. 1990. Society of control. *L'autre Journal* 1. No page numbers. Available at http://www.nadir.org/nadir/archiv/netzkritik/societyofcontrol.html. Last checked June 13, 2012.

Demerling, R. 2010. "Twitter me this, Twitter me that": The marketization of brands through social networking sites. *Stream: Culture, Politics, Technology* 3(1), 33–46.

Denning P., J. Horning, D. Parnas, and L. Weinstein. 2005. Inside risks: Wikipedia risks. *Communications of the ACM* 48(12), 152.

Deuze, M. 2009. Media industries, work and life. *European Journal of Communication* 24, 467–80.

Diakopoulos, N., and D. A. Shamma. 2010. Characterizing debate performance via aggregated Twitter sentiment. Paper presented at the CHI Conference, April 10–15, 2010, Atlanta, GA. Available at http://dl.acm.org/citation.cfm?id=1753504. Last checked June 13, 2012.

Dijck, J. van. 2007a. *Mediated Memories in the Digital Age*. Stanford: Stanford University Press.

———. 2007b. Homecasting: The End of Broadcasting? *Receiver* 18, April 2. No page numbers. Available at http://212.241.182.231/rcb1/?p=36. Last checked December 12, 2011.

———. 2009. Users like you: Theorizing agency in user-generated content. *Media, Culture & Society* 31(1), 41–58.

———. 2010. Search engines and the production of academic knowledge. *International Journal of Cultural Studies* 13(6), 574–92.

———. 2011. Flickr and the Culture of Connectivity: Sharing Views, Experiences, Memories. *Memory Studies* 4(4), 401–15.

———. 2012a. Facebook as a tool for producing sociality and connectivity. *Television & New Media* 13(2), 160–76.

———. 2012b. Social media platforms as producers. Tobias Olsson, ed., *Producing the Internet: Platforms, Communities, Actors*. Stockholm: Nordic Communication. Forthcoming.

Dijck, J. van, and D. Nieborg. 2009. Wikinomics and its discontents. A critical analysis of collaborative culture. *New Media & Society* 11(4), 855–74.

Ding, Y., Y. Du, Y. Hu, Z. Liu, L. Wang, K. W. Ross, and A. Ghose. 2011. Broadcast yourself: Understanding YouTube uploaders. Paper presented at the Internet Measurement Conference, IMC'11, November 2–4, Berlin. Available at http://conferences.sigcomm.org/imc/2011/program.htm. Last checked June 13, 2012.

Doherty, N., C. Coombs, and J. Loan-Clarke. 2006. A re-conceptualization of the interpretive flexibility of information technologies: Redressing the balance between the social and the technical. *European Journal of Information Systems* 15(6), 569–82.

Doyle, G. 2002. *Understanding Media Economics*. London: Sage.

Duhigg, C. 2012. *The Power of Habit: Why We Do What We Do in Life and Business*. New York: Random House.

Ellison, N. B., C. Steinfeld, and C. Lampe. 2007. The benefits of Facebook "friends": Exploring the relationship between college students' use of online social networks and social capital. *Journal of Computer-Mediated Communication* 12(1), 1143–68.

———. 2011. Connection strategies: Social capital implications of Facebook-enabled communication practices. *New Media & Society* 13(6), 873–92.

Emmett, A. 2008. Networking news. *American Journalism Review* 30, 40–43.

Enders, A., H. Hungenberg, H. P. Denker, and S. Mauch. 2008. The long tail of social networking: Revenue models of social networking sites. *European Management Journal* 26, 199–211.

Feenberg, A. 2009. Critical theory of communication technology: Introduction to the special section. *Information Society* 25(2), 77–83.

Foucault, M. 1980. *An Introduction*. Vol. 1 of *The History of Sexuality*. New York: Vintage.

Fuchs, C. 2009a. Information and communication technologies and society: A contribution to the critique of the political economy of the Internet. *European Journal of Communication* 24, 69–87.

———. 2009b. Some reflections on Manuel Castell's book *Communication Power*. *Triple C* 7(1), 94–108.

———. 2011a. An alternative view of privacy on Facebook. *Information* 2, 140–65.

———. 2011b. *Foundations of Critical Media and Information Studies*. London: Routledge.

Fuller, M. 2005. *Media Ecologies: Materialist Energies in Art and Technoculture*. Cambridge: MIT Press.

———. 2008. *Software Studies: A Lexicon*. Cambridge: MIT Press.

Fuster Morell, M. 2011. The Wikimedia Foundation and the governance of Wikipedia's infrastructure: Historical trajectories and its hybrid character. G. Lovink and N. Tkacz, eds., *Critical Point of View: A Wikipedia Reader*. Amsterdam: Institute for Network Cultures. 325–41.

Gaffney, D. 2010. #iranElection: Quantifying online activism. *Proceedings of the WebSci10: Extending the Frontiers of Society On-Line*, April, Raleigh, NC. Available at http://journal.webscience.org/295/. Last checked June 13, 2012.

Galloway, A. 2004. *Protocol: How Control Exists after Decentralization*. Cambridge: MIT Press.

Garde-Hansen, J. 2009. MyMemories? Personal digital archive fever and Facebook. J. Garde-Hansen, A. Hoskins, and A. Reading, eds., *Save As . . . Digital Memories*. Basingstoke: Palgrave. 135–50.

Gehl, R. 2009. YouTube as archive. Who will curate this digital Wunderkammer? *International Journal of Cultural Studies* 12(1), 43–60.

Geiger, R. S. 2011. The lives of bots. G. Lovink and N. Tkacz, eds., *Critical Point of View: A Wikipedia Reader*. Amsterdam: Institute for Network Cultures. 78–93.

Geiger, R. S., and D. Ribes. 2010. The work of sustaining order in Wikipedia: The banning of a vandal. *Proceedings of the 2010 ACM Conference on Computer Supported Cooperative Work*, February 6–10, Savannah, GA. Available at ACM portal, http://dl.acm.org/citation.cfm?id=1718941. Last checked June 13, 2012.

Ghosh, R. A., and V. V. Prakash. 2000. The Orbiten free software survey. *First Monday* 5(7). No page numbers. Available at http://www.firstmonday.org/issues/issue5_7/ghosh/. Last checked June 12, 2012.

Gilder, G. 1994. *Life after Television*. New York: Norton.

Giles, J. 2005. Internet encyclopaedias go head to head. *Nature* 438, 900–901. Available at http://www.nature.com/nature/journal/v438/n7070/full/438900a.html. Last checked December 12, 2011.

Gillespie, T. 2010. The politics of platforms. *New Media & Society* 12(3), 347–64.

Giroux, H. A. 2009. The Iranian uprisings and the challenge of the new media: Rethinking the politics of representation. *Fast Capitalism* 5(2). No page numbers. Available at http://www.uta.edu/huma/5_2/Giroux5_2.html. Last checked December 11, 2012.

Gitelman, L. 2008. *Always Already New: Media, History, and the Data of Culture*. Cambridge: MIT Press.

Gooyong, K. 2009. The future of YouTube: Critical reflections on YouTube users' discussions over its future. *Interactions: UCLA Journal of Education and Information Studies* 5(2), article no. 4. No page numbers. Available at http://escholarship.org/uc/item/9tn362r2. Last checked June 12, 2012.

Grimmelmann, J. 2009. Saving Facebook. *Iowa Law Review* 94, 1138–1206. Available at http://works.bepress.com/james_grimmelmann/20/. Last checked June 12, 2012.

Gripsrud, J. 2004. Broadcast television: The chances of its survival in a digital age. L. Spigel and J. Olsson, eds., *Television after TV: Essays on a Medium in Transition*. Durham: Duke University Press. 210–23.

Gross R., and A. Acquisti. 2005. Information revelation and privacy in online social networks. *Proceedings of the ACM WPES'05*. Alexandria, VA: ACM Press. 71–80.

Ha, J.-Y., S. Dick, and S. K. Ryu. 2003. Broadcast via the Internet: Technology, market, and the future. *Trends in Communication* 11(2), 155–68.

Habermas, J. 1989. *The Structural Transformation of the Public Sphere: An Inquiry into a Category of Bourgeois Society*. Cambridge: MIT Press.

Halatchliyski, I., J. Moskaliuk, J. Kimmerle, and U. Cress. 2010. Who integrates the networks of knowledge in Wikipedia? *Proceedings of the 6th International Symposium on Wikis and Open Collaboration WikiSym*, July 7–9, Gdansk, Poland. Available at ACM portal, http://dl.acm.org/citation.cfm?id=1832774. Last checked June 12, 2012.

Halavais, A., and D. Lackaff. 2008. An analysis of topical coverage of Wikipedia. *Journal of Computer-Mediated Communication* 13, 429–40.

Haythornthwaite, C., and L. Kendall. 2010. Internet and community. *American Behavioral Scientist* 53(8), 1083–94.

Heil, B., and M. Piskorski. 2009. New Twitter research: Men follow men and nobody tweets. *Harvard Business Review*, June 24. Available at http://blogs.hbr.org/cs/2009/06/new_twitter_research_men_follo.html. Last checked June 12, 2012.

Hendler, J., and T. Berners-Lee. 2010. From the Semantic Web to social machines: A research challenge for AI on the World Wide Web. *Artificial Intelligence* 174(2), 156–61.

Hermida, A. 2010. Twittering the news: The emergence of ambient journalism. *Journalism Practice* 4(3), 297–308.

Hetcher, S. A. 2004. *Norms in a Wired World*. Cambridge: Cambridge University Press.

Hirst, M. 2011. *News 2.0: Can Journalism Survive the Internet?* Sydney: Allen & Unwin.

Honeycutt, C., and S. Herring. 2009. Beyond microblogging: Conversation and collaboration via Twitter. *Proceedings of the 42nd Hawaii International Conference on System Sciences*. 1–10. Available at http://www.citeulike.org/user/imrchen/article/4033966. Last checked June 12, 2012.

Huang, J., K. M. Thornton, and E. N. Efthimidias. 2010. Conversational tagging in Twitter. *Proceedings of the Conference on Hypertext and Hypermedia*, June 13–16, Toronto. Available at http://dl.acm.org/citation.cfm?id=1810647. Last checked June 12, 2012.

Huang, T.-H., and J. Y. Hsu. 2006. Beyond memories: Weaving photos into personal networks. *Proceedings American Association for Artificial Intelligence*. No page numbers Available at www.aaai.org. Last checked June 12, 2012.

Huberman, B., D. Romero, and F. Wu. 2009. Social networks that matter: Twitter under the microscope. *First Monday* 14(1). No page numbers. Available at http://firstmonday.org/. Last checked June 12, 2012.

Hutchby, I. 2001. Technologies, texts, and affordances. *Sociology* 35(2), 441–56.

Isaacson, W. 2011. *Steve Jobs*. New York: Simon and Schuster.

Jakobsson, P. 2010. Cooperation and competition in open production. *Platform: Journal of Media and Communication* 12, 106–19.

Jakobsson, P., and F. Stiernstedt. 2010. Pirates of Silicon Valley: State of exception and dispossession in Web 2.0. *First Monday* 15(7). No page numbers. Available at http://firstmonday.org/htbin/cgiwrap/bin/ojs/index.php/fm/article/viewArticle/2799/2577.

Jarvis, J. 2009. *What Would Google Do?* New York: Harpers.

———. 2011. *Public Parts: How Sharing in the Digital Age Improves the Way We Work and Live*. New York: Simon and Schuster.

Java, A., T. Finin, X. Song, and B. Tseng. 2007. Why we Twitter: Understanding microblogging usage and communities. Paper presented at the ACM Social Network Mining and Analysis Workshop, San Jose, CA, August 12. Available at http://ebiquity.umbc.edu/paper/html/id/367/Why-We-Twitter-Understanding-Microblogging-Usage-and-Communities. Last checked June 12, 2012.

Jenkins, H. 2006. *Convergence Culture: Where Old and New Media Collide*. Cambridge: MIT Press.

Jin, X., A. Gallagher, L. Cao, J. Luo, and J. Han. 2010. The wisdom of social multimedia; Using Flickr for prediction and forecast. *Proceedings of the International Conference on Multimedia*, Florence, Italy, October 25–29. Available at http://dl.acm.org/citation.cfm?id=1874196. Last checked June 12, 2012.

Kamir, D., and J. Niesyto. 2011. User DrorK: A call for a free content alternative for sources. An interview with Dror Kamir. G. Lovink and N. Tkacz, eds., *Critical*

Point of View: A Wikipedia Reader. Amsterdam: Institute for Network Cultures. 288–95.

Kaplan, A. M., and M. Haenlein. 2010. Users of the world, unite! The challenges and opportunities of social media. *Business Horizons* 53(1), 59–68. Available online at http://www.sciencedirect.com/science/article/pii/S0007681309001232#sec4.1.3. Last checked June 12, 2012.

Keane, M., and A. Moran. 2008. Television's new engines. *New Media & Society* 9(2), 155–69.

Keen, A. 2008. *The Cult of the Amateur: How Blogs, MySpace, YouTube, and the Rest of Today's User-Generated Media Are Killing Our Culture and Economy*. London: Nicholas Brealey.

Kelly, R., ed. 2009. *Twitter Study Reveals Interesting Results about Usage*. San Antonio, TX: Pear Analytics. Available at http://www.pearanalytics.com/wp-content/uploads/2009/08/Twitter-Study-August-2009.pdf, Last checked February 26, 2011.

Kennedy, L., M. Namaan, S. Ahern, R. Nair, and T. Rattenbury. 2007. "How Flickr helps us make sense of the world: Context and content in community-contributed media collections. *Proceedings of the 15th International Conference on Multimedia* Augsburg, Germany, September 23–28. 631–40. Available at ACM portal, http://dl.acm.org/citation.cfm?id=1291384. Last checked June 12, 2012.

Kessler, F., and M. T. Schaefer. 2009. Navigating YouTube: Constituting a hybrid information management system. P. Snickars and P. Vondereau, eds., *The YouTube Reader*. Stockholm: National Library of Sweden. 275–91.

Kildall, S., and N. Stern. 2011. Wikipedia art: Citation as performative act. G. Lovink and N. Tkacz, eds., *Critical Point of View: A Wikipedia Reader*. Amsterdam: Institute for Network Cultures. 165–90.

Kirkpatrick, D. 2010. *The Facebook Effect: The Inside Story of the Company That Is Connecting the World*. New York: Simon and Schuster.

Kittler, F. 1999. *Gramophone, Film, Typewriter*. Stanford: Stanford University Press.

Kittur A., E. Chi, B. Pendleton, B. Sun, and T. Mytkowicz. 2007. Power of the few vs wisdom of the crowd: Wikipedia and the rise of the bourgeoisie. Paper presented at Conference on Human Computer Interfaces, CHI 2007, San Jose, CA, April 28–May 3. Available at http://www.parc.com/publication/1749/power-of-the-few-vs-wisdom-of-the-crowd.html. Last checked June 12, 2012.

Konieczny, P. 2010. Adhocratic Governance in the Internet age: A case of Wikipedia. *Journal of Information Technology & Politics* 7(4), 263–83.

Krishnamurthy, B., P. Gill, and M. Arlitt. 2008. A few chirps about Twitter. Paper presented at the ACM SIGCOMM Workshop for Online Social Networks, Seattle, WA, August 18. Available at http://www.citeulike.org/user/jobadge/article/3334885. Last checked June 12, 2012.

Kruitbosch, G., and F. Nack. 2008. Broadcast yourself on YouTube—Really? HCC '08: *Proceedings of the 3rd ACM International Workshop on Human-Centered Computing*. New York. Available at http://dl.acm.org/citation.cfm?id=1462029. Last checked June 12, 2012.

Kwak, H., C. Lee, H. Park, and S. Moon. 2010. What is Twitter, a social network or a news media? *Proceedings of the 19th International World Wide Web (WWW) Conference*, April 26–30, Raleigh NC, 591–600. Available at http://an.kaist.ac.kr/traces/WWW2010.html l. Last checked June 12, 2012.

Lange, P. G. 2007. Publicly private and privately public: Social networking on YouTube. *Journal of Computer-Mediated Communication* 1, 361–80.

————. 2008. (Mis)conceptions about YouTube. G. Lovink and S. Niederer, eds., *The Video Vortex Reader: Responses to YouTube*. Amsterdam: Institute of Network Cultures. 87–100.

Latour, B. 1996. *Aramis; or, The Love of Technology*. Cambridge: Harvard University Press.

————. 1998. On actor-network theory. A few clarifications. *Nettime List Archives*. Available at http://www.nettime.org/Lists-Archives/nettime-l-9801/msg00019.html. Last checked June 12, 2012.

————. 2005. *Reassembling the Social: An Introduction to Actor-Network Theory*. Oxford: Oxford University Press.

Ledoux Book, C., and B. Barnett. 2006. PCTV: Consumers, expectancy-value and likely adoption. *Convergence* 12(3), 325–39.

Lenhart, A., and S. Fox. 2009. *Twitter and Status Updating*. Pew Internet and American Life Project report. Available at www.pewinternet.org/Reports/2009/Twitter-and-status-updating.aspx. Last checked June 12, 2012.

Leon, P. G., B. Ur, R. Balebako, L. Cranor, R. Shay, and Y. Wang. 2011. *Why Johnny Can't Opt Out: A Usability Evaluation of Tools to Limit Online Behavioral Advertising*. Research report CMU-CyLab-11-017. Carnegie Mellon University, Pittsburgh, PA, October 31. Available at http://www.cylab.cmu.edu/research/techreports/2011/tr_cylab11017.html. Last checked June 12, 2012.

Lessig, L. 2008. *Remix. Making Art and Commerce Thrive in the Hybrid Economy*. New York: Penguin.

Levy, S. 2011. *In the Plex. How Google Thinks, Works, and Shapes Our Lives*. New York: Simon and Schuster.

Lipford, H. R., A. Besmer, and J. Watson. 2008. Understanding privacy settings in Facebook with an audience view. UPSEC'08: *Proceedings of the 1st Conference on Usability, Psychology, and Security*, Berkeley, CA. 1–8.

Liu, S. B., L. Palen, J. Sutton, A. L. Hughes, and S. Vieweg. 2008. In search of the bigger picture: The emergent role of online photo sharing in times of disaster. *Proceedings of the 5th International ISCRAM Conference*, Washington, DC, May. No page numbers. Available at http://www.citeulike.org/user/krisl/article/7150985. Last checked June 12, 2012.

Lovink, G. 2008. The art of watching databases. G. Lovink and S. Niederer, eds., *The Video Vortex Reader: Responses to YouTube*. Amsterdam: Institute of Network Cultures. 9–12.

————. 2012. *Networks without a Cause: A Critique of Social Media*. Cambridge: Polity Press.

Lovink, G., and S. Niederer, eds. 2008. *The Video Vortex Reader: Responses to YouTube*. Amsterdam: Institute for Network Cultures.

Lovink, G., and N. Tkacz, eds. 2011. *Critical Point of View: A Wikipedia Reader*. Amsterdam: Institute for Network Cultures.

Luders, M. 2008. Conceptualizing personal media. *New Media & Society* 10(5), 683–702.

Mackenzie, A. 2006. *Cutting Code: Software and Sociality*. New York: Peter Lang.

Madejski, M., M. Johnson, and S. M. Bellovin. 2011. The failure of online social network privacy settings. Research paper published by Columbia University (CUCS 010-11). Available at http://www.mendeley.com/research/failure-online-social-network-privacy-settings/. Last checked June 12, 2012.

Magnus, P. D. 2008. Early response to false claims in Wikipedia. *First Monday* 13(9). No page numbers. Available at http://www.uic.edu/htbin/cgiwrap/bin/ojs/index.php/fm/article/viewArticle/2115/2027. Last checked June 12, 2012.

Manovich, L. 2001. *The Language of New Media*. Cambridge: MIT Press.

———. 2009. The practice of everyday (media) life: From mass consumption to mass cultural production? *Critical Inquiry* 35(2). No page numbers. Available at http://www.citeulike.org/user/DrewMLoewe/article/3763782. Last checked June 12, 2012.

Manzuch, Z. 2009. Digitisation and communication of memory: From theory to practice. *Conference Proceedings: Cultural Heritage Online*. Empowering Users: An Active Role for User Communities. Florence, December 16–17, 2009. Pages 92–95. Available at www.rinascimento-digitale.it/eventi/conference2009/. . .2009/manzuch.pdf. Last checked June 12, 2012.

Marvin, C. 1988. *When Old Technologies Were New: Thinking about Communication in the Late Nineteenth Century*. New York: Oxford University Press.

Marwick, A., and d. boyd. 2011. I tweet honestly, I tweet passionately: Twitter users, context collapse and the imagined audience. *New Media & Society* 13(1), 114–33.

McDonald, P. 2009. Digital discords in the online media economy: Advertising versus content versus copyright. P. Snickars and P. Vondereau, eds., *The YouTube Reader*. Stockholm: National Library of Sweden. 387–405.

McGrath, R. G. 2009. Business models: A discovery driven approach. *Long Range Planning* 7, 1–15. Available at www.elsevier.com/locate/lrp. Last checked June 12, 2012.

Milberry, K., and S. Anderson. 2009. Open sourcing our way to an online commons: Contesting corporate impermeability in the new media ecology. *Journal of Communication Inquiry* 33(4), 393–412.

Miller, N., and R. Allen, eds. 1995. *The Post-broadcasting Age: New Technologies, New Communities*. Luton: University of Luton Press.

Miller, T. 2009. Cybertarians of the world, unite: You have nothing to lose but your tubes! P. Snickars and P. Vondereau, eds., *The YouTube Reader*. Stockholm: National Library of Sweden. 406–23.

Mintzberg, H. 2007. *Tracking Strategies: Toward a General Theory*. Oxford: Oxford University Press.

Mischaud, E. 2007. *Twitter: Expressions of the whole self*. An investigation into user appropriation of a Web-based communications platform. Dissertation, London School of Economics. Available at www.lse.ac.uk/collections/media@lse. Last checked June 12, 2012.

Mislove, A., H. S. Koppula, K. P. Gummadi, P. Druschei, and B. Bhattacharjee. 2008. Growth of the Flickr social network. *Proceedings on the First Workshop on Online Social Networks (SIGCOMM)*, August 18, Seattle. 25–30. Available at http://www.citeulike.org/article-posts/3271250. Last checked June 12, 2012.

Mitchem, M. 2008. Video social: Complex parasitical media. G. Lovink and S. Niederer, eds., *The Video Vortex Reader: Responses to YouTube*. Amsterdam: Institute of Network Cultures. 273–82.

Moran, J. 2002. *There Is No Place Like Home Video*. Minneapolis: University of Minnesota Press.

Morozov, E. 2011. *The Net Delusion: How Not to Liberate the World*. New York: Penguin.

Mortensen, M. 2011. When citizen photojournalism sets the news agenda: Neda Agha Soltan as a Web 2.0 icon of post-election unrest in Iran. *Global Media and Communication* 7(1), 4–16.

Mosco, V. 2004. *The Digital Sublime: Myth, Power and Cyberspace*. Cambridge: MIT Press.

———. 2009. *The Political Economy of Communication: Rethinking and Renewal*. London: Sage.

Muller, E. 2009. Where Quality Matters: Discourses on the art of making a YouTube video. P. Snickars and P. Vondereau, eds., *The YouTube Reader*. Stockholm: National Library of Sweden. 126–39.

Murray, S. 2008. Digital images, photo-sharing, and our shifting notions of everyday aesthetics. *Journal of Visual Culture* 7(2), 147–63.

Murthy, D. 2011. Twitter: Microphone for the masses? *Media, Culture & Society* 33(5), 779–89.

Negoescu, R.-A., and D. Gatica-Perez. 2008. Analyzing Flickr groups. Paper presented at Conference on Image and Video Retrieval, July 7–9, Niagara Falls, Canada. Available at http://people.idiap.ch/negora/civr08. Last checked June 12, 2012.

Niederer S., and J. van Dijck. 2010. Wisdom of the crowd or technicity of content? Wikipedia as a socio-technical system. *New Media & Society* 12(8), 1368–87.

Nissenbaum, H. 2010. *Privacy in Context: Technology, Policy, and the Integrity of Social Life*. Stanford: Stanford University Press.

Nov, O., and C. Ye. 2010. Why do people tag? Motivations for photo tagging. *Communications of the ACM* 53(7), 128–31.

Nussbaum, B. 2010. Facebook's culture problem may be fatal. *Harvard Business Review* 24. Available online at http://blogs.hbr.org/cs/2010/05/facebooks_culture_problem_may.html. Last checked June 12, 2012.

O'Brien, D., and B. Fitzgerald. 2006. Digital copyright law in a YouTube world. *Internet Law Bulletin* 9(6–7), 71–74.

O'Neil, M. 2011. Wikipedia and authority. G. Lovink and N. Tkacz, eds., *Critical Point of View: A Wikipedia Reader*. Amsterdam: Institute for Network Cultures. 309–24.

O'Sullivan, D. 2011. What is an encyclopedia? From Pliny to Wikipedia. G. Lovink and N. Tkacz, eds., *Critical Point of View: A Wikipedia Reader*. Amsterdam: Institute for Network Cultures. 34–49.

Orlikowski, W. J., and S. Iacono. 2001. Desperately seeking the "IT" in IT research: A call to theorizing the IT artefact. *Information Research* 12(2), 121–34.

Pak, A., and P. Paroubek. 2010. Twitter as a corpus for sentiment analysis and opinion mining. *Proceedings of the Seventh Conference on International Language Resources and Evaluation* LREC, Valletta, Malta, May. Available at http://www.bibsonomy.org/bibtex/25656c3bb1adf00c58a85e3204096961c/frederik. Last checked June 12, 2012.

Paolillo, J. C. 2008. Structure and network in the YouTube core. *Proceedings of the 41st Hawaii International Conference on System Sciences*, EEEC Computer Society, Washington, DC. Available at http://portal.acm.org/citation.cfm?id=1334977. Last checked June 12, 2012.

Papacharissi, Z. 2009. The virtual geographies of social networks: A comparative analysis of Facebook, LinkedIn and ASmallWorld. *New Media & Society* 11(1–2), 199–220.

———. 2010. *A Private Sphere: Democracy in a Digital Age*. Cambridge: Polity Press.

Pariser, E. 2011. *The Filter Bubble: What the Internet Is Hiding from You*. New York: Viking.

Parks, L. 2004. Flexible microcasting: Gender, generation, and television-Internet convergence. L. Spigel and J. Olsson, eds., *Television after TV: Essays on a Medium in Transition*. Durham: Duke University Press, 133–56.

Pauwels, L. 2008. A private visual practice going public? Social functions and sociological research opportunities of Web-based family photography. *Visual Studies* 23(1), 34–49.

Pentzold, C. 2011. Imagining the Wikipedia community: What do Wikipedia authors mean when they write about their "community"? *New Media & Society* 13(5), 704–21.

Peters, K., and A. Seiers. 2009. Home dance: Mediacy and aesthetics of the self on YouTube. P. Snickars and P. Vondereau, eds., *The YouTube Reader*. Stockholm: National Library of Sweden. 187–203.

Petersen, S. M. 2008. Loser-generated content: From participation to exploitation. *First Monday* 13(3). No page numbers. Available at http://firstmonday.org/ht-bin/cgiwrap/bin/ojs/index.php/fm/article/view/2141/1948.

Peuter, G. de, and N. Dyer-Witheford. 2005. Playful multitude? Mobilising and counter-mobilising immaterial game labour. *Fibreculture* 5. No page numbers. Available at http://journal.fibreculture.org/issue5/depeuter_dyerwitheford.html. Last checked June 12, 2012.

Pinch, T. J., and W. E. Bijker. 1984. The social construction of facts and artifacts: Or how the sociology of science and the sociology of technology might benefit each other. *Social Studies of Science* 14, 399–441.

Poell, T., and K. Darmoni. 2012. Twitter as a multilingual space: The articulation of the Tunisian revolution through #sidibouzid. *European Journal of Media Studies* 1(1). No page numbers. http://www.necsus-ejms.org/twitter-as-a-multilingual-space-the-articulation-of-the-tunisian-revolution-through-sidibouzid-by-thomas-poell-and-kaouthar-darmoni/.

Poritz, J. 2007. Who searches the searchers? Community privacy in the age of monolithic search engines. *Information Society* 23(5), 383–89.

Potts, J. 2009. Why creative industries matter to economic evolution. *Economics of Innovation and New Technology* 18(7), 663–73.

Preston, P. 2010. Manuel Castells, *Communication Power*. Book review. *Media, Culture & Society* 32(6), 1042–49.

Prieur, C., D. Cardon, J.-S. Beuscart, N. Pissard, and P. Pons. 2008. The strength of weak cooperation: A case study of Flickr. *Reseaux Archive*. Available at http://arxiv.org/abs/0802.2317. Last checked June 12, 2012.

Prince, D. L. 2010. *Get Rich with Twitter: Harness the Power of the Twitterverse and Reach More Customers Than Ever Before*. New York: McGraw Hill.

Raynes-Goldie, K. 2010. Aliases, creeping, and wall cleaning: Understanding privacy in the age of Facebook. *First Monday*, 15(1). No page numbers. Available at http://firstmonday.org/htbin/cgiwrap/bin/ojs/index.php/fm/article/view/2775. Last checked June 12, 2012.

Robertson, S. P., R. K. Vatapru, and R. Medina. 2009. The social life of networks: Facebook linkage patterns in the 2008 U.S. presidential elections. *Proceedings of the 10th International Digital Government Research Conference*. Available at http://dl.acm.org/citation.cfm?id=1556183. Last checked June 12, 2012.

Rosenzweig, R. 2006. Can history be open source? Wikipedia and the future of the past. *Journal of American History* 93(1), 117–46.

Rossiter, N., and G. Lovink. 2010. Urgent aphorisms: Notes on organized networks for the connected multitudes. M. Deuze, ed., *Managing Media Work*. London: Sage. 279–90.

Rotman, D., and J. Preece. 2010. The "WeTube" in YouTube. Creating an online community through video sharing. *International Journals of Web-Based Communities* 6(3), 317–33.

Sacchi, D. L., F. Agnoli, and E. Loftus. 2007. Changing history: Doctored photographs affect memory for past public events. *Applied Cognitive Psychology* 21, 1005–22.

Sakaki, T., M. Okazaki, and Y. Matsuo. 2010. Earthquake shakes Twitter users: Real-time event detection by social sensors. Paper presented at the World Wide Web Conference, April 26–30, Raleigh, NC. Available at http://dl.acm.org/citation.cfm?id=1772777. Last checked June 12, 2012.

Schaefer, M. T. 2011. *Bastard Culture! How User Participation Transforms Cultural Production*. Amsterdam: Amsterdam University Press.

Schewick, B. van. 2010. *Internet Architecture and Innovation*. Cambridge: MIT Press.

Schiller, D. 2007. *How to Think about Information*. Urbana: University of Illinois Press.

Schmidt, E., and J. Cohen. 2010. The digital disruption: Connectivity and the diffusion of power. *Foreign Affairs* 89(6), 75–85.

Shachaf, P., and N. Hara. 2010. Beyond vandalism: Wikipedia trolls. *Journal of Information Science* 36(3), 357–70.

Shapiro, C., and H. R. Varian. 1999. *Information Rules: A Strategic Guide to the Network Economy*. Boston: Harvard Business School Press.

Shirky, C. 2008. *Here Comes Everybody! How Change Happens When People Come Together*. London: Penguin.

Siegel, D. 2009. *Pull: The Power of the Semantic Web to Transform Your Business*. New York: Penguin.

Siersdorfer, S., S. Chelaru, W. Nejdl, and J. San Pedro. 2010. How useful are your comments? Analyzing and predicting YouTube comments and comment ratings. Paper presented at the World Wide Web Conference, April 26–30, Raleigh, NC. Available at http://malt.ml.cmu.edu/mw/index.php/Analyzing_and_Predicting_Youtube_Comments_Rating:_WWW2010. Last checked June 12, 2012.

Skageby, J. 2009. Exploring qualitative sharing practices of social metadata: Expanding the attention economy. *Information Society* 25(1), 60–72.

Smith-Shomade, B. 2004. Narrowcasting in the new world information order. A space for audience? *Television and New Media* 5(1), 69–81.

Snavely, N., S. M. Seitz, and R. Szeliski. 2008. Modeling the world from Internet photo collections. *International Journal of Computer Vision* 80(2), 189–210.

Solove, D. J. 2009. *Understanding Privacy*. Cambridge: Harvard University Press.

Springer, M., B. Dulabahn, P. Michel, B. Natanson, D. Reser, D. Woodward, and H. Zinkham. 2008. *For the Common Good: The Library of Congress Flickr Pilot Project*. Evaluation report for Library of Congress, available at www.loc.gov/rr/print/flickr_pilot.html. Last checked June 12, 2012.

Stutzman, F., and J. Kramer-Duffield. 2010. Friends only: Examining privacy enhancing behavior in Facebook. *Proceedings of the Computer-Human Interface Conference*, April 10–15, Atlanta, GA. Available at http://www.citeulike.org/user/isp/article/7028829. Last checked June 12, 2012.

Sunstein, C. R. 2006. *Infotopia: How Many Minds Produce Knowledge*. Oxford: Oxford University Press.

Surowiecki, J. 2004. *The Wisdom of Crowds: Why the Many Are Smarter Than the Few and How Collective Wisdom Shapes Business, Societies and Nations*. New York: Doubleday.

Tapscott, D., and A. D. Williams. 2006. *Wikinomics: How Mass Collaboration Changes Everything*. New York: Penguin.

Teece, D. J. 2010. Business models, business strategies and innovation. *Long Range Planning* 43, 172–94.

Tencati, A., and L. Zsolnai. 2008. The collaborative enterprise. *Journal of Business Ethics* 85, 367–76.

Terranova, T. 2004. *Network Culture: Politics for the Information Age*. London: Pluto Press.

Thompson, J. B. 1995. *The Media and Modernity: A Social Theory of the Media*. Cambridge: Polity Press.

———. 2005. The new visibility. *Theory, Culture and Society* 22(6), 31–51.

Tkacz, N. 2011. The politics of forking paths. G. Lovink and N. Tkacz, eds., *Critical Point of View: A Wikipedia Reader*. Amsterdam: Institute for Network Cultures. 94–109.

Toffler, A. 1970. *Future Shock*. New York: Random House.

Turner, F. 2006. *From Counterculture to Cyberculture: Stewart Brand, the Whole Earth Network, and the Rise of Digital Utopianism*. Chicago: University of Chicago Press.

Turow, J. 2006. *Niche Envy: Marketing Discrimination in the Digital Age*. Cambridge: MIT Press.

Uricchio, W. 2004. Television's next generation: Technology/interface culture/flow. L. Spigel and J. Olsson, eds., *Television after TV: Essays on a Medium in Transition*. Durham: Duke University Press. 163–82.

———. 2009. The future of a medium once known as television. P. Snickars and P. Vondereau, eds., *The YouTube Reader*. Stockholm: National Library of Sweden. 24–39.

———. 2011. The algorithmic turn: Photosynth, augmented reality and the changing implications of the image. *Visual Studies* 26(1), 25–35.

Vaidhyanathan, S. 2011. *The Googlization of Everything (and Why We Should Worry)*. Berkeley: University of California Press.

Valenzuela, S., N. Park, and K. F. Kee. 2009. Is there social capital in a social network site? Facebook use and college students' life satisfaction, trust, and participation. *Journal of Computer-Mediated Communication* 14, 875–901.

Van House, N. 2007. Flickr and public image-sharing: Distant closeness and photo exhibition. *SIGCHI Work-in-progress*, April 28–May 3, San Francisco. 2717–22. Available at http://www.ischool.berkeley.edu/research/publications/vanhouse/2007/flickr. Last checked June 12, 2012.

Vukanovic, Z. 2009. Global paradigm shift: Strategic management of new and digital media in new and digital economics. *International Journal on Media Management* 11(2), 81–90.

Wellman, B., A. Quan-Haase, J. Boase, and W. Chen. 2003. The social affordances of the Internet for networked individualism. *Journal of Computer-Mediated Culture* 8(3). No page numbers. Available at http://homes.chass.utoronto.ca/~wellman/publications/index.html. Last checked June 12, 2012.

Winston, B. 1998. *Media Technology and Society: A History. From the Telegraph to the Internet*. New York: Routledge.

Wirtz, B. W., O. Schilke, and S. Ullrich. 2010. Strategic development of business models. Implications of the Web 2.0 for creating value on the Internet. *Long Range Planning* 43, 272–90.

Wu, T. 2010. *The Master Switch: The Rise and Fall of Information Empires*. New York: Knopf.

Yang, H.-L., and C. Lai. 2010. Motivations of Wikipedia content contributors. *Computers in Human Behavior* 26, 1377–83.

Zhao, D., and M. B. Rosson. 2009. How and why people Twitter: The role that microblogging plays in informal communication at work. *Proceedings of the GROUP'04 Conference*, May, Sanibel Island, FL. Available at http://portal.acm.org/citation.cfm?id=1531710&dl=GUIDE&coll=GUIDE&CFID=79835132&CFTOKEN=99251838. Last checked June 12, 2012.

Zheleva, E., and L. Getoor. 2009. To join or not to join: The illusion of privacy in social networks with mixed public and private user profiles. *Proceedings of the World*

Wide Web Conference Committee, April 20–24, Madrid, Spain. 531–40. Available at http://www2009.eprints.org/54/. Last checked June 12, 2012.

Zielinski, S. 1999. *Audiovisions: Cinema and Television as Entr'actes in History*. Amsterdam: Amsterdam University Press.

Zittrain, J. 2008. *The Future of the Internet and How to Stop It*. New York: Penguin.

Zott, C., and R. H. Amit. 2009. Designing your future business model: An activity system perspective. IESE Business School Working Paper no. 781. Available at SSRN: http://ssrn.com/abstract=135651. Last checked June 12, 2012.

INDEX

Made in the USA
San Bernardino, CA
26 July 2013

Betty Grable

The Girl with the Million Dollar Legs

TOM McGEE

WELCOME RAIN PUBLISHERS

NEW YORK

Dedication

For my mother, Mamie, whose love of the
Hollywood musical has never deserted her.

Originally published by Vestal Press, Ltd., Vestal, NY 13851
Text design by Don Bell

First Welcome Rain edition 2010

Manufactured in the U.S.A.

The Library of Congress catalogued the original edition as follows:
McGee, Tom.
Betty Grable : the girl with the million dollar legs / by Tom McGee.
    p. cm.
    Includes bibliographical references.
    1. Grable, Betty, 1916-1973. 2. Motion pictures actors and actresses—
United States—Biography. I. Title.
PN2287.G66M35   1995
791.43'028'092—dc20
[B] 94-31145

ISBN 978-1-56649-956-9